Approaches to Global Sustainability, Markets, and Governance

Approaches to Global Sustainability, Markets, and Governance takes a fresh and global approach to issues of corporate social responsibility, regulation, governance, and sustainability. It encompasses such issues as: environmental sustainability and managing the resources of the world; geopolitics and sustainability; global markets and their regulation; governance and the role of supranational bodies; sustainable production and resource acquisition; society and sustainability.

Although primarily a business and management series, it is interdisciplinary and includes contributions from the social sciences, technology, engineering, politics, philosophy, and other disciplines. It focuses on the issues at a meta-level, and investigates the ideas, organisation, and infrastructure required to address them.

The series is grounded in the belief that any global consideration of sustainability must include such issues as governance, regulation, geopolitics, the environment, and economic activity in combination to recognise the issues and develop solutions for the planet. At present such global meta-analysis is rare as current research assumes that the identification of local best practice will lead to solutions, and individual disciplines act in isolation rather than being combined to identify truly global issues and solutions.

David Crowther · Shahla Seifi
Editors

Corporate Social Responsibility in Difficult Times

Springer

Editors
David Crowther
Social Responsibility Research Network
www.SRRNet.org, UK

Shahla Seifi
Social Responsibility Research Network
www.SRRNet.org, UK

ISSN 2520-8772 ISSN 2520-8780 (electronic)
Approaches to Global Sustainability, Markets, and Governance
ISBN 978-981-99-2590-2 ISBN 978-981-99-2591-9 (eBook)
https://doi.org/10.1007/978-981-99-2591-9

This Springer imprint is published by the registered company Springer Nature Singapore Pte Ltd.
The registered company address is: 152 Beach Road, #21-01/04 Gateway East, Singapore 189721, Singapore

Introduction

There are changes happening in the world, and arguably, it is entering an era in which we need to deal with the consequences of climate change and environmental problems while also recovering from the global pandemic. The United Nations, however, has declared that the climate is the greatest problem facing the world. This can be extended to an overarching concern with sustainability. There have been many who have recounted the problems but much fewer who have proposed solutions which can be adopted at a local level. What has been proposed can generally be found in selected journals such as New Scientist, Technological Sustainability, Social Responsibility Journal and Sustainability. But the field is vast as these individual papers published only deal with individual issues. In general, most papers being published at present focus upon how the past crisis has been dealt with rather than the effect upon CSR of past, current and future crises. This book is intended to add to the discourse by the various contributions.

It has been fairly traumatic for everyone and every organisation over the last couple of years as we have had to deal with the coronavirus pandemic. It has certainly been a shock to the economic system of the world from which many are still recovering. Equally, it has affected social systems and the environment, the effects of which are still being felt and will be felt for some time to come. Corporations therefore need to be resilient to deal with these effects and to develop plans for the future. More worryingly, the World Health Organisation has predicted that future pandemics are inevitable and it is fairly certain that everyone would prefer that we deal with these in a better way than the one just past. Other serious threats also fill the horizon linked to climate change and sustainability and the UN has forecast that this is an even bigger threat which must be dealt with. Hence the need for resilience to deal with present and future shocks becomes apparant.

In addition, there has been a fairly general economic crisis around the world as people struggle and adapt to the new environment. Firms have responded to the pressures created by all of these events in a number of ways—some very positive and innovative while others have retrenched and cut down on CSR activities. Moreover, actions in different parts of the world have differed as governments have reacted differently to the pandemic crisis and introduced differing requirements for the businesses operating within their sphere of influence. For many, this has created additional difficulties or has given short-term relief at the expense of future problems. Now, we have emerged from the pandemic crisis and are seeking to restore normality—in whatever way this might in future manifest itself. Certainly, there have been and will be changes which are likely to become permanent.

While recovering from one crisis, however, another is becoming more significant as climate change and its effects start to become ever more apparent. Consequently, corporations need to adapt further and to deal with the past while also preparing for the future. So it seems inevitable that difficult times will continue into the future.

This book therefore sets out to examine aspects of the changes to corporate and institutional behaviour which have come about the difficult times of needing to deal with past and future crises. Thus, we focus upon the current situation with respect to CSR while also considering the extent to which the focus has changed so much that we need to think about new approaches to our understanding of corporate behaviour and differing effects in practice. The international origins of the contributors to this volume make this an original contribution taking some of the best ideas from around the world.

This approach is based on the tradition of the Social Responsibility Research Network (a worldwide body of scholars with membership of several thousand), which in its 20-year history has sought to broaden the discourse and to treat all research as inter-related and relevant to business. This tradition has always been to explore the subject widely and to seek relevant solutions, while also sharing best practice. This book is based upon some of the contributions from the Network at our recent conference and shows both commonality and diversity in approaches and effects. Accordingly, the audience of this book is wide and includes but is not limited to academics in different fields including politics, industrial engineering, business, science and social science. This is a multidisciplinary topic.

You will find that the book describes a range of approaches to managing resilience in difficult times which have been adopted around the world. While taking a future orientation, the book addresses a wide range of issues concerning corporate social responsibility in difficult times at both a global level and a more local level. It takes an interdisciplinary global perspective on corporate social responsibility to offer new insights. It is a unique work both in the method used to investigate and also in the implications. Besides, the book can be used in diverse coursework including advanced courses dealing with sustainability—main or supplementary text and supplementary reading for many MBA/DBA courses. Based on the diversity of the chapters, they are divided into three main sections.

The first section deals with global approaches of the theme. These include a view point regarding the role of executive officers and senior executives in CSR communication on social media as a driver of the non-financial performance of the firm. Another chapter is a philosophical approach towards multiple simultaneous natural/unnatural disasters with a view of their aesthetics, philosophy of religion and ethics. The other chapter investigates the Impact of Corporate Social Responsibility on Market Value Creation bearing in mind the Moderating Role of Pressure-sensitive institutional investors. And the last chapter in this section explores the hybridity dilemma considering the role of personal values.

This section is followed by a second one which deals with the regional approach of the topic. Digital transformation of banking systems in Eurasian Economic Union countries is the matter of discussion for the first chapter while the second one investigates the role of whistleblowing as an element of corporate governance in Mauritius. It is then followed by another chapter which evaluates training corporate social responsibility context in a new university out there. The extent of assistance of telecommunicating in businesses during the COVID-19 pandemic is evaluated on the last chapter in this section.

Finally, the last section covers the corporate approaches of the matter. So the section starts with a chapter which questions if companies in Madagascar are sensitive to SCR. The integrated reporting (IR) concept has been emerged with a global coalition in order to make up for the failure of traditional reporting to meet the needs of stakeholders in the aftermath of the global financial crisis. So the second paper in this section evaluates the determinants of integrated reporting assurance in Australian companies. And this chapter is followed by another one which goes to Portuguese companies to analyse the implications of considering the environmental variables into the companies' strategy, management and accounting information systems. And the very last chapter finds out the impact of the COVID-19 pandemic on the strategies and corporate social responsibility of companies in Mauritius.

Shahla Seifi
David Crowther

Contents

Contributors

Muhammad Jahangir Ali Discipline in Accounting and Finance, The University of Newcastle, Callaghan, Australia

Justin Nathanaël Andrianaivoarimanga ISCAM Research Centre, Antananarivo, Madagascar

Nirmal Kumar Betchoo Université des Mascareignes, Pamplemousses, Mauritius

Sudipta Bose Discipline in Accounting and Finance, The University of Newcastle, Callaghan, Australia

Sheistah Bundhoo-Deenoo Charles Telfair Institute, Moka, Mauritius

Raghda El Ebrashi The German University in Cairo, New Cairo, Egypt; Management & Organization, German University in Cairo, Cairo, Egypt

Mohammad Kaleem Galamali Université des Mascareignes, Beau Plan, Mauritius

Kristijan Krkač Zagreb School of Economics and Management, Zagreb, Croatia

Muhammad Hishaam Ibn Afzal Lauthan Rabindranath Tagore Secondary School, Ilot, Mauritius

Shameera Lauthan Department of Software Engineering, Université des Mascareignes, Beau Plan, Mauritius

Ilya V. Maltsevich Institute of Economics of the National Academy of Sciences of Belarus, Business of School of the Belarusian State University, Minsk, Belarus

Natallia V. Maltsevich Institute of Economics of the National Academy of Sciences of Belarus, Business of School of the Belarusian State University, Minsk, Belarus

Dessalegn Mihret Discipline in Accounting and Finance, The University of Newcastle, Callaghan, Australia

Amira Magdy Mirghani The German University in Cairo, New Cairo, Egypt; Management & Organization, German University in Cairo, Cairo, Egypt

Sónia Monteiro Research Centre on Accounting and Taxation (CICF), Polytechnic Institute of Cavado and Ave, Barcelos, Portugal

Girish Napaul University of Mauritius, Reduit, Mauritius

Mahejabeen Peermamode-Mohaboob Université des Mascareignes, Beau Plan, Mauritius

Tatiana V. Proharava Institute of Economics of the National Academy of Sciences of Belarus, Business of School of the Belarusian State University, Minsk, Belarus

Lantoniaina Béatrice Ralijerson ISCAM Research Centre, Antananarivo, Madagascar

Dineshwar Ramdhony University of Mauritius, Reduit, Mauritius

Hajaina Ravoaja ISCAM Research Centre, Antananarivo, Madagascar

Verónica Ribeiro Research Centre on Accounting and Taxation (CICF), Polytechnic Institute of Cavado and Ave, Barcelos, Portugal

Syed Shams Discipline in Accounting and Finance, The University of Newcastle, Callaghan, Australia

Shivani Thakur Dayalbagh Educational Institute, Agra, India;
Janki Devi Memorial College, University of Delhi, Delhi, India

Part I
Global Approaches

Chapter 1
CSR Communication on Social Media as a Driver of the Non-financial Performance of the Firm: Role of Chief Executive Officers and Senior Executives in CSR Communication: A Viewpoint

Shivani Thakur

Abstract CEOs can improve the non-financial performance of the firm by posting CSR initiatives of their firms on social media. CEOs can enhance stakeholder support behaviours and their perspective towards them by disseminating information about their corporate social responsibility (CSR) activities. A company's reputation, stakeholder-company relationships, and other non-financial performance are all improved over time through these actions. This chapter highlights the necessity for CEOs to more actively involve stakeholders in CSR activities using social media because stakeholder's inadequate awareness of and negative perception towards firm's CSR activities continue to be significantly hampered in the firm's attempts to maximize the non-financial performance of the firm through their CSR initiatives. This chapter highlights the importance of social media usage for CSR communication. This chapter presents five action plans that define how CEOs and senior executives can use social media platforms for CSR communication. The chapter highlights that the success of CSR communication can be influenced by many factors, including message content, social media communication platforms, and communication strategies (one-way or two-way communication).

Keywords CEOs · Social media · Non-financial performance · CSR · Communication · Senior executives · Managers

S. Thakur (✉)
Dayalbagh Educational Institute, Agra, India

Janki Devi Memorial College, University of Delhi, Delhi, India

D. Crowther and S. Seifi (eds.), *Corporate Social Responsibility in Difficult Times*, Approaches to Global Sustainability, Markets, and Governance,
https://doi.org/10.1007/978-981-99-2591-9_1

1.1 Corporate Social Responsibility Communication on Social Media: Significant, but not on the Agenda of Chief Executive Officers and Senior Executives

Many CEOs are not making good use of social media platforms for communication purposes (Capriotti & Ruesja, 2018; Malhotra Kubowicz & Malhotra, 2016). Past research (Capriotti & Ruesja, 2018; Parveen et al., 2015) has shown that social media usage among corporations is rapidly expanding. Firms are now building and maintaining public social media profiles in order to boost the social media engagement of their organization, their social network visibility, and their capacity to connect with the online public (Parveen et al., 2015). Many studies also show that CSR communication on social media leads to provide numerous non-financial benefits to the firm, such as stakeholder support, enhanced corporate reputation, positive word of mouth, e-reputation, consumer engagement, enhanced social capital, higher level of content diffusion, and a higher level of endorsement (Araujo & Kollat, 2018; Chen et al., 2017; Fatma et al., 2020; Grover et al., 2019; Jiang & Park, 2022; K. Lee et al., 2013; Zizka, 2017). Companies are under intense pressure to communicate their views and CSR (corporate social responsibility) initiatives, as well as to tell clients of their good deeds in order to appear trustworthy (Kollat & Farache, 2018). CEOs should write more about their company's CSR activities, missions, and visions to establish their corporate image among the public, which could improve their company's reputation (Yue et al., 2019). Fatma and Rahman (2014) found that the majority of banks in India employ CSR measures in their daily operations and disseminate information about these activities on their websites. The actions of the stakeholders are used to categorize the dimensions and sub-dimensions. Results show that banks give their stakeholders more thought and consideration in their corporate statements, which helps them develop their unique identities.

CEOs and senior leaders do not place CSR communication on social media at the top of their priority lists. The number of chief executives of prominent corporations who are engaged on social media remains low. CEOs can influence the impression of their companies through social media, as opposed to waiting for others to drive an image of their companies. Among the Fortune 500 CEOs, just 42 had Twitter accounts in September 2014. Only around 70% of those were actually active and tweeting in a meaningful manner (Malhotra Kubowicz & Malhotra, 2016). Therefore, we are left with this question: How can chief executive officers and senior executives use social media for CSR communication to increase the non-financial performance of the firm?

Elon Musk, the founder and CEO of SpaceX and Tesla Motors Inc., is one prominent Twitter user. Musk regularly tweets several times per month, and his tweets occasionally include interesting and novel information. He tweeted, for instance, on 30 March 2015 that a huge new line of Tesla products would be introduced the following month and that it was "not a car". There was no other way to share the news outside Musk's tweet, which attracted a lot of attention. Additionally, there was a lot of speculative hype surrounding the new product (Malhotra Kubowicz &

Malhotra, 2016). Social media engagement between CEOs and the public strongly impacted how people saw the CEO's approachability and authenticity, leading to improved public satisfaction and trust (Men & Tsai, 2016). According to the upper echelons theory, a CEO's personality will affect an organization's performance (S. Wang & Chen, 2020). When CEOs communicate with empathy and confidence, their followers are more likely to see them as supportive friends and role models, which improves their enthusiasm for the company (Tsai & Men, 2017).

1.2 Corporate Social Responsibility Communication on Social Media: The Hidden Treasure

The past study research also showed that firms on Twitter that tweeted very persistently about CSR were linked with increased intensity of content diffusion and endorsement in general (Araujo & Kollat, 2018). CSR communication efforts, such as notifying, retweeting, and mentioning, strengthen a firm by consolidating its network position and earning support from the public (i.e. emotional, influencer, and knowledge support) (Jiang & Park, 2022). The most widely used channels for CSR communications were company websites and CSR reports; nevertheless, only general corporate Facebook pages and press releases, which had an impact on news headlines, were successful in developing CSR reputation (S. Y. Lee, 2016). Communication about corporate social responsibility (CSR) on social media is connected with stakeholder involvement (Kucukusta et al., 2019). Findings revealed that internal CSR practices, such as employment security, a positive work environment, skills enhancement, diversity and inclusion, and work-life balance, enhance interpersonal connections and employee engagement; the positive correlation between internal CSR and engagement and pro-social behaviour is mediated through social exchange relationships; additionally, employee engagement mediates the relationship between internal CSR and employees' advocacy and scouting behaviours (Y. Lee, 2022). Framing strategies can be useful in crafting CSR messaging that will be favourably seen by young consumers. CSR messages may stress company competence with less emphasis on moral concepts and commitments (Schmeltz, 2014).

Further, past research indicates that managers of enterprises operating in the credibility goods market should give serious consideration to the expansion of their use of various dialogical CSR communication tactics in order to boost the level of customer confidence and positive attitudes towards brands (Dai & Reich, 2022). Participation in a CSR programme can improve an organization's sense of its own value and its social standing. Consequently, participants' intentions to spread positive word of mouth regarding the company's CSR initiatives become stronger as a direct result of these increases (Park & Kim, 2022). Consumer's electronic word of mouth is correlated with the level of CSR activity on social media (Fatma et al., 2020). The KLD ratings of the 500 most successful companies in the United States were gathered, and regression was used to analyse the results. According to the research conducted on the Twitter accounts of Fortune 500 companies, a higher CSR rating is a significant predictor of an earlier adoption of Twitter, speedier development of online presence (following), a higher receptiveness to the company's identity (replies and mentions), and higher popularity of the messages and retweets (K. Lee et al., 2013). Community issues and environmental challenges were the two most often disclosed topics by the companies (Anadol et al., 2015).

According to R. Wang and Huang (2018), in comparison with the exterior CSR message and the CEO's personal life message, the internal CSR message was found to elicit superior views, trust, contentment, control reciprocity, and loyalty towards the firm from the firm's stakeholders. It was discovered that there was a significant two-way relationship between the information's source and the CSR communication's format and behaviour intentions towards the organization. This interaction was found to have an effect on behaviour intention towards the organization. Participatory discussion, which may be had in both directions, is essential to effective communication via social media (Zizka, 2017). Engaging customers in message-sharing actions to achieve the desired results presents its own unique set of challenges, despite the fact that digital channels make it possible to reach huge audiences in a relatively short amount of time. Because of the large number of consumers who get their information from social media, businesses have begun using these platforms to communicate their commitment to social responsibility. Companies have a responsibility to learn what factors increase the spread of their messages about sustainability; however, they must also be careful not to exaggerate their commitment to sustainability, as this could be misconducted as a form of greenwashing (Adi & Grigore, 2015). Consumers have a tendency to form their perceptions about an organization through the use of two associations: corporate ability (CA), which focuses on expertise in providing high-quality products, and corporate social responsibility (CSR), which tends to focus on social obligations (Chen et al., 2017). Positive attitudes towards an organization are more likely to merge when consumers are aware of the charitable and socially responsible actions taken by that organization (Naatu et al., 2022).

According to Dai and Reich (2022), a dialogical communication strategy is significantly more effective than a monological communication strategy at increasing consumer confidence in the brand of credibility items, as well as the consumer's desire to purchase the goods and positive word of mouth. A company's corporate reputation and performance factors, such as likeability, performance, competence, and quality, can be improved via CSR communication on social media (Dai & Reich, 2022). When it comes to social media sharing, internal CSR messaging does matter. The internal CSR message generated stronger views of trust, satisfaction, control mutuality, and organizational commitment among stakeholders than the outward CSR messages and the CEOs' personal life messages (R. Wang & Huang, 2018).

The use of social media for corporate disclosures has several significant implications, and the first one is that it helps to minimize the knowledge gap that exists between a company and its investors (Nuseir & Qasim, 2021). According to social capital theory, social networks, norms, and trust enable public cooperation and coordination for mutual benefits. CSR disclosure via social media is that it is helpful in building social capital, which in turn leads to enhanced corporate reputation (Grover et al., 2019). The public is evolving into responsible customers that encourage businesses to work towards societal betterment. The use of social media in corporate social actions has the potential to influence an organization's online reputation and commitment (Dutot et al., 2016). A social network is a collection of social actors, such as people, organizations, and interest groups, that are connected by "a rule that specifies whether, how, and to what extent any two units are associated to each other", according to the network theory of stakeholder management. Jiang and Park (2022) investigated how a company was able to build its network power through a number of different types of CSR communication activities, which led to the subsequent generation of support from stakeholders. Maiorescu-Murphy (2022) analysed five American companies' diversity communications that were both business- and CSR-focused, as well as the responses those organizations received on Twitter. Companies that spoke more about how diversity affects their bottom line had higher levels of user agreement than those who just discussed diversity from the perspective of corporate social responsibility.

A company's reputation, brand attitude, and purchase intention can all be positively impacted by CSR communication on social media; nevertheless, consumer interaction with CSR posts has been underwhelming (Fernández et al., 2022). Additionally, managers of firms should seriously consider increasing the usage of a variety of dialogical CSR communication tactics in order to raise the amount of confidence that consumers have in brands and the supporting behaviours that they exhibit towards those brands (Dai & Reich, 2022). Simply communicating messages related to corporate social responsibility may result in beneficial effects for companies (Harrison et al., 2022). Park and Kim (2022) studied the impact of participatory corporate social responsibility on customer feedback in a social media setting and evaluated it as a strategy for consumer empowerment. Results show that a company's CSR programme increases people's perceptions of their social value and self-efficacy, which strengthens their intentions to spread the news about the company's CSR initiatives. This is a key finding in support of the social cognitive theory. The findings imply that customer empowerment through participatory corporate social responsibility has the potential to increase a business's reputation as a "admired" corporation.

The stakeholder theory defines CSR as a corporation that simultaneously assumes necessary duties to its creditors, government, consumers, employees, communities, and other stakeholders while bearing economic responsibilities to its stakeholders. Therefore, it is possible to increase consumers' intention to remain loyal to brands by deliberately utilizing emotional appeals in CSR messaging on social media platforms (He et al., 2022). Communication about corporate social responsibility on social networking sites is an effective way to engage customers, as it not only helps customers identify with organizations but also encourages them to spread positive word of mouth online. It is important for managers to post on social media about their organizations' CSR activity in order to have a positive influence on identification and electronic word of mouth (Fatma et al., 2020). According to CSR communication theory, this is consistent with simply spreading CSR messages which could have a good impact on businesses (Harrison et al., 2022). The comments left by customers on a company's post—both favourable and negative—reflect their opinions of the company's actions. As a result, these comments may, to some extent, indicate whether or not the company's claims are consistent with what it actually does (Chen et al., 2017). This is consistent with the attribution theory. According to the attribution theory, when a consumer views a company favourably and perceives it to be socially responsible, they are motivated to reciprocate favourably (Wei et al., 2021).

Furthermore, two-way, interactive conversation is the foundation of successful communication through social media. Strategic CSR communication should initially concentrate on two stakeholder groups, namely employees and consumers (Zizka, 2017). Significant shifts have occurred in the production and dissemination of corporate information as a result of the advent of social media as a corporate disclosure channel (Lei et al., 2019). Colleoni (2013) explored which corporate communication tactics used in online social media are most successful at bridging the gap between businesses' corporate social responsibility agenda and stakeholders' societal expectations, boosting businesses' legitimacy.

Elon Musk, the founder and CEO of SpaceX and Tesla Motors Inc., is one prominent Twitter user. Musk regularly tweets several times per month, and his tweets occasionally include interesting and novel information. He frequently interacts with other Twitter users on Twitter (Fig. 1.1).

(Elon Musk, CEO of Tesla) "Population collapse due to low birth rates is a much bigger risk to civilization than global warming" on 26th August 2022.

(Elon Musk, CEO of Tesla) "Despite Tesla doing more for the environment than any company ever!" on 18th May 2022.

Similarly, Chuck Robbins, CEO of Cisco Systems and Rich Handler, CEO of Jefferies group, regularly tweeted several times about the CSR initiatives of their firms (Fig. 1.2).

(Chuck Robbins, CEO of Cisco Systems) "I believe every day should be #WomensEqualityDay. Today, we commemorate the adoption of the 19th amendment

Fig. 1.1 Elon Musk, CEO of Tesla, replying to a Twitter user* (*https://twitter.com/elonmusk/status/1564023672737828865)

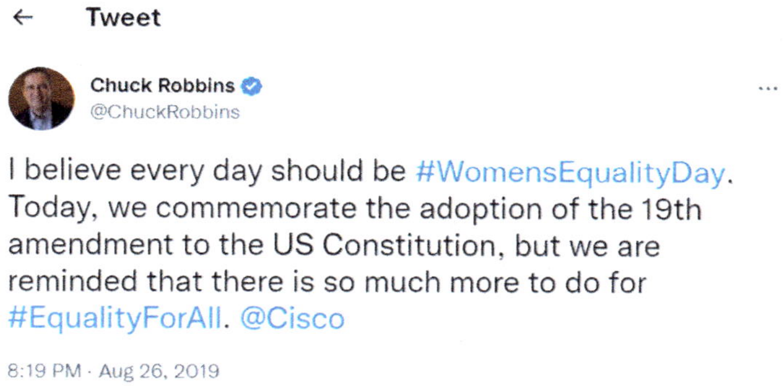

Fig. 1.2 Chuck Robbins, CEO of Cisco systems, sharing tweets related to women equality* (*https://twitter.com/ChuckRobbins/status/1165999823431987201)

to the US Constitution, but we are reminded that there is so much more to do for #EqualityForAll. @Cisco".

(Rich Handler, CEO of Jefferies Group) "Celebrating the biggest contributors to #jwin #breastcancerawareness! #jefferies #culture #tribestrong #tilmanserves-greatfood https://t.co/mr5uY2woFH".

This article presents five essential action plans that CEOs and senior C-suite executives can use in order to enhance the non-financial performance of the firm and to adopt a visionary long-term strategy for CSR communication using social media platforms.

1.3 An Agenda for CEOs and Senior-Level Executives: Five Essential Actions to Drive the Non-Financial Performance of the Firm via CSR Communication on Social Media

1.3.1 Action 1: Pay Close Attention to CSR Communication on Social Media

The first step for CEOs who are still afraid to use social media should be to listen and observe. It is possible to obtain information about stakeholders and determine what is being said about their businesses by keeping an eye on the online dialogue. Apply the "rule of five" by following five additional accounts and five additional persons (such as colleagues and business executives) (e.g. trade publications and competitors) (Ross, 2015). CEOs can find out which type of CSR information must be shared on social media and which type of CSR information leads to higher stakeholder engagement, enhanced purchase intention, promote customer trust, customer loyalty, public relations, brand admiration, corporate reputation, e-reputation, higher levels of content diffusion and endorsement, and positive word of mouth. Past studies (Uzunoğlu et al., 2017) indicate that product/economic and ethical CSR-related tweets are associated with increased purchase intention than product-related CSR tweets. Firms can successfully improve consumer's CSR awareness using face-to-face, electronic, and interactive internet channels, which can persuade consumers to think and act more favourably towards the company's product and brand (Dai & Reich, 2022). Consumer engagement and identification with brands are facilitated by CSR communication on SNSs, which also increases eWOM (Fatma et al., 2020). Promoting CSR initiatives that are suitable for the company increases the credibility of its CSR communication (Go & Bortree, 2017).

The usage of interactive organizational communication has the potential to increase message credibility and sentiments of engagement with the organization (Eberle et al., 2013). In addition to service quality and value for money, clients have other concerns. Communication of both social CSR and environmental CSR is helpful in increasing PWOM while decreasing MWOM and offers a safety net that is helpful in reducing NWOM about the company (Vo et al., 2019). Customer loyalty is influenced by CSR communication both directly and through admiration. Customers get a sense of admiration for their company when they learn that it shares information about its CSR initiatives with them on social media, and this admiration significantly boosts customer loyalty (Ahmad et al., 2021).

Gaining the trust of highly engaged customers, especially when they are young, can be accomplished by using symmetric communication tactics (two-way communication) (Kollat & Farache, 2018). Business communication used to be one way, but as the digital era has developed, this model is being overtaken by an open communication framework in which interested parties, especially customers, have a voice and participate in the choices of an organization (Ahmad et al., 2021). Usage of a response and involvement strategy to communicate the CSR activities of companies is helpful in eliminating the effect of negative and sceptical comments on social media about the companies (Song & Wen, 2020). Involvement strategy includes responding and replying to stakeholder's comments on social media platforms.

1.3.2 Action 2: Make Sensible Platform Selections for CSR Communication

CEOs can find the appropriate social media platform if they are scared to share their identity online. Internally or on the firm's website, CEOs can begin by posting a brief welcome video on firm's careers page. Alternatively, CEOs might start with a basic LinkedIn profile and then advance to a lengthy influencer article (Ross, 2015). Past studies (S. Y. Lee, 2016) indicate that the most popular CSR communication channels were corporate websites and CSR reports, but only press releases, which had an impact on news items, and general business Facebook pages were useful for building CSR reputation. If misused, social media may be a two-edged sword. They may have a favourable, negative, or no impact on how CSR initiatives affect the company's reputation (Benitez et al., 2020).

The features of various social networking platforms vary. For example, Twitter is one of the best social media platforms for CSR communication for the following reasons: (a) through the Twitter application programming interface. Twitter data can be accessed without charge. The tweets can be extracted based on topics, key phrases, or timelines and then objectively analysed. (b) Twitter is one of the most rapidly expanding social media platforms due to its massive user base and broad exposure. (c) Thirdly, in comparison with other social media sites like Facebook, Twitter users are more likely to actively engage in the following actions: following other users, posting, liking, and publicly sharing information. (d) The fourth benefit of user-generated information on Twitter is that it is more visible because it is indexed in organic search results (Grover et al., 2019). A CEO can communicate directly and personally with their network of followers on Twitter. Stakeholders can show their support for a CEO and the firm by following them on Twitter. The CEO's ability to influence and reach out to others grows along with the extent of the CEO's network. CSR-dedicated Facebook pages are also helpful in engaging stakeholders (Shane-Simpson et al., 2018). The general audience was more interested in posts that included multimedia elements like links, photographs, and graphics, as well as interactive messages that prompted participation on social media (Abitbol & Lee, 2017).

Due to the fact that information on LinkedIn can be text-only and the average posting frequency is not high, it is one of the easiest social media platforms to maintain a presence on. Additionally, LinkedIn provides a number of platform-specific advantages, like the chance to connect with a niche professional audience and simple access to information that is popular within a given field. Instagram and YouTube are still unpopular among CEOs (Ross, 2015).

1.3.3 Action 3: Adopt a "Mindset of a Media Firm" and Involve Followers

CEOs should use the company website or YouTube channel as a media platform to promote thought leadership or CSR content and seize the trend of telling the firm's narrative. Even a brief clip from a town hall meeting or video of a CEO giving a speech about firm's CSR initiatives should be shown frequently (Ross, 2015).

It's one thing for a firm to declare its commitment to change but quite another to provide individuals with the resources they need to carry out the change for themselves. The latter fosters a sense of connection and community, while the former can come out as self-promotion. Making it possible for people to get involved in a company's CSR initiatives is crucial. Social media users have the power to increase involvement, strengthen the impact, and reshape public conversation to be more consumer-driven, which impacts the validity of an organization's actions beyond simply raising knowledge of those programmes among the wider public (Andersen, 2021).

1.3.4 Action 4: Learn to Accept Criticism and Use the Storytelling Approach

Everyone dislikes criticism; CEOs have to learn to accept both the good and the bad. As the CEO, do your best not to take it personally and remind yourself that your role is one of listening and learning (Andersen, 2021). The perceived authenticity and approachability of the CEO were significantly improved through CEO-public engagement, which in turn led to improved public satisfaction and trust. Social media interaction between the general public and CEOs directly impacts company-public relations (Men & Tsai, 2016).

Every CEO's communications plan should include storytelling, and CSR campaigns may be the one area where it is most crucial. The foundation of social responsibility is in the charitable work that a company does, and if a brand has the chance to streamline its messaging and highlight its own initiatives, its followers are more likely to support them. Effective ways to tell these stories include heavily utilizing photos and videos, sharing testimonies from those the initiatives have aided, creating calls to action using the voices of volunteers and those providing the services, or emphasizing the organization's inherent difficulties and how they are being overcome (Anderson, 2021).

1.3.5 Action 5: Make it on Your Own and Post Frequently

Although outsourcing sociability may save time, staff members are quick to detect deception. Although CEOs can ask for help, it is always better to serve as the editor-in-chief. The use of CSR on social media requires a careful balance. While excessive information can be unappealing, ineffective promotion will fall flat. According to a 2017 IBM survey, specific businesses that advertise their CSR actions on social media gain increased fan loyalty (Anderson, 2021) (Table 1.1).

Table 1.1 Essential action plans that CEOs and senior C-suite executives can use in order to enhance the non-financial performance of the firm

Recommendations	Benefits	How does CSR communication on social media provide non-financial benefits?
CEOs should use a network approach for CSR communication	Stakeholder support	As opposed to conventional message-centric or organization-centric communication approaches, CEOs who adopt the network approach consistently inform, retweet, and make mention of the company's CSR initiatives on social media. Then, a company will be empowered by the CEO's CSR communication efforts by consolidating its network position and winning public support (Jiang & Park, 2022)
CEOs should select appropriate CSR policies, create compelling CSR content, increase network virality, and combat and avoid social media opposition through unfavourable reviews	Enhanced purchase intention	Customers get a sense of appreciation (admiration) for the company when they see an organization's CSR communication on social media. Additionally, people experience admiration for choosing to support a socially conscious brand. As a result, these pleasant feelings and emotions encourage consumers to show greater loyalty and raise their likelihood of making purchases (Gupta et al., 2021)
CEOs of businesses in the consumer products sector ought to think about using more dialogic CSR communication techniques, which is helpful in improving consumer trust and supportive behaviour towards brands	Promote customer trust, positive word of mouth, stakeholder engagement and supportive behaviour towards brands	When CEOs use dialogic CSR communication while communicating CSR activities of the firm, then consumers feel more encouraged and act more favourably towards brands which in turn leads to enhanced customer trust, positive word of mouth about the company, enhanced stakeholder engagement, and supportive behaviour towards a brand (Chu & Chen, 2019; Dai & Reich, 2022; Grover et al., 2019)
CEOs should respond to stakeholder's comments on social media and should use appropriate use of mentions and hashtags on social media platforms	Higher levels of content diffusion and endorsement	When CEOs use a two-way communication strategy on social media. Reply and interact with stakeholders (including customers) on the social media platform, and then the stakeholders feel connected with CEOs. They retweet and like CEOs' tweets, which leads to higher levels of information diffusion and content endorsement (Araujo & Kollat, 2018; Etter, 2014; Grover et al., 2019)
CEOs should use CSR communication from the marketing perspective, which helps increase consumer loyalty and brand admiration	Enhanced public relations, customer loyalty and consumer brand admiration	When CEOs use social media to share information about their CSR initiatives with many stakeholders, including customers, it fosters positive consumer perceptions of the brand and ultimately promotes customer loyalty and brand admiration (Ahmad et al., 2021; Laroche et al., 2012; Wei et al., 2021)

(continued)

Table 1.1 (continued)

Recommendations	Benefits	How does CSR communication on social media provide non-financial benefits?
CEOs should strategically communicate about all dimensions of CSR, i.e. economic, legal, ethical, and discretionary	E-Reputation and corporate reputation	When CEOs post CSR messages related to all dimensions of CSR, such as economic, legal, ethical, and discretionary, on social media, it enhances awareness among the stakeholders, which leads to improved social capital, and better social capital leads to higher corporate reputation or e-reputation (Grover et al., 2019)

1.4 Conclusion

Academics have paid a lot of consideration to how CSR communication on social media is important, but less emphasis has been paid to how CEOs' usage of social media for CSR communication influences the non-financial performance of the firm. This article highlights the importance of understanding how social media platforms can be used by CEOs for CSR communication in order to enhance the non-financial performance of the firm. Our study is relevant for researchers, practitioners, and regulators. This paper highlights the importance of CSR communication via social media in order to identify the association between CSR communication on social media and non-financial performance of the firm.

A CEO recognizes a critical issue that the organization does not consider to be significant, raises it to receive widespread attention, and coaches the organization towards change by developing the necessary infrastructure, competencies, behaviours, context, and ambitions. Utilizing social media for CSR communication is one such burning platform where the flames are not clearly visible to all organizational members. Six crucial steps have been outlined in this article: senior executives and CEOs should (1) pay close attention towards CSR communication on social media, (2) make sensible platform selections for CSR communication, (3) adopt a "mindset of a media firm" and involve followers, (4) learn to accept criticism and use storytelling approach, and (5) make it on your own and post frequently.

This article highlights that CEOs' CSR communication plays an important role in stakeholder engagement. This article is an instrument used by CEOs who can play a dedicated role in CSR activities through social media platforms. CEOs should post CSR messages on Twitter because social capital from online communities can help build a company's reputation. The article raises the significance of two-way CSR communication on social media by CEOs. CEOs can improve stakeholder support behaviours (such as increased purchase intention, reputation, and investment in the company) as well as their point of view towards them by engaging in corporate social responsibility (CSR) activities. In the long run, these activities also help to improve the company's reputation, the relationships it has with its stakeholders, and the advocacy of its stakeholders. Future research can investigate how CEOs' CSR communication on social media improves financial performance of the firm.

References

Abitbol, A., & Lee, S. Y. (2017). Messages on CSR-dedicated Facebook pages: What works and what doesn't. *Public Relations Review, 43*(4), 796–808. https://doi.org/10.1016/j.pubrev.2017.05.002

Adi, A., & Grigore, G. (2015). Communicating csr on social media: The case of pfizer's social media communications in Europe. *Developments in Corporate Governance and Responsibility, 7*, 143–163. https://doi.org/10.1108/S2043-052320150000007009

Ahmad, N., Naveed, R. T., Scholz, M., Irfan, M., Usman, M., & Ahmad, I. (2021). CSR communication through social media: A litmus test for banking consumers' loyalty. *Sustainability (Switzerland), 13*(4), 1–16. https://doi.org/10.3390/su13042319

Anadol, Y., Youssef, M. A., & Thiruvattal, E. (2015). Consumer reaction towards corporate social responsibility in United Arab Emirates. *Social Responsibility Journal, 11*(1), 19–35. https://doi.org/10.1108/SRJ-07-2013-0081

Andersen, E. (2021). How should companies communicate CSR on social media? Forbes. Retrieved February 17, 2021 from https://www.forbes.com/sites/forbescommunicationscouncil/2021/02/17/how-should-companies-communicate-csr-on-social-media/?sh=498b5dd42c2d

Araujo, T., & Kollat, J. (2018). Communicating effectively about CSR on Twitter: The power of engaging strategies and storytelling elements. *Internet Research, 28*(2), 419–431. https://doi.org/10.1108/IntR-04-2017-0172

Benitez, J., Ruiz, L., Castillo, A., & Llorens, J. (2020). How corporate social responsibility activities influence employer reputation: The role of social media capability. *Decision Support Systems, 129*(May 2019), 113223. https://doi.org/10.1016/j.dss.2019.113223

Capriotti, P., & Ruesja, L. (2018). How CEOs use Twitter: A comparative analysis of Global and Latin American companies. *International Journal of Information Management, 39*(December 2017), 242–248. https://doi.org/10.1016/j.ijinfomgt.2018.01.003

Chen, Z. F., Hong, C., & Li, C. (2017). The joint effect of association-based corporate posting strategy and eWOM comment valence on social media. *Internet Research, 27*(5), 1039–1057. https://doi.org/10.1108/IntR-05-2016-0140

Chu, S. C., & Chen, H. T. (2019). Impact of consumers' corporate social responsibility-related activities in social media on brand attitude, electronic word-of-mouth intention, and purchase intention: A study of Chinese consumer behavior. *Journal of Consumer Behaviour, 18*(6), 453–462. https://doi.org/10.1002/cb.1784

Colleoni, E. (2013). CSR communication strategies for organizational legitimacy in social media. *Corporate Communications, 18*(2), 228–248. https://doi.org/10.1108/13563281311319508

Dai, W., & Reich, A. Z. (2022). The differential impact of monological and dialogical corporate social responsibility communication strategies on brand trust in the credence goods market. *Asia Pacific Journal of Marketing and Logistics*. https://doi.org/10.1108/APJML-08-2021-0583

Dutot, V., Lacalle Galvez, E., & Versailles, D. W. (2016). CSR communications strategies through social media and influence on e-reputation: An exploratory study. *C, 54*(2), 363–389. https://doi.org/10.1108/MD-01-2015-0015

Eberle, D., Berens, G., & Li, T. (2013). The impact of interactive corporate social responsibility communication on corporate reputation. *Journal of Business Ethics, 118*(4), 731–746. https://doi.org/10.1007/s10551-013-1957-y

Etter, M. (2014). Broadcasting, reacting, engaging – three strategies for CSR communication in twitter. *Journal of Communication Management, 18*(4), 322–342. https://doi.org/10.1108/JCOM-01-2013-0007

Fatma, M., & Rahman, Z. (2014). Building a corporate identity using corporate social responsibility: A website based study of Indian banks. *Social Responsibility Journal, 10*(4), 591–601. https://doi.org/10.1108/SRJ-01-2013-0002

Fatma, M., Ruiz, A. P., Khan, I., & Rahman, Z. (2020). The effect of CSR engagement on eWOM on social media. *International Journal of Organizational Analysis, 28*(4), 941–956. https://doi.org/10.1108/IJOA-10-2019-1895

Fernández, P., Hartmann, P., & Apaolaza, V. (2022). What drives CSR communication effectiveness on social media? A process-based theoretical framework and research agenda. *International Journal of Advertising, 41*(3), 385–413. https://doi.org/10.1080/02650487.2021.1947016

Go, E., & Bortree, D. S. (2017). What and How to Communicate CSR? The Role of CSR fit, Modality Interactivity, and Message Interactivity on Social Networking Sites. *Journal of Promotion Management, 23*(5), 727–747. https://doi.org/10.1080/10496491.2017.1297983

Grover, P., Kar, A. K., & Ilavarasan, P. V. (2019). Impact of corporate social responsibility on reputation—Insights from tweets on sustainable development goals by CEOs. *International Journal of Information Management, 48*(November 2018), 39–52. https://doi.org/10.1016/j.ijinfomgt.2019.01.009

Gupta, S., Nawaz, N., Alfalah, A. A., Naveed, R. T., Muneer, S., & Ahmad, N. (2021). The relationship of csr communication on social media with consumer purchase intention and brand admiration. *Journal of Theoretical and Applied Electronic Commerce Research, 16*(5), 1217–1230. https://doi.org/10.3390/jtaer16050068

Harrison, V., Vafeiadis, M., Diddi, P., & Conlin, J. (2022). The impact of CSR on nonprofit outcomes: How the choice of corporate partner influences reputation and supportive intentions. *Corporate Communications, 27*(2), 205–225. https://doi.org/10.1108/CCIJ-02-2021-0020

He, Z., Liu, S., & Countryman, C. C. (2022). Pride or empathy ? *Exploring Effective CSR Communication Strategies on Social Media Strategies.* https://doi.org/10.1108/IJCHM-09-2021-1182

Jiang, Y. (Nicole), & Park, H. (2022). Mapping networks in corporate social responsibility communication on social media: A new approach to exploring the influence of communication tactics on public responses. *Public Relations Review, 48*(1), 102143. https://doi.org/10.1016/j.pubrev.2021.102143

Kollat, J., & Farache, F. (2018). Achieving consumer trust on Twitter via CSR communication. *Journal of Consumer Marketing, 34*(6), 505–514. https://doi.org/10.1108/JCM-03-2017-2127

Kucukusta, D., Perelygina, M., & Lam, W. S. (2019). CSR communication strategies and stakeholder engagement of upscale hotels in social media. *International Journal of Contemporary Hospitality Management, 31*(5), 2129–2148. https://doi.org/10.1108/IJCHM-06-2018-0484

Laroche, M., Habibi, M. R., Richard, M. O., & Sankaranarayanan, R. (2012). The effects of social media based brand communities on brand community markers, value creation practices, brand trust and brand loyalty. *Computers in Human Behavior, 28*(5), 1755–1767. https://doi.org/10.1016/j.chb.2012.04.016

Lee, K., Oh, W. Y., & Kim, N. (2013). Social Media for Socially Responsible Firms: Analysis of Fortune 500's Twitter Profiles and their CSR/CSIR Ratings. *Journal of Business Ethics, 118*(4), 791–806. https://doi.org/10.1007/s10551-013-1961-2

Lee, S. Y. (2016). How can companies succeed in forming CSR reputation? *Corporate Communications, 21*(4), 435–449. https://doi.org/10.1108/CCIJ-01-2016-0009

Lee, Y. (2022). Linking internal CSR with the positive communicative behaviors of employees: The role of social exchange relationships and employee engagement. *Social Responsibility Journal, 18*(2), 348–367. https://doi.org/10.1108/SRJ-04-2020-0121

Lei, L. (Gillian), Li, Y., & Luo, Y. (2019). Production and dissemination of corporate information in social media: A review. *Journal of Accounting Literature, 42*(January), 29–43. https://doi.org/10.1016/j.acclit.2019.02.002

Maiorescu-Murphy, R. D. (2022). Business-centered versus socially responsible corporate diversity communication. An assessment of stakeholder (dis)agreement on Twitter. *Public Relations Review, 48*(1), 102138. https://doi.org/10.1016/j.pubrev.2021.102138

Malhotra Kubowicz, C., & Malhotra, A. (2016). How CEOs Can Leverage Twitter: University of Warwick eResources. *MIT Sloan Management Review, 57*(2).

Men, L. R., & Tsai, W. H. S. (2016). Public engagement with CEOs on social media: Motivations and relational outcomes. *Public Relations Review, 42*(5), 932–942. https://doi.org/10.1016/j.pubrev.2016.08.001

Naatu, F., Nyarko, S. A., Munim, Z. H., & Alon, I. (2022). Crowd-out effect on consumers attitude towards corporate social responsibility communication. *Technological Forecasting and Social Change, 177*(July 2021), 121544. https://doi.org/10.1016/j.techfore.2022.121544

Nuseir, M., & Qasim, A. (2021). Investor relations in the era of social media: Systematic literature review of social media as a strategic corporate disclosure tool. *Journal of Financial Reporting and Accounting, 19*(5), 819–838. https://doi.org/10.1108/JFRA-06-2020-0160

Park, H., & Kim, S. Y. (2022). Consumer empowerment in corporate social responsibility: The effect of participatory CSR on company admiration and word-of-mouth communications. *Corporate Communications, 27*(2), 346–367. https://doi.org/10.1108/CCIJ-02-2021-0025

Parveen, F., Jaafar, N. I., & Ainin, S. (2015). Social media usage and organizational performance: Reflections of Malaysian social media managers. *Telematics and Informatics, 32*(1), 67–78. https://doi.org/10.1016/j.tele.2014.03.001

Ross, L. (2015). What CEOs have learned about social media. Harvard Business Review, Published on HBR.org on May 18 2015 https://hbr.org/2015/05/what-ceos-have-learned-about-social-media

Schmeltz, L. (2014). Introducing value-based framing as a strategy for communicating CSR. *Social Responsibility Journal, 10*(1), 184–206. https://doi.org/10.1108/SRJ-06-2012-0065

Shane-Simpson, C., Manago, A., Gaggi, N., & Gillespie-Lynch, K. (2018). Why do college students prefer Facebook, Twitter, or Instagram? Site affordances, tensions between privacy and self-expression, and implications for social capital. *Computers in Human Behavior, 86*, 276–288. https://doi.org/10.1016/j.chb.2018.04.041

Song, B., & Wen, J. (2020). Online corporate social responsibility communication strategies and stakeholder engagements: A comparison of controversial versus noncontroversial industries. *Corporate Social Responsibility and Environmental Management, 27*(2), 881–896. https://doi.org/10.1002/csr.1852

Tsai, W. H. S., & Men, L. R. (2017). Social CEOs: The effects of CEOs' communication styles and parasocial interaction on social networking sites. *New Media and Society, 19*(11), 1848–1867. https://doi.org/10.1177/1461444816643922

Uzunoğlu, E., Türkel, S., & Yaman Akyar, B. (2017). Engaging consumers through corporate social responsibility messages on social media: An experimental study. *Public Relations Review, 43*(5), 989–997. https://doi.org/10.1016/j.pubrev.2017.03.013

Vo, T. T., Xiao, X., & Ho, S. Y. (2019). How does corporate social responsibility engagement influence word of mouth on twitter? Evidence from the airline industry. *Journal of Business Ethics, 157*(2), 525–542. https://doi.org/10.1007/s10551-017-3679-z

Wang, R., & Huang, Y. (2018). Communicating corporate social responsibility (CSR) on social media: How do message source and types of CSR messages influence stakeholders' perceptions? *Corporate Communications, 23*(3), 326–341. https://doi.org/10.1108/CCIJ-07-2017-0067

Wang, S., & Chen, X. (2020). Recognizing CEO personality and its impact on business performance: Mining linguistic cues from social media. *Information and Management, 57*(5), 103173. https://doi.org/10.1016/j.im.2019.103173

Wei, G., Lin, W., Yanxiong, W., Jingdong, Y., & Musse, S. Y. (2021). The relationship of sustainability communication on social media with banking consumers' loyalty through e-WOM. *Sustainability (Switzerland), 13*(7), 1–13. https://doi.org/10.3390/su13073832

Yue, C. A., Thelen, P., Robinson, K., & Men, L. R. (2019). How do CEOs communicate on Twitter? A comparative study between Fortune 200 companies and top startup companies. *Corporate Communications, 24*(3), 532–552. https://doi.org/10.1108/CCIJ-03-2019-0031

Zizka, L. (2017). The (mis)use of social media to communicate CSR in hospitality: Increasing stakeholders' (dis)engagement through social media. *Journal of Hospitality and Tourism Technology, 8*(1), 73–86. https://doi.org/10.1108/JHTT-07-2016-0037

Chapter 2
Un/natural Disasters III: Aesthetics, Religion, and Ethics and of Multiple Simultaneous Un/natural Disasters

Kristijan Krkač

Abstract In this paper, the author continues with developing a philosophy of *multiple simultaneous un/natural disasters* (MSDs) in terms of the basic development of aesthetics, philosophy of religion, and ethics of MSDs. The paper is a continuation of the research from the initial papers, namely "Un/natural disasters, Philosophy of multiple simultaneous un/natural disasters" (Krkač, 2022a) and Un/natural disasters II, Epistemology and ontology of multiple simultaneous un/natural disasters (Krkač, 2022b). The main issues in this text are aesthetics, philosophy of religion, and ethics of and in multiple simultaneous un/natural disasters in terms of setting the scene. These are being analyzed in conceptual-morphological terms. The critical finding concerned with the three mentioned aspects is the following: concerning aesthetics that the dichotomy of disaster-ugly vs. non-disaster-beautiful doesn't apply universally; concerning religion that it can produce a lot of confusion and wrong beliefs and actions if misused during MSDs; and concerning ethics that morality and ethics of MSDs are determined by concepts that are not available in traditional moral and ethical theories, namely by proper attention, adaptation, and responsiveness (AAR) of human action before, during, and after an MSD.

Keywords Un/natural disasters · Multiple simultaneous disasters · Aesthetics · Philosophy of religion · Ethics

2.1 Introduction

2.1.1 A Remark on the Method and Structure of Analysis

Things are rarely simple. This is why we know so little. Especially in philosophy. Twentieth century philosophy is at least partly marked by challenging its own traditional necessary and sufficient conditions, namely its *genus* and *differentia*. Concerning the *genus* of philosophy, moving from it as something that *falls under*

K. Krkač (✉)
Zagreb School of Economics and Management, Zagreb, Croatia

D. Crowther and S. Seifi (eds.), *Corporate Social Responsibility in Difficult Times*, Approaches to Global Sustainability, Markets, and Governance,
https://doi.org/10.1007/978-981-99-2591-9_2

the humanities toward something that *falls under the sciences* is obvious as well as moving other way around toward art in general. However, not so much regarding the results of these movements, philosophy became neither science, nor art, not even resembling them sufficiently.

Concerning the *differentia*, various obvious moves were made, for instance, the movement from *abstract and universal* toward *concrete and particular* issues resembling more and more to old-school casuistry manuals, or modern case studies. Also, obvious is the move from *theory* to *practice*, from *thought* to *action* (no matter if the movement from *models* to *modeling* was actually made decades ago by Wittgenstein, see Điri et al., 2016). Under this movement especially interesting are those changes in its *differentia* which fall under the movement from *reason* to *experiment*, despite the fact that beyond *Gedanken experiment* it is pretty unclear what a *philosophical experiment* is, and move from *theoretical* to *clinical* aspects of philosophical activity almost as if it resembles medicine. Last but not least, there is a movement from *unpopular* to *popular* issues almost as if philosophy so keenly tries to be *liked* (papers and books on various topics in popular philosophy come in great amounts nowadays, but their quality is far from unquestionable). This diversity in its *differentia* can be described by analogy with the interest of parents or grandparents in what their children and grandchildren are learning and studying. If there are many children and grandchildren, there will be many interests. If all of this stands for philosophy, then it surely stands for aesthetics, philosophy of religion, and ethics as well.

In light of previously described, to deal with moral, religious, and aesthetical issues of multiple simultaneous un/natural disasters (MSDs) is perhaps expected to go along with these new movements in philosophy. However, I don't have the slightest motive to engage in them. At the same time, I don't regard the traditional concept of philosophy useful, and therefore, it wouldn't be used in what follows as well. Being educated in Wittgenstein's philosophy, I think that philosophy isn't just some *abstract concept of activity*, but primarily the *practice of actually doing something*, perhaps of reaching some level of clarity of our *concepts* which are *manifested* in and by our *actions* (because "*In the beginning was the deed*". Wittgenstein, 1969 OC 402).

The sole motive to resemble something different, say sciences, poetry, or popular issues because somebody *likes* them, or even thinks that they are a merit of philosophy, will not do. If something is highly abstract, universal, theoretical, model-related, and not applicable in practice, it should be abandoned. This is how sometimes things stand in philosophy and that's it. Why should anyone try to make the most abstract ontological questions more particular, practical, or popular? We can imagine one wanting to sell his/her discipline, theory, or more bluntly a lecture, or a book? If one thinks that there is a series of examples of, for instance, an abstract question, as Wittgenstein did, and thinks that the whole philosophy is in this series of examples, then this is an important matter of method and style.

In exactly this way, I will approach to ethical, religious, and aesthetical issues of MSDs because this is the method that I consider to be the right one and my goal is *conceptual clarity* as far as we *manifest* it by our actions. Popularizing ethics by dealing with popular phenomena or practices and *making ethics great again* is the worst way of doing philosophy. It seems important to say that when I thought of doing ethics, religion, and aesthetics of MSDs I wasn't thinking of what philosophy can do for MSDs, rather what MSDs can do for philosophy. MSDs are fairly new phenomena and philosophers aren't much concerned with them perhaps because there is nothing philosophically relevant to be said about them (Krkač, 2022a, 2022b). This possibility hangs over one's head if one starts to do something new regardless of the fact that some similar issues were and are topics of contemporary ethics; issues such as war, climate change, and *global* warming.

To cut long story short, the idea is to formulate the right question concerning the possibility that MSDs are influencing our lives and consequently our philosophies. Perhaps philosophy will remain the same even under MSDs, but in a different form. Namely, as clinical medicine, because the process of publishing the results in medical journals was too slow in the face of the ongoing pandemic, turned to social networks during the pandemic in order to quickly share valuable information between MDs in order to save lives, so perhaps philosophy of MSDs should also turn to new forms which will partly influence its contents and style. This of course stands for all disciplines of philosophy and therefore for ethics, religious, and aesthetical philosophy as well. Here, we have a sketch of the general structure of explications given all the remarks.

2.1.2 A Remark on the Current Global Situation Concerning MSDs

Since this is the 3rd paper in a series of papers with the general title *Un/natural disasters,* i.e. *On multiple simultaneous un/natural disasters*, and since it was written mostly during 2022, it should be noted that the topic gained extremely unfortunate evidence because of the Russian invasion on Ukraine which as an unnatural (or human-made) disaster (see "2022 Russian invasion of Ukraine") at this moment (25 April 2022) entering its 3rd month overlaps not only with humanitarian crisis in Europe given that there are around 4.000.000 mostly Ukrainian women and children refugees in neighboring countries, humanitarian crises in Ukraine because of Russian war crimes, but also with economic crises (in terms of *galloping inflation*), and still ongoing COVID-19 pandemic which is in terms of current data not confirmed either by Russia or by Ukraine during the invasion for obvious security reasons (although some sources confirm that both have at least 500.000 current cases, 25/April/2022, ULR: https://covid19.who.int/).

Further on, and in light of the philosophy of MSDs in terms of the theory of action, epistemology, and ontology (discussed in Krkač, 2022a, 2022b), all the elements of philosophy of natural disasters repeat themselves in the case of unnatural disaster, e.g. in the case of war ranging from the denial of invasion to the various obvious and measurable effects of it on Russia, Ukraine, Europe, and the whole world.

Finally, given the present topic, and also in view of the mentioned invasion, namely aesthetical in terms of Russian destruction of whole cities, ethical in terms of immorality of Russian obvious war crimes, and religious in terms of completely irreligious and quasi-political supporting and inciting Russian invasion by highest Orthodox Church officials in Russia support the general hypotheses supplied hereafter; that is, these aspects of MSDs are highly important.

I am fully aware that I am starting here from my own manner of philosophical analysis which is, given my previous texts that dealt with the same issue from general, ontological, and epistemological aspects of MSDs, now directed toward aesthetics, religion, and ethics of MSDs. In other words, I am fully aware that there are probable manners of dealing with the same issue which would exclude some of these aspects or which would defend different order of analysis. Yet, I don't see how these would affect my general conclusions neither in previous texts nor in the present one. Concerning the distinction between natural, unnatural, and mixed disasters, i.e. their categorization, I made this sufficiently clear for present purposes in my previous texts (see Krkač, 2022a, 2022b, I am grateful to the blind reviewer for bringing these points up).

2.1.3 A Remark on the Relation of Values

Initially, concerning facts, individuals, cultures, and societies have particular hierarchies of the mentioned values, namely, at least 2/3 of world population is religious and may put religion at the top, so maximum 1/3 would put non-religious ethics at the top (see Hackett & McClendon, 2017), and for sure the group that would put aesthetical value at the top is the smallest. However, this doesn't support a valid analysis of these values and their hierarchy.

Secondly, concerning worldviews, religious universalists would always put religiosity at the top, moralizers as those who are exaggeratedly anxious to make moral judgments would always put morality at the top, and proponents of *aestheticism* in terms of the primacy of beauty over other values (i.e. *art for art's sake*, *l'art pour l'art*, *ars gratia artis*, and similar) would always put beauty at the top.

Thirdly, concerning the present order of explication, aesthetics, religion, and ethics of MSDs given in Diagram 2.1 may be interconnected in some way beyond simply being similar as normative and value phenomena of beauty, sacred, and good. It is not necessary that they have any special mutual connection, and if they have it, for the present purposes it isn't necessary to explicate it (one can imagine them interconnected like *three realms of value*, or like three *Stages on life's Way*, namely philosophical work by Søren Kierkegaard written in 1845 which was written as a continuation of *Either/Or* which is about the aesthetic and ethical realms, while *Stages on life's Way* consider the religious realm).

However, the present hierarchy of explication is given by two criteria. One is the value in MSDs being more or less paradoxical which means that beauty is the most paradoxical, religious faith is less paradoxical but still is, and morality isn't

Diagram 2.1 The structure of remarks, analyses, and argument (by the author)

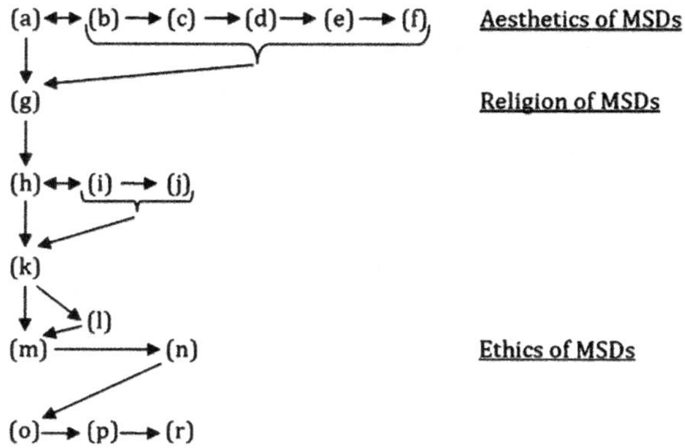

paradoxical, but has even more than one ethical justification of various aspects of proper actions under MSDs. Another is the universalizability principle (Kant, 2005). Namely, aesthetical judgments aren't easily made universal. Further on, religious beliefs cannot be reduced to one. Moral values and ethical analyses can be made universal, especially within limits of a particular ethical system, but this doesn't mean that they in any particular ethical system don't create various paradoxes especially under MSDs.

2.2 Aesthetics of MSDs

In case of both beauty and sacred, i.e. aesthetics and religion, in relation to disasters and MSDs I am relying on anecdotal evidence which at best can be turned into case studies, but to be on the safe side it is necessary to say that no statistical or factual evidence is available especially concerning MSDs (concerning terminology one should bear in mind that "beauty disaster" and "beauty of a disaster" are two different expressions meaning two different phenomena). Therefore, let me start with the seemingly clear remark:

(a) There is nothing beautiful in disasters, because disasters mean destructions and destructions aren't beautiful.

The evidence for remark (a) is indirect since common perception of disasters' ugliness in most cases can be drawn from loses in human lives, infrastructure, or particularly beautiful natural landscape (see: "Natural disaster deaths by country 1990–2019", in: Our world in Data, https://ourworldindata.org/grapher/natural-disaster-deaths-ihme?time=1990, accessed: 10 September 2022). Generally speaking, the combination of words disaster + beauty is much more rare than combination of words disaster + ugly. Are they ugly by themselves or by their consequences on humans, infrastructure, and nature it is not clear. Remark (a) may seem obvious and possibly it works for many cases, but perhaps it has exceptions. Exceptions may be divided according to different criteria, but natural/unnatural disasters, and disaster itself/consequences of a disaster seem to be reasonable criteria for the present purposes (as shown in Table 2.1). In short, there are possibilities that challenge the remark (a). Let me list some.

(b) For example, a strong earthquake can crash the whole top of the mountain (which actually happened during the 1952 Severo-Kurilsk earthquake) and create new beautiful landscape.
(c) Another example may be a human-made destruction of some ugly urban site in order to create a beautiful one. In such examples, the destruction itself could be considered beautiful (on April 27 Radio Free Europe published text "Soviet Monuments Come Down Across Europe" in which there are examples of removal of Soviet monuments which is considered beautiful, RFE 2022, see Illustration 2.1).

So, generally, the *consequences of disasters*, natural as well as unnatural, may not be always or necessarily ugly. However, what about *disasters themselves*? Besides being first and foremost frightening, some disasters may be in the same time at least partially beautiful.

(d) Some would say that the visual image of an explosion of nuclear bomb may appear beautiful; namely a mushroom cloud formation.

Concerning (d) I can supply an interesting personal example. My friend, academic painter Goran Novaković, for his final thesis made a huge painting of mushroom cloud made solely of computer keyboard keys entitled "They are coming ... beginning of the end" (see Illustration 2.2, for the interview with the author see Krkač, 2015). The paradox of this artwork is revealed when a viewer comes close to it and finds

Table 2.1 Division of exceptions to (a) according to two criteria, i.e. natural/unnatural and disaster itself/consequences of a disaster (by the author)

Beauty of a disaster, exceptions to (a):		Types of disaster	
		Natural	Unnatural
Stages of a disaster	Disaster itself	(b)	(c), (d)
	Consequence of a disaster	(b), (e)	(c), (d), (f)

Illustration 2.1 Destruction of Kyiv monument symbolizing friendship between Russia and Ukraine by the order of Kyiv mayor (https://mediumpublishers.com/ukraine-topples-statue-symbolizing-bond-with-russia-its-no-friendship-anymore/, free use, accessed 28 April 2022)

in the middle of it the quote by Chuck Palahniuk (the author of *Fight Club*) which says: "We all die. The goal isn't to live forever. The goal is to create something that will" (Palahniuk in Krkač, 2015). So something which is a part of nuclear explosion and a symbol of ultimate destruction is created as the artwork itself with the quote inside of it which points exactly to opposite phenomenon of everlasting creation in the middle of representation of an everlasting destruction.

(e) Similar situation is with some natural disasters like tornados, volcano eruptions, and similarly they may appear beautiful (aesthetically speaking, i.e. one could argue that they are really beautiful in terms of shape, color, size, movement, etc.).

Concerning (e), a photographer Aric Mayer discussed the problems and possibilities in photographing New Orleans in the aftermath of *Hurricane Katrina* supplying a series of beautiful photographs of the consequences of the hurricane (Mayer, 2010).

(f) Last but not the least, an example can be *The Dresden Frauenkirche*, i.e. *Church of Our Lady* in case of which one could say that ruins after British-American bombing are more beautiful than rebuilt church. However, this example isn't clear. Let me explicate it in order to show how it can be interpreted as going along with (a), but also against it.

The old church was made by Catholics, but during the Reformation it was a Protestant church. It was devastated during British-American World War II bombing of Dresden, and ruins were kept as a memorial in DDR (East Germany during Communist period). The church exterior and interior were rebuilt in 2004 and 2005 by local government after reunification of Germany.

The question concerning (f) is not was bombing beautiful because it was not (and because it remains controversial under the view of its military purpose). The

Illustration 2.2 Goran Novaković: "They are coming… beginning of the end" (see Krkač, 2015, photo by the author)

question is about the dichotomy between ruins as a memorial of bombing and rebuilt church as a memorial of the old church before the bombing. Reconstructed church may be beautiful, but also were the ruins. Now, someone obviously thought that reconstructed church will be more beautiful than the ruins. There are other voices too which claim that ruins were more beautiful, and that the reconstructed church is *kitsch* compared to the ruins (see Illustration 2.3).

As being opposite to (a), the possibilities from (b) to (f) suggest that there are aspects of disasters and their effects that can be considered beautiful. All the mentioned possibilities can be arranged by use of two following criteria (as shown in Table 2.1).

However, nature may appear beautiful and balanced, but for humans in most cases it is unsafe, dangerous, and hostile environment. On the other hand, disasters, especially natural ones, may seem ugly under their effects on humans because they kill people, but they can be seen as beautiful representations of natural forces in action.

(g) The point of these examples (b) to (f) in contrast to (a) is to say that it is not necessarily that disasters are ugly and non-disasters are beautiful in themselves. They appear such only under our human anthropocentric perspective, but as far as disasters are concerned, they don't care. This seeming tension between (a) and (b)–(f) may be resolved by saying that in (a) disasters are considered "ugly" by their "ugly" consequences for humans (in terms of casualties), infrastructure (especially valuable one), and natural beauty, while they are considered "beautiful" in (b)–(f) by their natural appearance and proceeding without taking into account their consequences.

More to that, the issue of beauty is one thing, but the issue of aesthetics is another. Aesthetical judgment on beauty or ugliness of a disaster or its effects must be properly

Illustration 2.3 *Dresden Frauenkirche* ruins before reconstruction (left) and reconstructed church (right), Wikipedia, free use https://en.wikipedia.org/wiki/Frauenkirche,_Dresden, (free use, Accessed 01 February 2022)

justified. However, this point goes beyond the scope of the present paper. It seems sufficient to say that beauty and ugliness and affirmative and negative aesthetical judgments of disasters are possible and that if this is the case, it seems it applies *ceteris paribus* to MSDs as well.

In addition, some philosophical aesthetical theories, namely those which discuss beauty of *kitsch* or beauty of *ugliness*, seem to be more applicable here. Also, the distinction between natural and man-made beauty also seems to be important here. In short, aesthetical and philosophical aspect of MSDs obviously requires much more analysis and clarification in order to formulate unproblematic statements.

For one thing, if beauty of an un/natural disaster exists at all, it doesn't seem to be based on or causing the same emotions as in the case of beauty of an artwork. Before a great artwork, a viewer may feel various positive emotions, even an awe, but it doesn't feel in the same time fear or isn't terrified which one may feel before, for example, a scene of industrial explosion or a volcano eruption.

2.3 Religion and MSDs

Before we explicate paradoxes that can occur in the relation of religion and MSDs, we must make at least a short remark on literature review and probable literature gap.

A note on literature review: Again, as in case of aesthetics, and generally of MSDs, the literature is scarce. Of course, there is a lot of literature concerning particular and individual disasters and disasters in general but assuming that MSDs are more complicated than individual disasters, perhaps the religious aspect would be similarly complicated, and therefore, it would be hard to explicate it simply by means of analogy. Perhaps it would be more appropriate to research the relation of religion and COVID-19 pandemic especially in MSDs hotspots around the world, but again the research is awfully scarce. Given that majority of religions include social and physical contacts, and many religious officials were openly against ban of such contacts during the COVID-19 pandemic (see Druckman et al., 2021), many researches identify religion as contributing to the virus spread, but also pluses and minuses of online religious meetings (see Wildman et al., 2020). However, there are spiritual and physical loses of such bans as well (see Hart & Koenig, 2020). Due to various factual clashes between religious people and epidemiologists, especially concerning vaccination hesitancy promoted by particular members of clergy while official leaders promoted vaccination, some propose collaboration (for such collaboration in terms of vaccination, see Galang, 2021). Now, there is no research on the relation of religion and COVID-19 pandemic in MSD hotspots, and therefore, the mentioned researches should be used cautiously because clear conclusions cannot be drawn.

Let us start with the tension between religion and MSDs based on an analogy with the proven tension between religion and COVID-19 pandemic as an individual disaster. One thing concerning the relation of religions and MSDs seems to be obvious, namely the following.

h. Religions and religious people do help, or ought to help, others in times of crises. They help them bodily and spiritually giving them water, food, shelter, but also comfort and hope to sustain and move on. Concerning this seemingly true remark, some evidence supports it. For example, some data suggest that "religious people are more into charity and volunteering then secular ones" (see Brooks, 2003).

However, concerning (h) there is little good to be said on the matter of religion of MSD if the analogy with COVID-19 pandemic works, but based on available evidence it would be reasonable to hypothesize that religious people would be more into volunteering concerning say COVID-19. And here again as in the case of beauty and ugliness of disaster we may found some tension between religiously motivated "good" and a series of quite disturbing opposite or even counterexamples.

(i) Given the ongoing MSDs around the world, religion didn't do much, and concerning what it actually did, perhaps it was better that it didn't do anything at all (this kind of religious damage to MSDs is obvious in the case of Russian Patriarch Kirill's support for the Russian invasion of Ukraine (see: Wikipedia entry: "Russian Orthodox Church").

The remark (i) goes primarily on the account of misuse of religion during the pandemic and war. For example, many priests, theologians, and publicly influential Catholics in Croatia during the pandemic quite aggressively manifested various anti-vaxxers statements and actions and were accusing epidemiologists and the state of *Devil's work* and similar regardless of the fact that the Pope actually said that taking a vaccine is "an act of love" and "a duty" (see Illustration 2.4). Nonetheless, these are concrete moments which may or may not be relevant for the overall relation of religion to MSDs. On the other hand, there are more abstract negative aspects of the relation of religions to MSDs.

(j) A more abstract aspect is the misuse of *religious apocalypticism* (as opposed to profane apocalypticism) in terms that since the apocalypse or the end of the world is inevitable and near, we cannot do anything about it, and so we shouldn't do anything concerning MSDs.

Interpreting current MSD events as an apocalypse as in (j), as an *extinction level events* (ELE), or as a *longtermism* (idea which says that since, for example, Sun will someday *die*, we must act now under this fact), is not just huge exaggeration vastly ignorant of currently known facts, but also harmful because it results either in non-action or omission of actions in situations in which there are obviously reasonable things to do, or in improper actions given the situation. There are more abstract examples, but examples given in (i) and (j) seem to be sufficient at least to create a tension if compared to (h).

On 22 April 2022, a strong earthquake (6.1M) hit Stolac region in Bosnia and Herzegovina. At least one person died due to the escarpment of rocks on the house, and several were injured. However, one among Facebook commentaries of an ex-Franciscan priest (he was expelled from the order and suspended as a priest) was the following: "What earthquake?! I haven't enjoyed this for a long time because, I just prayed: Jesus is with me. Still shaking … I think it's above 6 degrees. Glory to God Almighty!" (Bože Radoš, see the Illustration 2.5). This kind of enjoyment in a natural disaster I cannot comment because I am not a psychiatrist, but a kind

Illustration 2.4 Anti-vaxxers among Croatian Catholic priests and members of religious orders (collected by the author from various Croatian media and social networks): a priest violating quarantine measures and accusing journalists and epidemiologist as Freemasons (up left), a priest claiming that the COVID-19 vaccine leads to slavery (up right), a priest attacking a minister of health in front of a hospital (down left), and a priest posting on social network claim that he is ready "to shoot those who force him if epidemiologist introduce mandatory vaccination" (down, right) (print screens of the news web pages, free use)

of *religious apocalypticism* is obviously harmful. In some of the commentaries to the post, there is obvious relation to Apocalypse, Last Judgment, sins of humans to which an earthquake is God's response, and similar.

Religion which should go along with science and technology (as it went all the way through most of its history), and supply calmness, belief, trust, and hope to religious people and *people of good* will which are often under stress during MSDs by not doing so, and by tolerating *religious apocalypticism* in its own ranks makes a huge mistake contributing to fear, stress, panic, and lack of minimal level of reasonableness necessary for proper actions. MSDs are not caused by the *envious and angry Gods* or by *the lack of faith* or by *the plenty of sin* among humans. They are natural cosmic and earthly events some of which are partly caused by human improper actions.

(k) So, starting intuition which says that religions go along with MSDs in (h) as well as other services (like medical, firemen, etc.) obviously has its exceptions in (i) and (j) which create a tension or even a contradiction. This tension cannot be resolved by appeal to the difference between MSDs in themselves and MSDs regarding their impact on humans (or perhaps it could). Namely, what we have here is the fact that religion generally has a positive social impact on society,

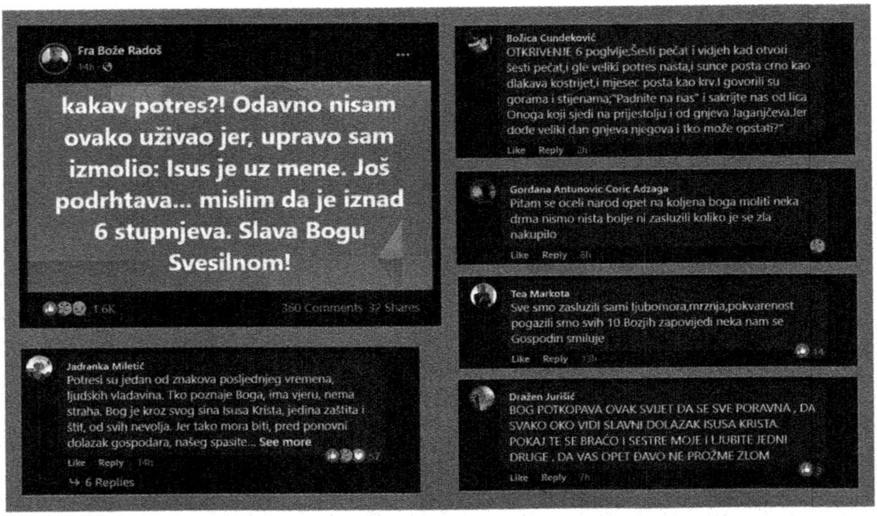

Illustration 2.5 The Facebook post by an ex-Franciscan priest Bože Radoš after an earthquake in Bosnia and Herzegovina on 22 April 2022 around 23:00 hours. In my opinion, there are elements of probable disaster denial, strange enjoyment in disaster, and thanking God for the disaster in the post and in commentaries to it (https://www.facebook.com/profile.php?id=100050155763911, free use)

especially in times of disasters and MSDs, but also fact that some religious people (ranging from believers, parish priests, and theologians to bishops) show negative social impact on society for various reasons, causes, and motives which are not of our present concern. This tension can be solved by saying that what we have here is a model of a rule and its violation (e.g. Pope Francis promoted vaccination against SARS-CoV-2, while series of believers, priests, etc., went directly against this).

Further on, problems concerned with a philosophy of religion which may be of importance here are only few. Perhaps the most important is the problem of evil but in a new shroud. The traditional question on the origin of human moral evil under the assumption that God is good or omnibenevolent in the case of MSDs has a new meaning.

(l) Namely, the question now takes the form of one about the origin of natural evil that is partly or completely caused by human improper actions again under the assumption that God is good, and that religious people motivated by their faith will do more good in social terms than non-religious people. However, some allegedly religious people would do things that cannot be regarded as sacred, rather as profane, as in given examples. Do these counterexamples (i)–(j) refute the universality of proposition (h) it is not clear since it is not clear are they rare exceptions or do they constitute a relevant part of action of religious people under MSDs?

In (l), the old problems of human-caused moral evil and of natural evil here merge into one and multiply in the case of MSDs. Last but not the least, the theological explication of natural evil (natural disasters) as opposed to natural law explications still uses various strange arguments (which were present during the pandemic, wildfires, earthquakes, floods, and similar disasters in period 2020–2022) such as the argument from the revenge of God or Gods to the argument that such disasters were caused by various evil forces and demonic powers, or even by genuinely evil humans (see Illustration 2.4). Such arguments go hand in hand with the apocalyptic explications of current situation around the world, and they are very hard to dismiss especially if they are combined with a series of conspiracy theories (not only anti-religion conspiracies explicated by religious people, but conspiracies in general). The whole issue is far too complicated to be further explicated.

2.4 Morality and Ethics of MSDs

Let me now move to the third aspect of the present research, namely morality and ethics. First, I will make a short remark on available literature.

A note on literature review: *Articles and manuals*: Traditional ethical theories probably wouldn't do concerning the AAR. Virtue, duty ethics, and utilitarian ethics perchance only to a degree and insofar as it overlaps with pragmatist ethics and ethics of responsibility for example. However, there are different arguments, for example for a defense of virtue ethics in disaster see Geale, 2012). Leider et al. (2017) in the results claim that "triage" is important, and it can be regarded as means to utilitarian ethical principles. Some sources remain neutral concerning the choice of the most suitable ethics for disasters (see Jenson, 1997). *Books*: In her book *Ethics for Disaster* (2009), Zack discusses utilitarian, virtue, and lifeboat ethics, and at the end, she supplies the *Code of Ethics for Disasters* in which she claims "The addition of virtue ethics may fill in gaps left by both consequentialism and extensions of deontology, but we need to think critically about our preferred virtues" (Zack, 2009: 125–126). Rigby (2015) emphasizes ethics of empathy, which could possibly go under the altruistic consequentialist ethics (see also Dieter & Bergmann, 2010). Slim (2015) in his book *Humanitarian Ethics A Guide to the Morality of Aid in War and Disaster* advances as it seems ethics of struggle (Slim, 2015: 111–125). Traczykowski (2021) in her book *Ethics, Law and Natural Hazards* emphasizes well-being in various ethical, legal, and political contexts (Traczykowski, 2021). Generally speaking, it seems that there is no consensus on the issue of the best ethics for disasters. Therefore, it seems that all the issues from general ethical theories simply repeat in the context of disasters. In the context of MSDs, there is almost no literature on ethics of them, but it can be reasonably assumed that the same issues would repeat if there would be any literature on ethics of MSDs.

In light of the literature review, here a different approach will be made, namely the one which can be regarded the closest to a middle ground between pragmatist ethics and ethics of responsibility (for Dewey, see Hickman & Alexander, 1998; for commentary of Dewey, see Frega & Levin, 2021; Krkač, 2006).

(m) Given that ethics is *reasoning about morality*, and that morality is a *feature of comparative rightness (goodness)* or *wrongness* of an action that can be more or less *proper* or *improper then x*, morality of MSDs is a feature of rightness of action that can be more or less *proper* or *improper then x under an MSD*. Here, in (m), we do not have the similar tension as in cases of aesthetics and religion of MSDs, rather what we have is the issue of finding the right accommodation for any ethical theory for human actions under MSDs. It is by all means possible that no ethical theory could be accommodated to human actions under MSDs, but this has to be shown. Methodologically, since it seems hard to eliminate or confirm each and every ethical theory here, it seems more plausible to search for morally right features of human actions under an MSD and see to which ethical theory they fit most clearly and directly.

Given that one of the basic features of an MSD is uncertainty, said in (m) seems to influence morality of action under an MSD. The space of possible *proper actions* under an MSD seems to be limited to few sets of possibilities. Namely, given the complexity of MSDs, actions can be: (1) analogous to non-MSD actions (to a certain degree of comparability), (2) adapted to an MSD (if such adaptation is known and can be performed), (3) invented for a new MSD (given the level of novelty of situation of an MSD), or (d) some amalgam of (1), (2), and (3). So, basically (1) are actions under an MSD analogous to actions under a non-MSD as far as such analogous action-model works, (2) are actions which are adapted to an MSD (being partly (1) and partly (3)), and (3) are actions that are invented for a particular new MSD. All of them, namely (1)–(4), are in fact reactions to an MSD. However, in order to react properly, to have proper reaction, or ability to *response* properly to an MSD which is a feature of *responsiveness*, one seems to need two more features, namely *adaptability* and *attention* to an MSD. Without an attention to MSD, it seems impossible to adapt or adjust to it, i.e. to its sudden and radical changes, and without adaptation, it seems impossible to react or response to it.

(n) Therefore, morality of an MSD comes down in terms of necessary conditions of an action under an MSD, to the morality of *proper attention*, *adaptation*, and *responsiveness* (in short AAR). In other words, *proper actions* under an MSD have *proper features* of AAR. Now, proper features of AAR are hard to further analyze, but the concept of (at least instrumental) *responsibility* as moral feature of AAR seems to be sufficient so far (and without entering into the discussion on the feature of a responsible action) (see Vargas, 2022: 3–27, especially for coping see: Beaudry & Pinsonneault, 2005, 2010).

Let us assume that responsible means having causal relation (i.e. being liable to be called to account as the primary cause), power, control, or authority over an action. So, a being performing an action (which in a way belongs to this being) is responsible for that action and its direct effects (sometimes to other effects even if they are indirect). If one's action is responsible, one can be praised for it, and if it is irresponsible, one can be blamed for it. Responsibility for an action simply belongs to the doer of it regardless of the fact does one accepts it or not, or do others call upon it or not.

In *Culture and Value*, Wittgenstein writes: "Denying responsibility means, not holding anyone responsible" (Wittgenstein CV, 1998:78, MS 135 110: 28 July 1947). In his "Moral responsibility," Talbert writes: "Making judgments about whether a person is morally responsible for her behavior, and holding others and ourselves responsible for actions and the consequences of actions, is a fundamental and familiar part of our moral practices and our interpersonal relationships" (Talbert, 2019). Here by responsibility it is implied both *taking responsibility* for an action and *holding responsible* for an action (by a doer or by somebody else). So, affirming and taking responsibility and holding responsible seem to be at least something that we do regardless of the *theory* of responsibility or of the *fact* is there a free will or not (there are theories of moral responsibility that don't imply free will).

However, in which ways are AAR responsible features of our actions, under an MSD, aren't clear? One possibility seems to be a good starting description, namely the description using the analogy of proper action and/or professional action. An action is performed professionally if it is performed under the rules of a profession (*lege artis*), and performing under the rules of a profession implies and manifests the responsibility of doing so and not otherwise. By analogy, an action is performed properly if it is performed under the rules of a proper action. Consequently, a professional or a simply proper action under an MSD if performed professionally or properly is implying and manifesting responsibility if it manifests *optimal* AAR. The addition of *optimality* under an MSD seems to be reasonable since doing too much as well as doing too little or non-proper (or unprofessional) can be equally irresponsible (e.g. doing too much under the severe influence of shock or panic before or during an MSD can lead to a lot of irresponsible actions).

By probably being necessary conditions of a morally proper (responsible) action, it isn't clear are the AAR also necessary. One possibility is that AAR can be reduced to two or even one condition. Another possibility is that they are necessary if taken individually, but in a conjunction they are sufficient. The last possibility is that other conditions are needed to make it sufficient, namely fourth, fifth, etc. Nevertheless, if suggested in (n) is acceptable in terms of necessary conditions of moral or proper action under an MSD, this seems enough for the present purposes. However, what does it mean to have *proper* (also *responsible*) AAR it is not clear, and clarifying what it means belongs to the ethics of AAR.

For one thing, AAR may differ regarding different MSD stages, namely before, during, and after an MSD. To act properly in terms of AAR before, during, and after an MSD may mean different things. An order of importance of A, A, and R within AAR is different before, during, and after an MSD (as shown in Table 2.2 in terms of possible order of importance).

Table 2.2 An order of importance of A, A, and R within AAR before, during, and after an MSD (by the author)

Ethics of:		MSD		
		Before	During	After
AAR	Attention	1	3	2
	Adaptation	2	1	3
	Responsiveness	3	2	1

Table 2.2 a priori or *ex termini* assumes that there is a different order of importance within AAR before, during, and after an MSD based on the nature of an MSD as a disaster (see Krkač, 2022a).

(o) Given that an MSD is a type of a disaster which is determined among other things by inability of the affected community to response to it by the use of its own means, i.e. the harm of a disaster exceeds the community's ability to response autonomously, the level of inability to response is in principle lower if AAR is higher before, but also during, and after an MSD.

However, the order of elements of AAR is such only before an MSD, while during, and after it is again *ex termini* different, namely the adaptation is the first during an MSD, and responsiveness is the first after it given the fact that for example during an MSD there is not much concerning paying attention is there or isn't there an MSD because an affected community is directly confronted to it. Similarly, after an MSD responsiveness is the most important because everybody already adapted to it to a certain degree (e.g. after the availability of a vaccine against the SARS-CoV-2 a section of affected community which freely and deliberately didn't get vaccinated (*anti-vaxxers* and *hesitant vaxxers*) created the vast majority of severely sick, patients on ventilators, and deceased (sometimes even 80% and more) of all hospitalized patients).

Another issue here is the relation of the AAR to ontological, epistemological, and habitual aspects of an MSD (as shown in Table 2.3). Namely, the original order of elements in AAR is given under the ontological, specifically appearance-reality aspect of an MSD since attention is the most important feature of proper reasoning and acting. It concerns not only discriminating between non-MSD and MSD, but also recognizing the actual (vs. *fictive*) beginning of an MSD which is a clear prerequisite of other features (see Krkač, 2022a). However, in view of epistemology, i.e. know-how in relation to AAR the feature of adaptation is the first in order of importance, and finally, in view of philosophical anthropology, i.e. habitual action in relation to AAR, the feature of responsiveness is the most important.

All of the mentioned orders seem to be clear and trivial, but their violation is often the most common cause of high level of cost in terms of human lives and infrastructure in an MSD and therefore of high level of inability of an affected community to respond.

Table 2.3 An order of importance of A, A, and R within AAR in relation to appearance-reality, know-how, and habits in an MSD (by the author)

		MSD		
		Appearance-reality	Know-how	Habits
AAR	Attention	1	3	2
	Adaptation	2	1	3
	Responsiveness	3	2	1

Concerning Table 2.3 let us take an example of responsiveness and habits in an MSD. It seems obvious that high level of MSD habitual actions means high level of responsiveness to an MSD and vice versa.

However, and given that all these elements are descriptive and procedural, let us turn to the most important aspect of AAR in relation to its normative, i.e. moral feature.

(p) AAR features of human action under an MSD are being proper or morally correct (*responsible*) simply by being AAR and not non-AAR or insufficiently AAR. In other words, being (*optimally*) attentive, adaptive, and responsive before, during, and after an MSD under the ontological, epistemological, and action aspect of human action is by itself morally correct.

Remark (p) deals with AAR as the matter of degree, not kind meaning that there are certain levels of A, A, and R which are necessary for a particular MSD. However, what is an ethical explication and justification of AAR is another issue (therefore, the notion of *optimality*).

The closest candidate for an ethical explication of morality of AAR would perhaps be *ethics of responsibility* because it covers individuals and groups in the same time compared to mentioned traditional theories. Namely, the same concept of responsibility spreads from individuals to groups and from general population and volunteers to professionals (e.g. concerning flood-fighting or firefighting). Also, responsibility concerns in the same time individual and collective actions which are both equally important concerning AAR in an MSD.

(r) In short and in terms of suggestion, it can be said that a certain combination of pragmatist ethics and ethics of responsibility could be tried as an ethical explication and justification of AAR features of proper human action in an MSD.

Remark (r) doesn't supply ethical explication or justification of AAR in MSD, but it suggests the probable direction in which these could be done. Certain combination of ethics of moral responsibility (of individuals and groups) and pragmatist ethics suggests choosing an action from the point of our future self and/or future world that is in making by performing such action (see Dewey, 1998, for an excellent analysis Frega & Levin, 2021). Ethics of responsibility gives individuals and groups a "sense" of their optimal contribution, and pragmatist ethics gives a kind of "meaning" to their contribution in the wider pattern of optimal AAR regarding an MSD.

Since under MSDs human action probably will be changed more or less radically, it seems that the moral valuation of human action probably will be changed as well. A series of "new" habits, perhaps even ways of life and forms of live had to be invented; perhaps whole new "patterns" of life (as suggested in Table 2.4). This much can be concluded based on known facts about current and probably future MSDs.

Table 2.4 Possible rubrics for describing a pattern of AAR in MSDs in which the value of each variable combining with values of other variables creates a particular pattern of human action and the moral valuation of it (by the author)

AAR in MSDs (ethics of responsibility/pragmatist ethics)							
Responsibility of who / in relation		To magnitude and scope of MSDs (no. of individual disasters, their relations, and effects)		To geo-climatological features (terrain, transnational)		To period (short, medium, long term)	
Of individuals	Non-professionals (civilians, citizens)						
	Professionals (various)						
Of groups	Non-professionals (civilians, citizens)						
	Professionals (various)						

2.5 Conclusion

Since we humans don't know much about MSDs concerning their descriptive elements, it is highly unlikely that some reasonable philosophy in terms of ontology and epistemology as theoretical issues, philosophy of action as a borderline issue, and ethics as practical issue could be done. We simply do not know what kind of MSDs awaits us in the near or far future, in which regions of the world, and of which strength, suddenness, and magnitude. Therefore, it would be extremely if not extremist action to claim that we completely understand what we are dealing with, how it will affect Earth and humans, and how much we would have to change our *Lebensformen* to barely survive.

The present research in terms of conclusions gives little space.

- Concerning aesthetics and religion of MSDs, it was suggested that there are some contradictions that aren't easy to resolve.
- In the case of morality and ethics of MSDs, it was said as much as presently available ethical theories allow. The ethics of AAR was suggested as a possible pragmatist starting point given that AAR are explicated from the nature of MSDs and appropriate human actions as response to them in terms of ethics of responsibility.

In all three aspects of the research, much is left unsaid because there is little reasonable that can be said, and so this conclusion is rather poor and uninformative. The general motive was simple: *It is better to be safe than sorry.* I can only hope that it is not wrong.

- The research simply repeated what majority of humans have as their common sense intuitions about MSDs, and some of them were partially refuted (aesthetical and religious) by facts, and some of them were at least partially explicated and an attempt of their justification was supplied (moral and ethical).

Anything more goes beyond my present philosophical powers, and it is important to be said that saying too much which is in most cases unwarranted either by clear concepts (which we don't have) or by our experiences (which majority of us don't have) can create more damage than good. This is why we know so little. However, things are rarely simple. And multiple, simultaneous un/natural disasters aren't simple especially under the view of their aesthetical, religious, and moral values.

Acknowledgements I would like to thank Professor David Crowther from University of Bedfordshire, London School of Commerce, and University of Northampton for initial discussion on analyzed philosophical aspects of MSDs, and Professors Alain Cucchi from Université de La Réunion and Calin Gurau from Montpellier Business School for criticism, objections, and comments after my presentation of this research during the 19th International Conference on CSR by SRRNet in Mauritius 2022, especially to Alain who pointed me toward different possible description of my AAR model. I must also thank formal blind reviewers and informal objections by my colleagues from ZSEM which I took into account and made suitable corrections, cuts, and additions.

References

Beaudry, A., & Pinsonneault, A. (2005). Understanding user responses to information technology: A coping model of user adaptation. *MIS Quarterly, 9*(1), 493–524.

Beaudry, A., & Pinsonneault, A. (2010). The other side of acceptance: Studying the direct and indirect effects of emotions on information technology use. *MIS Quarterly, 12*(1), 689–710.

Brooks, A. C. (2003). Religious faith and charitable giving. *Policy Review, 121*, 39. http://www.hoover.org/research/religious-faith-and-charitable-giving

Dewey, J. (1998). *The essential Dewey: Ethics, logic, psychology* (Vol. 2, L. A. Hickman & T. M. Alexander, Eds.). Indiana University Press.

Dieter, G., & Bergmann, S. (Eds.). (2010). *Religion and dangerous climate change: Transdisciplinary perspectives on the ethics of climate and sustainability*. LIT.

Điri, J., Lukin, J., & Krkač, K. (2016). Modeling axis by rotation. In S. Majetschak & A. Weiberg (Eds.), *Aesthetics today, Contemporary approaches to the aesthetics of nature and of art, contributions of the 39th international wittgenstein symposium* (pp. 57–60). Kirchberg am Wechsel, ALWS.

Druckman, J. N., et al. (2021). The role of race, religion, and partisanship in misperceptions about COVID-19. *Group Processes & and Intergroup Relations, 24*(4), 638–657. https://doi.org/10.1177/1368430220985912

Frega, R., & Levin, S. (2021). *John Dewey's ethical theory, the 1932 ethics*. Routledge.

Galang, J. R. F. (2021). Science and religion for COVID-19 vaccine promotion. *Journal of Public Health, 43*(3), e513–e514. https://doi.org/10.1093/pubmed/fdab128

Geale, S. K. (2012). The ethics of disaster management. *Disaster Prevention and Management, 21*(4), 445–462. https://doi.org/10.1108/09653561211256152

Hackett, C., & McClendon, D. (2017, April 5). *Christians remain world's largest religious group, but they are declining in Europe.* Pew Research Center. https://www.pewresearch.org/fact-tank/2017/04/05/christians-remain-worlds-largest-religious-group-but-they-are-declining-in-europe/. Accessed 6 February 2022.

Hart, C. W., & Koenig, H. G. (2020). Religion and health during the COVID-19 pandemic. *Journal of Religion and Health, 59*, 1141–1143.

Hickman, A., & Alexander, T. M. (Eds.). (1998). *The essential Dewey, volume 2, ethics, logic, psychology*. Indiana University Press.

Jenson, E. (1997). *Disaster management ethics.* UNDP, DHA, Disaster Management Training Programme. http://www.disaster-info.net/lideres/spanish/mexico/biblio/eng/doc13980.pdf. Accessed 5 February 2022.

Kant, I. (2005). *Groundwork for the metaphysics of morals* (T. K. Abbott Trans., edited with revisions by Lara Denis). Broadview Press.

Krkač, K. (2006). *Rutina, moral i pragmatizam* [*Routine, morality and pragmatism*]. Vlastita naklada.

Krkač, K. (2015). Goran Novaković: *The are coming ... Beginning of the end.* Interview, *Hrvatska danas.* https://blog.vecernji.hr/konceptualna-kirurgija/goran-novakovic-oni-dolaze-beginning-of-the-end-7172. Accessed 1 February 2022.

Krkač, K. (2022a). Un/natural disasters: Philosophy of multiple simultaneous un/natural disasters. In D. Crowther & S. Sheifi (Eds.), *The equal pillars of sustainability, developments in corporate governance and responsibility* (Vol. 17, pp. 241–255). Emerald Publishing Limited.

Krkač, K. (2022b). Un/natural disasters II, Epistemology and ontology of multiple simultaneous un/natural disasters. *International Studies, 22*(1), 13–41.

Leider, J. P., DeBruin, D., Reynolds, N., & Seaberg, J. (2017, September). Ethical guidance for disaster response, specifically around crisis standards of care: A systematic review. *American Journal of Public Health, 107*(9), e1–e9.

Mayer, A. (2010, August 31). Aesthetics of catastrophe. *Bomb Magazine.* https://bombmagazine.org/articles/aesthetics-of-catastrophe/. Accessed 1 February 2022.

Radio Free Europe. (2022, April 27). *Soviet monuments come down across Europe.* https://www.rferl.org/a/soviet-monument-destroyed-war-ukraine-russia/31823629.html. Accessed 28 April 2022.

Rigby, K. (2015). *Dancing with disaster*. University of Virginia Press.

Russian Invasion of Ukraine. (2022). *Wikipedia.* https://en.wikipedia.org/wiki/2022_Russian_invasion_of_Ukraine. Accessed 25 April 2022.

Russian Orthodox Church. *Wikipedia.* https://en.wikipedia.org/wiki/Russian_Orthodox_Church. Accessed 25 April 2022.

Slim. (2015). *Humanitarian ethics: A guide to the morality of aid in war and disaster.* Oxford University Press.

Talbert, M. (2019). Moral responsibility. In E. N. Zalta (Ed.), *The Stanford encyclopedia of philosophy* (Winter 2019 ed.). https://plato.stanford.edu/archives/win2019/entries/moral-responsibility/

Traczykowski, L. (2021). *Ethics, law and natural hazards: The moral imperative for international intervention post-disaster*. Routledge.

Vargas, M. (2022). Instrumentalist theories of moral responsibility. In D. K. Nelkin & D. Pereboom (Eds.), *The Oxford handbook of moral responsibility* (pp. 3–27). Oxford University Press.

Wildman, W. J., Bulbulia, J., Sosis, R., & Schjoedt, U. (2020). Religion and the COVID-19 pandemic. *Religion, Brain & Behavior, 10*(2), 115–117.

Wittgenstein, L. (1969). *On certainty* (OC). Routledge.

Wittgenstein, L. (1998). *Culture and value* (CV). Routledge.

Zack, N. (2009). *Ethics for disaster*. Rowman & Littlefield.

Chapter 3
Environmental Sustainability, Governance, National Culture and COVID-19 Impact: International Evidence and Implications

Sudipta Bose, Dessalegn Mihret, Muhammad Jahangir Ali, and Syed Shams

Abstract This study examines the association between environmental sustainability, governance factors and national culture with COVID-19 impact. We aim to draw implications for thinking and researching environmental accountability at a higher level than the organisation. We draw on the conceptual lens of deep ecology. Using a sample of 44 countries, we find that countries with a higher level of corporate carbon emissions experienced a greater impact from COVID-19. Moreover, countries with higher accountability and government effectiveness are associated with a lower COVID-19 impact, implying that productive policy responses to the pandemic were employed in such settings. The study also finds that the positive association between carbon emissions and COVID-19 impact is less pronounced for countries with an individualism culture. This suggests that policy responses, such as social distancing, may have yielded better results in these cultural contexts. Furthermore, it is found that the positive impact of carbon emissions on COVID-19 impact is lower for countries having long-term orientation and environmental value orientation cultures.

Keywords COVID-19 · Coronavirus · Climate change · Carbon emissions · Deep ecology · Governance effectiveness · National culture

3.1 Introduction

Numerous countries grappled with the challenges of the global COVID-19 (also known as coronavirus) pandemic, which traces its origin to environmental destruction (World Economic Forum [WEF], 2020; World Health Organization [WHO], 2020) thereby inviting a critical look into the human interaction with the natural environment. Besides, people's death from COVID-19 tends to be significantly related to areas with high air pollution (Wu et al., 2020). The pandemic has reinvigorated the debate surrounding the relationship between human society and the natural environment. At the epistemological level, Gray (2010) critiqued the commonly adopted

S. Bose (✉) · D. Mihret · M. J. Ali · S. Shams
Discipline in Accounting and Finance, The University of Newcastle, Callaghan, Australia

D. Crowther and S. Seifi (eds.), *Corporate Social Responsibility in Difficult Times*, Approaches to Global Sustainability, Markets, and Governance,
https://doi.org/10.1007/978-981-99-2591-9_3

view of conceptualising corporate environmental accountability at the organisational level, arguing that sustainability is ontologically a planetary concept that needs to be researched as such. He called for a shift in the locus of scholarly effort from the organisational to the ecological level (Russell et al., 2017), which bodes well with the deep ecological view of the relationship between mankind and the environment (Devall, 1991; Le Grange, 2018; Naess, 1973). The COVID-19 pandemic—that emanated from environmental destruction permit extending this genre of critical studies through further empirical examination.

The origin of COVID-19 is traced to the "ecological disasters of the Anthropocene" (Ferguson, 2020, p. 3), the contemporary epoch in human history that emphasises the instrumental value of natural environment (Bebbington et al., 2019). Heeding Gray's (2010) advice on the imperative to study environmental issues as planetary matter, we adopt the deep ecology perspective (Le Grange, 2018; Naess, 1973) to empirically examine the link between environmental sustainability and COVID-19 impact. Compared to the "human-centred worldview" of the anthropocentric thinking, deep ecology advocates "ways of living that are best for all living beings" (Devall, 1991, pp. 248–249). It is widely accepted that carbon emissions are responsible for global warming, and scientists argue that global warming is driven by intense EL-Nino phenomena (Geladari et al., 2020) that drives the movement of animals to new places.[1] Such movements facilitate encounters of different species of animals outside their native environment, thereby providing the opportunity for pathogens to invade new hosts and share germs. Scientists believe that the spread of the COVID-19 pandemic occurred through zoonotic transmission (infected either directly through the bites or saliva of infected animals) accompanied by human-to-human transmission, connected to a large seafood market in Wuhan (Geladari et al., 2020). Yet, while the origin of COVID-19 is traced to climate change, the overall impact of the pandemic may also be influenced by cultural and governance factors.

We seek to examine the link between a country's environmental sustainability (proxied by the level of carbon emissions) and COVID-19 impact (i.e., death and infections) using corporate carbon emissions as a proxy for national-level emissions as the corporate sector remains the primary driver of environmental destruction (Bakan, 2012) responsible for 71% of global carbon emissions (*The Guardian*, 2017). Further, we consider accountability and government effectiveness of countries (World Bank, 2020) as potential determinants of the design and implementation of COVID-19 protection policies. Moreover, we examine the impact of individualism/collectivism, long-term orientation (Hofstede et al., 2010) and national cultural orientations of environmental focus (Schwartz, 1994, 2003) as moderator since better environmental focus in such cultures may minimise adverse consequences of environmental destruction.

Based on a sample of 44 countries, our results show that corporate carbon emissions are positively associated with country-level COVID-19 impact. Further, the

[1] https://www.hsph.harvard.edu/c-change/subtopics/coronavirus-and-climate-change/ [accessed on 10 May 2022].

study provides some evidence that countries with higher accountability and government effectiveness are associated with lower COVID-19 impact suggesting such countries' agility to effectively respond to the crisis. The study also finds that the positive association between carbon emissions and COVID-19 impact is less pronounced for countries with individualism culture, suggesting that COVID-19 response strategies were more effective in such cultures than in collectivist ones. Countries that exhibit long-term orientation and higher environmental value focus in their culture tend to have a lower COVID-19 impact supporting the argument that such cultures afford priority to long-term sustainability of society. This study contributes to the literature by offering empirical insights that extend the critical literature on methodological thinking about corporate accountability for the environment. The findings suggest that scholarly and policy engagement on environmental sustainability needs to be undertaken at a higher level of analysis than the organisation.

The rest of the paper proceeds as follows. The following section develops conceptual arguments linking environmental sustainability and country-level COVID-19 impact to formulate research questions. Section 3.3 outlines the research methods employed, and Section 3.4 reports the findings. Section 3.5 draws conclusion and implications.

3.2 Literature Review

The COVID-19 pandemic has spurred numerous studies investigating the potential role of corporate social responsibility (CSR) in shaping firm-level outcomes during the crisis. Huang and Ye (2021) examine the joint effect of capital structure and CSR activities on firm risk during the COVID-19 pandemic, demonstrating that firms with poor CSR performance have higher financial risk during the pandemic. Similarly, Bose et al. (2022) investigate the impact of COVID-19 on changes in firm value and the moderating role of firm-level sustainability performance on this relationship. They find that firms in countries with more severe COVID-19 impact experienced greater declines in firm value, but this negative impact was less pronounced for firms with better sustainability performance. Additionally, the study found that firms domiciled in countries with higher levels of environmental- and stakeholder-value-oriented culture experience less decline in firm value due to the pandemic. These results suggest that sustainability performance can serve as a valuable tool for firms to mitigate the negative impact of COVID-19 on firm value, particularly in countries where the pandemic has had a more significant impact.

Another study by Huang and Liu (2021) investigates whether the stock price crash risk of energy firms is reduced after COVID-19 outbreaks, finding that this reduction is more pronounced for energy firms with higher CSR performance. Furthermore, Sun and Li (2021) explore the link between the COVID-19 outbreak and financial performance using corporate culture and CSR, and they revealed that while the outbreak has a negative influence on the financial performance of travel and entertainment companies, the financial performance of the medical industry has improved during the pandemic period. Similarly, Lee et al. (2022) documented that socially responsible firms have higher stock returns and lower volatility of returns during the COVID-19 pandemic. Chen et al. (2022) investigate the relationship between firms' engagement in social responsibility activities and stock prices during the pandemic, finding an inverted U-shaped association between CSR and stock prices. Arora et al. (2022) also explore the impact of CSR on firm value during the pandemic, reporting that firms engaged in more CSR activities improve shareholder value compared to other firms. Lastly, Lassoued and Khanchel (2023) investigate the influence of the COVID-19 outbreak on the French stock market and whether firms committed to CSR are less affected, finding that active CSR adopters earned positive returns during the event date and were less influenced overall. Taken together, these studies provide important insights into the potential impact of CSR on firm-level outcomes during the COVID-19 pandemic.

In addition, prior research has investigated the impact of COVID-19 on global stock markets, revealing a strong reaction to pandemic shocks. For instance, Chatjuthamard et al. (2021) examine the impact of COVID-19 on the global stock market and showed that the growth rate of the number of confirmed cases is associated with stock return volatility. Xu et al. (2021) investigate the influence of COVID-19 on the Chinese stock market and found that the COVID-19 outbreak had a negative influence on the stock returns and price sensitivity to firm-specific information. Pham et al. (2021) examine the association between COVID-19 outbreaks and stock returns during the pandemic period from January to June 2020. They found a negative relationship between the daily increase in the number of infection, hospitalised cases, and deaths and the next day stock returns. These studies support the conjecture that the global stock market reacted strongly to the COVID-19 pandemic shocks.

Moreover, another line of literature highlights the impact of COVID-19 outbreaks on accounting practices and disclosures. For example, Cui et al. (2021) examine the association between conditionally conservative accounting practices and stock returns during the COVID-19 outbreak in China. They find that listed companies employed more conditionally conservative reporting practices during the COVID-19 outbreak. Subsequently, Hao and Pham (2022) investigate the association between the quarterly filing of COVID-19 disclosures and stock returns volatility, demonstrating a negative association between COVID-19 disclosure and return volatility. BC and Simpson (2022) explore the influence of COVID-19 on US corporate cash holdings and find that pandemic exposure was related to higher corporate cash holdings. Zhai et al. (2022) examine the cumulative abnormal returns around the event date and find negative abnormal returns around the event dates for firms located far from the Hubei province in China.

3.3 Theoretical Background and Research Questions

3.3.1 Deep Ecology and Global Health Pandemic

Compared to the human-centric—i.e., anthropocentric worldview—deep ecology is an eco-centric view in which individuals identify themselves with the natural environment (Fox, 1989). It attaches intrinsic value to the natural environment that transcends the utilitarian consideration of the environment to human existence (Devall, 1991; Le Grange, 2018; Naess, 1973). While the anthropocentric view considers environmental issues in terms of future generations in a narrow sense, the eco-centric view that underpins deep ecology conceives "future generations include generations of all living beings [whereby] "beings" are broadly defined to include living rivers as well as living species" (Devall, 1991, pp. 248–249). It provides a long-term perspective to issues of environmental sustainability and considers human life as integral to life on earth (Naess, 1973).

Consistent with the thoughts of deep ecology, Gray (1992) advocated the need for sustainability accounting that renders the environment at the centre of analysis. Further, Gray's (2010) call for a planetary view of environmental sustainability research is consistent with the deep ecology perspective. Indeed, such a holistic consideration is also acknowledged as sustainable for "human health and well-being" (Devall, 1991, p. 249) as would be inferred from the COVID-19 pandemic. While the deep ecology perspective is a normative attitude, it can be argued that societies with cultural and governance orientations closer to the eco-centric (deep ecological) than anthropogenic end would exhibit better environmental sustainability practices and—by implication—be exposed to a lesser extent to societal health crises such as COVID-19.

3.3.2 Human Health, Environmental Sustainability and COVID-19 Impact

The World Health Organization [WHO] (2020) states that climate change is associated with infectious disease occurrence and changes in infectious disease transmission patterns are considered as the consequence of climate change. Similarly, the European Parliament (2020) presents that rapid urbanisation, increasing international travel and climate change lead to global epidemic outbreaks. COVID-19 has severely impacted the world economy and health substantially since its first outbreak in China (European Parliament, 2020; Liu et al., 2020). The impact of COVID-19 is closely linked to climate and biodiversity crises. That is, habitat loss and shifting climate zones originating from climate change cause migration of animals to new places, where they interact with other new species, possibly leading to increased risk of new diseases (Armstrong et al., 2020). Health threats, including the COVID-19 pandemic, are associated with environmental degradation and climate destabilisation while associated health threats are severe for cities and people exposed to higher levels of pollution (World Economic Forum [WEF], 2020). Wu et al. (2020) reported empirical evidence that people's death from COVID-19 is significantly related to areas in the United States (US) where air pollution is high. They find that particle pollution level in the year prior to the pandemic is associated with an increase in death rate.

However, prior environmental and social research on the corporate sector is largely focused on the organisational level analysis or stock market-based research largely considering financial metrics (Ashforth & Gibbs, 1990), which suggests general anthropocentric orientation. Given the planetary nature of environmental sustainability issues (Gray, 2010), environmental research that transcends the organisation level has merit. The COVID-19 pandemic has produced a shock that triggered a re-thinking of organised human activity. We pursue the following research question (RQ) with a cross-country design:

RQ 1. Is environmental sustainability associated with COVID-19 impact?

3.3.3 Governance Factors and National Culture

While the origin of the COVID-19 virus and its transmission rate are linked to environmental destruction, cultural and governance factors may influence the way countries responded to the pandemic. Further, such factors may influence a country's propensity to behave in eco-centric ways, and thus the effectiveness of a country's policy response to the impact of COVID-19. The World Bank (2020) provides ratings of countries on several governance factors, of which two are relevant to our study: *Voice and accountability* and *Government Effectiveness*. That is, these factors may determine the extent to which governments competently take policy measures (Basrija & Handoyo, 2019) that minimise the impact of the pandemic through effective health governance. Thus, we pursue the following research question:

RQ 2. Are a country's governance ratings associated with COVID-19 impact?

National culture is another possible factor that could influence environmental sustainability and thus societal health risks, including those of COVID-19. Cultural orientations may influence the effectiveness of policy responses to the pandemic, such as social distancing, self-isolation and staying at home. Individualist cultures tend to hold values that are focused on the self rather than the collective interests (Hofstede et al., 2010). From an environmental thinking perspective, controlling for other national-level factors, individualist cultures may be focused less on sustainability issues than collectivist cultures (Gallén & Peraita, 2018). On the other hand, it could be argued that individualist cultures are associated with lower COVID-19 effect because COVID-19-related restrictions such as social distancing and self-isolation may be better implemented in such cultures (Tallis, 2020). Another cultural dimension is long-term orientation, in which individuals tend to hold values that afford priority to long-term benefits (Hofstede et al., 2010), which is compatible with the notion of maintaining a more sustainable society (Disli et al., 2016; Garcia-Sanchez et al., 2016; Halkos & Skouloudis, 2017) and thus potentially leading to reduced COVID-19 impact. Based on the foregoing arguments, we pursue the following research question:

RQ 3. Are cultural dimensions of individualism and long-term orientation associated with a country's COVID-19 impact?

Similarly, Schwartz's (1994, 2003) international study on social values of countries suggests potential variations in the extent to which societies afford importance to protecting the natural environment. He identified ten value types, of which *universality* pertains to the society's tendency to focus on protecting the environment.[2] It signifies the society's focus on "[u]nderstanding, appreciation, tolerance, and protection for the welfare of all people and for nature", which are manifested in "social justice" and "protecting the environment" and "unity with nature" (p. 31), which is compatible with the deep ecology orientation. It could be argued that countries with a universalistic value orientation are likely to prioritise environmental-friendly policies and practices. Therefore, the link between *environmental sustainability* practices and COVID-19 impact could be influenced by the extent of commitment to the environmental value in a country's culture. We, therefore, pursue the following research question:

RQ 4. Does a focus on environmental value in a country's culture influence the association between environmental sustainability and a country's COVID-19 impact?

3.4 Methods

3.4.1 Sample and Data

Our sample comprises 44 countries, and we use corporate carbon emissions as a proxy for a country's environmental sustainability. We covered all companies that responded to the CDP (previously, Carbon Disclosure Project) questionnaire in 2019. CDP is an independent global not-for-profit organisation running the global environmental disclosure systems for investors through which companies disclose their climate change-related information. Carbon emissions data is collected from the CDP database. We select the sample countries based on the availability of the carbon emissions data from CDP2019 database. We collected COVID-19 death and infection data from ourworldindata.org (Roser et al., 2020) and global country-level societal health risk data from the Knoema (2020) database. We collected country-level

[2] Other value types include power, achievement, hedonism, stimulation, self-direction, benevolence, tradition, conformity and security (Schwartz, 1994, p. 22).

global climate change risk index data from the reports published by the Germanwatch and Climate Action Network,[3] country-level individualism vs. collectivism and long-term vs. short-term orientation culture data from (Hofstede et al., 2010), and country-level environmental value orientation of culture from the World Value Survey database.

3.4.2 Measure of the Dependent Variable and Societal Health Risk

COVID-19 impact is proxied by the country-level death and infection numbers. We collect the total number of COVID-19 death and infections data as at 31st October 2020 from ourworldindata.org database (Roser et al., 2020). This database, which is updated daily, is maintained through a collaborative effort between researchers at the University of Oxford and Global Change Data Lab.

3.4.3 Measurement of Corporate Carbon Emissions and Societal Health Risk

We measure corporate carbon emissions as a firm's total amount of carbon emissions scaled by the industry average of carbon emissions within a country. We compute the five-year average of each company's relative carbon emissions. Then, we calculate country-level average carbon emissions (*EMISSION*) using all firms in our sample for each country which is used as a proxy for carbon emissions (*EMISSION*) in the study. We checked the soundness of this proxy by testing how well it is correlated with country-level emissions, for which latest data is available only up to 2016 from the World Bank database. We find the statistically significant correlation between the two variables, suggesting that corporate emissions provide a reasonable proxy for country-level emissions. This correlation is also consistent with the Guardian's (2017) reflection that the corporate sector is responsible for 71% of emissions.

Societal health risk (*SOC_HEALTH_RISK*) is measured by an index developed at the country level by Knoema (2020). It is computed based on a country's: (a) quality of healthcare systems and availability of healthcare resources; (b) economic interconnectedness (external and internal); (c) digital infrastructure; (d) demographic susceptibility; and (e) trust in government.

[3] https://germanwatch.org/en/8139 [accessed on 05 May 2022].

3.4.4 Model Specification

The following model is estimated to test the association of carbon emissions with COVID-19 deaths and infections:

$$\begin{aligned} COVID19\_IMPACT_{j,t+\tau} = &\beta_0 + \beta_1 EMISSION_{j,t} + \beta_2 VAE + \beta_3 GEE \\ &+ \beta_4 SOC\_HEALTH\_RISK_{j,t} + \beta_5 LNPOP_{j,t} \\ &+ \beta_6 LIFE\_EXPECT_{j,t} + \beta_7 65YR\_OLD_{j,t} \\ &+ \beta_8 GCRI_{j,t} + \beta_9 STAKE_{j,t} \\ &+ \beta_{10} ENFORCE_{j,t} + \beta_{11} SDG_{j,t,t} + \varepsilon_{i,t} \end{aligned} \quad (3.1)$$

where *EMISSION* is the carbon emissions which is used to proxy environmental sustainability. A higher level of *EMISSION* indicates lower environmental sustainability. All variables are defined in Appendix A.

3.5 Results

Table 3.1 provides country-wise descriptive statistics of our dependent and independent variables of interest. The results indicate that Belgium experienced the highest number of deaths per million population (1007.37) followed by Spain (767.37) and Mexico (708.04) while Thailand (0.845) experienced the lowest. Qatar had the highest number of infections per million population (45,935.52), while Thailand (54.16) had the lowest. Firms located in Russia (39.70 CO_2-e) and Czech Republic (25.20 CO_2-e) were the highest carbon emitters, while those in Malta were the lowest. Regarding societal health risk, China has the highest risk, followed by India while Norway has the lowest. Further, the Philippines suffers most from the global climate risk while Qatar had the lowest.

Panel A of Table 3.2 provides descriptive statistics. The natural logarithm of mean COVID-19 deaths and infections is 4.845 and 8.768, respectively implying that, on average, 285.73 per million of population are died, and 12,829.19 per million of population are infected due to COVID-19. Mean score for the country-level accountability (*VAE*) and government effectiveness (*GEE*) is 0.678 and 0.946, respectively. The natural logarithm of the average population size (*LNPOP*) and average country-level climate change risk index (*GCRI*) is 17.071 and 4.322, respectively. About 54.50% of our sample countries have stakeholder orientation.

Panel B of Table 3.2 provides the mean and median test. The results suggest that companies having a higher level of *EMISSION* located in countries with higher COVID-19 impact. Correlation results, not reported for brevity, show that *EMISSION* is positively correlated with COVID-19 deaths and infections.

Table 3.1 Country descriptive

	Total deaths (per million)	Total infection (per million)	Societal health risk	EMISSION (in Million CO_2-e)	GCRI
Australia	35.57	1,081.65	28.00	0.11	50.17
Austria	119.80	11,263.43	30.70	0.24	55.67
Belgium	1,007.37	38,159.59	37.10	1.21	63.83
Brazil	750.27	25,953.49	49.40	0.66	83.17
Canada	267.87	6,146.95	34.40	2.89	88.17
Chile	74.063	26,604.18	42.40	1.92	87.83
China	3.29	63.43	72.90	3.96	55.50
Columbia	611.90	20,894.08	49.70	1.66	55.67
Cyprus	28.54	4,814.48	40.60	0.40	129.67
Czech Republic	287.42	30,224.44	37.80	25.20	79.67
Denmark	124.132	7,807.91	39.10	0.18	112.83
Egypt	61.152	1,049.27	55.50	0.01	143.67
Finland	64.613	2,871.47	30.10	0.24	155.67
France	560.18	20,406.20	34.30	0.10	38.00
Germany	124.75	6,191.56	38.30	6.48	38.67
Greece	59.484	3,568.63	41.40	0.10	78.83
Hungry	181.15	7,796.92	39.40	0.04	69.00
India	88.15	5,896.44	68.90	16.10	38.67
Ireland	386.41	12,365.64	38.10	2.41	119.17
Israel	290.45	36,242.80	43.20	0.93	120.50
Italy	633.81	10,712.11	49.50	2.85	43.67
Japan	13.88	793.76	37.80	0.48	69.83
Mexico	708.04	7,126.28	55.20	5.31	61.83
Malta	138.15	13,457.47	37.30	0.00	152.83
Malaysia	7.693	954.68	50.20	0.08	103.33
Netherlands	428.07	19,899.42	38.30	3.63	71.83
Norway	52.02	3,608.58	25.10	0.05	138.83
New Zealand	5.18	332.00	33.70	0.20	84.17
Panama	622.98	30,793.54	48.80	2.39	106.50
Philippines	65.57	3,458.02	61.10	2.04	17.67
Portugal	242.04	13,462.38	42.40	0.92	38.83
Qatar	80.526	45,935.52	44.50	0.02	173.67
Russia	189.51	10,963.66	38.80	39.70	47.67
South Africa	324.236	12,201.96	49.10	1.88	77.33
South Korea	9.05	517.09	32.30	0.45	82.83
Singapore	4.786	9,914.46	45.50	1.10	172.17

(continued)

Table 3.1 (continued)

	Total deaths (per million)	Total infection (per million)	Societal health risk	EMISSION (in Million CO_2-e)	GCRI
Spain	767.37	25,359.50	42.90	4.27	47.33
Sweden	593.51	12,777.26	33.70	0.16	129.50
Switzerland	235.135	17,762.54	36.90	3.30	52.33
Thailand	0.845	54.16	53.90	2.66	31.00
Turkey	120.67	4,424.45	52.60	0.69	115.17
Ukraine	160.99	8,659.88	39.70	0.32	88.00
United Kingdom	680.98	14,579.51	44.40	0.42	65.00
United States	*693.976*	*27,333.40*	*48.40*	*4.38*	*44.17*
Average	**285.73**	**12,829.19**	**42.20**	**2.75**	**83.63**

Table 3.3 reports the regression results. The coefficient on *EMISSION* is positive and statistically significant in Models (1) and (2), suggesting that a country's COVID-19 deaths and infections are higher in countries with high carbon emissions. Further, the coefficients on *VAE* and *GEE* are negative and statistically significant in Models (1) and (2), suggesting that countries having higher level of voice and accountability and government effectiveness have lower COVID-19 impact. Regarding control variables, country-level societal health risk (*SOC_HEALTH_RISK*), percentage of population aged over 65 years (*65YR_OLD*) stakeholder orientation (*STAKE*) and legal environment (*ENFORCE*) are positively whereas life expectancy (*LIFE_EXPECT*) is negatively associated with COVID-19 deaths and infections.

Further, this study examines the effect of a country's individualism vs. collectivism and long-term vs. short-term orientation culture on the association of corporate carbon emissions with COVID-19 deaths and infections. We created an indicator variable of individualism *(HIGH_IND)* that takes a value of 1 if the country's individualism vs. collectivism score is above the median, and 0 otherwise. We also created an indicator variable of *HIGH_LTO* that takes a value of 1 if the country's long-term orientation culture score is above the median, and 0 otherwise. Model (1) and (2) of Table 3.4 report the regression results of the individualism vs. collectivism culture, while Model (3) and (4) report the results of the long-term vs. short-term orientation culture. The coefficient on the interaction term *EMISSION* × *HIGH_IND* and *EMISSION* × *HIGH_LTO* is negative and statistically significant in Models (1) to (4), suggesting that the positive impact of *EMISSION* on the COVID-19 death and infections is lower for countries with individualism and long-term orientation in their culture.

Regarding the impact of environmental value orientation of a country's culture on the association of carbon emission with COVID-19 deaths and infections, we created an indicator variable of higher environmental value culture that takes a value

Table 3.2 Descriptive statistics

Panel A: Descriptive statistics

	Mean	**Std. Dev**	**Median**
COVID-19 Deaths	4.845	1.631	5.146
COVID-19 Infections	8.768	1.581	9.241
VAE	0.678	0.899	1.030
GEE	0.946	0.774	1.080
LNPOP	17.071	1.693	17.173
LIFE_EXPECT	79.408	4.520	81.325
65YR_OLD	14.585	5.975	15.459
GCRI	4.322	0.503	4.370
STAKE	0.545	0.504	1.000
ENFORCE	1.481	1.561	1.688
SDG	74.613	6.117	75.790

Panel B: Mean and Median Test

	HIGH EMISSION		LOW EMISSION		Mean test	Median test
	Mean	Median	Mean	Median		
COVID-19 Deaths	5.258	5.579	4.247	4.156	2.100^{**}	2.339^{**}
COVID-19 Infections	9.323	9.508	7.965	8.186	3.062^{***}	3.008^{***}

Superscript ***, ** and * represent significance levels at 1%, 5% and 10%, respectively

Table 3.3 Regression results of environmental sustainability with the total number of COVID-19 deaths and infections

	Dependent variable = COVID-19 deaths	Dependent variable = COVID-19 infections
	Model (1)	Model (2)
EMISSION	0.140*	0.203***
	(1.687)	(2.814)
VAE	−0.676**	−1.154***
	(−2.067)	(−3.181)
GEE	−1.113**	−1.061***
	(−2.564)	(−3.158)
SOC_HEALTH_RISK	0.466***	0.245
	(2.950)	(1.629)
LNPOP	−0.128	−0.250*
	(−0.859)	(−1.816)
LIFE_EXPECT	−0.191***	−0.142***
	(−3.368)	(−2.750)
65YR_OLD	0.089*	0.062
	(1.987)	(1.561)
GCRI	0.167	0.292
	(0.334)	(0.616)
STAKE	0.988**	0.713*
	(2.284)	(1.856)
ENFORCE	0.894***	1.121***
	(3.502)	(4.276)
SDG	0.066	−0.332
	(0.138)	(−0.659)
Intercept	18.484***	21.026***
	(2.731)	(3.665)
Observations	44	44
R-square	0.483	0.483

Notes This table presents regression results of the association between carbon emissions and COVID-19 impact. Models (1) and (2) present regression results of the association of the carbon emissions with COVID-19 deaths and infections. Superscript ***, ** and * represent significance levels at 1%, 5% and 10%, respectively

of 1 if the country's environmental value orientation score is above the median, and 0 otherwise. The coefficient on *EMISSION* × *HIGH_ENV_VALUE* is negative and significant as shown in Model (5) and (6) of Table 3.4, suggesting that the positive impact of *EMISSION* on the COVID-19 death and infections is lower for countries with higher environmental value orientation in their culture.

Table 3.4 Regression results of environmental sustainability with the total number of COVID-19 deaths and infections: role of cultures

	Dependent Variable = COVID-19 Deaths	Dependent Variable = COVID-19 Infections	Dependent Variable = COVID-19 Deaths	Dependent Variable = COVID-19 Infections	Dependent Variable = COVID-19 Deaths	Dependent Variable = COVID-19 Infections
	Model (1)	Model (2)	Model (3)	Model (4)	Model (5)	Model (6)
EMISSION	0.204***	0.259***	0.147	0.296**	0.133*	0.251***
	(2.799)	(3.469)	(1.019)	(2.547)	(1.869)	(3.118)
EMISSION × HIGH_IND	−0.290***	−0.230**				
	(−3.116)	(−2.404)				
HIGH_IND	1.514***	0.363				
	(2.976)	(0.694)				
EMISSION × HIGH_LTO			−0.219*	−0.168*		
			(−1.810)	(−1.728)		
HIGH_LTO			0.495	0.899		
			(0.675)	(1.519)		
EMISSION × HIGH_ENV_VALUE					−0.436***	− 0.251**
					(−4.502)	(−2.282)
HIGH_ENV_VALUE					−0.165	− 0.323
					(−0.423)	(−0.729)
SOC_HEALTH_RISK	0.318	0.175	1.050*	0.655	0.192	0.119
	(1.469)	(0.787)	(1.730)	(1.338)	(0.820)	(0.447)
Intercept	12.207	20.945**	15.407	30.846	18.215***	19.220***
	(1.391)	(2.325)	(0.602)	(1.494)	(2.813)	(2.613)
Control variables	Included	Included	Included	Included	Included	Included
R-square	0.765	0.724	0.733	0.811	0.868	0.815

Notes This table presents regression results of the moderating role of individualism vs. collectivism culture, long-term vs. short-term orientation culture, and the environmental value orientation culture in the association between carbon emissions and COVID-19 impact. Models (1)–(2) and (3)–(4) present the regression results of the moderating role of individualism vs. collectivism culture and long-term vs. short-term orientation culture, while Models (3) and (4) present regression results of the moderating role of the environmental value orientation culture in the association of carbon emissions with COVID-19 deaths and infections. Superscript ***, ** and * represent significance levels at 1%, 5% and 10%, respectively

3.6 Conclusion and Implications

The main thrust of this study has been to examine whether environmental sustainability (proxied by carbon emission levels) of societies is associated with COVID-19 impact and identify country-level factors that influence this association. We adopted a cross-country research design and drew on the concept of deep ecology to undertake a study with a higher unit of analysis than the organisation to explore the association of carbon emissions with the impact of COVID-19. Our findings show that carbon emissions are positively associated with country-level COVID-19 impact. This association is weaker for countries with individualistic and long-term orientated culture as well as stronger focus on environmental value in their culture. As the philosophical view of deep ecology focuses the way we think about the relationship between humans and the environment, culture is an apt consideration in our model as culture shapes thoughts and actions of individuals. Our analysis also offers evidence that countries with good governance as shown in voice and accountability as well as government effectiveness tended to be successful in minimising the effect of the COVID-19 pandemic.

Communitarian behaviours, which bode well with the concept of deep ecology (Devall, 1991; Gray, 1992), attach importance to the natural environment beyond its instrumental value. Deep ecology challenges anthropocentric bias in environmental thinking (Devall, 1991) and proffers a view of the environment as having intrinsic value. Broadly informed by the idea of deep ecology, the methodological approach of this study responds to Gray's (2010) call for conceptualising environmental sustainability as a planetary matter. Gray (2010) called for empirical research to focus on a unit of analysis higher than the level of an organisation. Indeed, his call for emphasis on the planetary level is theoretically an ideal level of analysis for research issues surrounding the natural environment as this is a global—rather than a corporate—or even national-level issue. In view of this methodological consideration, our choice of a cross-country design with a unit of analysis that transcends the organisational level goes a step in the right direction to respond to Gray's (2010) call. As Russell et al. (2017) argue, there is a need to rethink research approaches on the link between corporations and the natural environment to focus on a locus away from the organisation and instead on the consequences of corporate activities on the environment.

Given our research aim to lay out insights that extend the ontological and methodological thinking about environmental sustainability, it is apposite to outline implications of the findings to thinking about, researching and regulating environmental sustainability. Predominantly, the study suggests that scholarly effort on environmental accountability should be anchored at a higher level of analysis than the organisation. In this respect, the findings have three key implications. First, environmental value orientation of culture merits consideration as a key concept in the thinking about environmental accountability. The nexus between the firm's corporate environmental sustainability practices and the consequential substantive impact on society would offer a fruitful avenue for future research. Second, it offers insights into the need for methodological and theoretical diversity in environmental accounting research. In addition, cross-country studies of numerous types could be undertaken, including qualitative comparative case studies to develop theory, or large-sample quantitative studies aimed at testing theory.

Third, our study contributes to the scholarly and policy discussions by offering insights into the link between environmental sustainability and COVID-19 impact. It is increasingly acknowledged that human health heavily relies on healthy ecosystems, and reducing carbon emissions and environmental degradation are imperative to reduce the impact of pandemics such as COVID-19 (Armstrong et al., 2020). As the World Health Organization [WHO] (2020) stated, reducing "environmental and social risk factors" can enable preventing "nearly a quarter of the global health burden (measured as loss from sickness, death and financial costs)". More broadly, environmental sustainability is one of the top priorities in global policy discussions (Bebbington et al., 2019). Our findings suggest deep ecological deliberations need to be considered in environmental policy setting as mere anthropocentric focus would rarely guarantee societal well-being. Such broad perspectives to environmental accountability issues merit policy attention in the post-COVID-19 world.

Appendix A: Variable Description

Variable(s)		Explanation
COVID-19 Deaths	COVID-19 Impact	The natural logarithm of the total number of deaths per million of population due to COVID-19
COVID-19 Infections	COVID-19 Impact	The natural logarithm of the total number of infections per million of population due to COVID-19
EMISSION	Carbon emissions	The average of the industry-adjusted carbon emissions of all sample firms in a country. Industry-adjusted carbon emissions is computed as the five-year average of the industry-adjusted carbon emissions emitted by a company
VAE	Voice and accountability	Country-level voice and accountability score from the Worldwide Governance Indicator (World Bank)
GEE	Government effectiveness	Country-level government effectiveness score from the Worldwide Governance Indicator (World Bank)
SOC_HEALTH_RISK	Societal health risk	Country-level societal health risk score. Higher value indicates higher risk
LNPOP	Population size	The natural logarithm of total populations of a country

(continued)

(continued)

Variable(s)		Explanation
LIFE_EXPECT	Life expectancy	Country-level average life expectancy
65YR_OLD	65 years old people	The percentage of population aged over 65 years
GCRI	Global climate change risk	The natural logarithm of the country-level long-term accumulated global climate change risk from 1999 to 2018 and released on 2020. Lower index scores indicate greater risk
STAKE	Stakeholder orientation	An indicator variable of 1 if the country has code law, and 0 otherwise
ENFORCE	Enforcement	Principal component of "Rule of Law", "Regulatory Quality" and "Control of Corruption" from the Worldwide Governance Indicator (World Bank)
SDG	Sustainable development goals	Sustainable development goals score rated by the United Nations
HIGH_IND	Individualism vs. collectivism culture	Country-level individualism vs. collectivism culture collected from Hofstede. We convert individualism vs. collectivism culture score as an indicator variable of 1 if the country's individualism vs. collectivism culture score is greater than the median individualism vs. collectivism culture, and 0 otherwise
HIGH_LTO	Long-term orientation index	Country-level long-term orientation culture collected from Hofstede. We convert long-term orientation culture score as an indicator variable of 1 if the country's long-term orientation culture score is greater than the median-term orientation culture score, and 0 otherwise
HIGH_ENV_VALUE	Environmental culture/awareness	Country-level environmental value collected from World Value Survey (WVA)

References

Armstrong, F., Capon, A., & McFarlane, R. (2020). Coronavirus is a wake-up call: Our war with the environment is leading to pandemics. *The Conversation*. https://theconversation.com/coronavirus-is-a-wake-up-call-our-war-with-the-environment-is-leading-to-pandemics-135023. Accessed on 9 December 2020.

Arora, S., Sur, J. K., & Chauhan, Y. (2022). Does corporate social responsibility affect shareholder value? Evidence from the COVID-19 crisis. *International Review of Finance, 22*(2), 325–334.

Ashforth, B., & Gibbs, B. (1990). The double-edge of organizational legitimation. *Organization Science, 1*(2), 177–194.

Bakan, J. (2012). *The corporation: The pathological pursuit of profit and power*. Hachette UK.

Basrija, A., & Handoyo, S. (2019). The relevance of public governance to national environmental performance. *Journal of Accounting Auditing and Business, 2*(2), 1–13.

BC, B., & Simpson, T. (2022). How do firms learn? Evidence from corporate cash holdings during the COVID-19 pandemic. *Accounting & Finance*. https://onlinelibrary.wiley.com/doi/abs/10.1111/acfi.13031

Bebbington, J., Österblom, H., Crona, B., Jouffray, J.-B., Larrinaga, C., Russell, S., & Scholtens, B. (2019). Accounting and accountability in the Anthropocene. *Accounting, Auditing & Accountability Journal, 33*(1), 152–177.

Bose, S., Shams, S., Ali, M. J., & Mihret, D. (2022). COVID-19 impact, sustainability performance and firm value: International evidence. *Accounting & Finance, 62*(1), 597–643.

Chatjuthamard, P., Jindahra, P., Sarajoti, P., & Treepongkaruna, S. (2021). The effect of COVID-19 on the global stock market. *Accounting & Finance, 61*(3), 4923–4953.

Chen, D., Chen, X., & Sun, H. (2022). Does corporate social responsibility protect shareholder value from the shock of COVID-19? Evidence from China. *Accounting & Finance*. https://doi.org/10.1111/acfi.13017

Cui, L., Kent, P., Kim, S., & Li, S. (2021). Accounting conservatism and firm performance during the COVID-19 pandemic. *Accounting & Finance, 61*(4), 5543–5579.

Devall, B. (1991). Deep ecology and radical environmentalism. *Society & Natural Resources, 4*(3), 247–258.

Disli, M., Ng, A., & Askari, H. (2016). Culture, income, and CO_2 emission. *Renewable and Sustainable Energy Reviews, 62*, 418–428.

European Parliament. (2020). *Economic impact of epidemics and pandemics*. https://www.europarl.europa.eu/RegData/etudes/BRIE/2020/646195/EPRS_BRI(2020)646195_EN.pdf. Accessed on 8 December 2020.

Ferguson, K. E. (2020). Anthropocene alerts in the Covid-scene. *New Political Science, 42*(4), 631–636.

Fox, W. (1989). The deep ecology-ecofeminism debate and its parallels. *Environmental Ethics, 11*(1), 5–25.

Gallén, M. L., & Peraita, C. (2018). The effects of national culture on corporate social responsibility disclosure: A cross-country comparison. *Applied Economics, 50*(27), 2967–2979.

Garcia-Sanchez, I.-M., Cuadrado-Ballesteros, B., & Frias-Aceituno, J.-V. (2016). Impact of the institutional macro context on the voluntary disclosure of CSR information. *Long Range Planning, 49*(1), 15–35.

Geladari, C., Andreadis, E., Dourakis, S., Geladari, E., Papademetriou, V., Tsioufis, C., Vallianou, N., Margellou, E., Psounis, K., Jahaj, E., Skourtis, A., Tsoura, M., Lavrentaki, A., Georgantoni, A., Kounatidis, D., Moragianni, V., Vlachos, K., & Aronis, K. (2020). *Is the COVID-19 pandemic linked to climate change?* https://www.researchgate.net/publication/340581324_Is_the_COVID-19_pandemic_linked_to_climate_change. Accessed on 8 December 2020.

Gray, R. (1992). Accounting and environmentalism: An exploration of the challenge of gently accounting for accountability, transparency and sustainability. *Accounting, Organizations and Society, 17*(5), 399–425.

Gray, R. (2010). A re-evaluation of social, environmental and sustainability accounting. *Sustainability Accounting, Management and Policy Journal, 1*(1), 11–32.
Halkos, G., & Skouloudis, A. (2017). Revisiting the relationship between corporate social responsibility and national culture. *Management Decision, 55*(3), 595–613.
Hao, J., & Pham, V. T. (2022). COVID-19 disclosures and market uncertainty: Evidence from 10-Q filings. *Australian Accounting Review, 32*(2), 238–266.
Hofstede, G., Hofstede, G. J., & Minkov, M. (2010). *Cultures and organizations: Software of the mind.* McGraw-Hill.
Huang, H., & Ye, Y. (2021). Rethinking capital structure decision and corporate social responsibility in response to COVID-19. *Accounting & Finance, 61*(3), 4757–4788.
Huang, S., & Liu, H. (2021). Impact of COVID-19 on stock price crash risk: Evidence from Chinese energy firms. *Energy Economics, 101*, 105431.
Knoema. (2020). *Global coronavirus susceptibility index.* https://knoema.com/xtkvoxc/global-coronavirus-susceptibility-index-by-knoema. Accessed on 9 December 2020.
Lassoued, N., & Khanchel, I. (2023). Impact of COVID-19 pandemic on earnings management: An evidence from financial reporting in European firms. *Global Business Review.* https://doi.org/10.1177/09721509211053491
Le Grange, L. (2018). Spinoza, deep ecology and education informed by a (post) human sensibility. *Educational Philosophy and Theory, 50*(9), 878–887.
Lee, S., Lee, D., Hong, C., & Park, M.-H. (2022). Performance of socially responsible firms during the COVID-19 crisis and trading behavior by investor type: Evidence from the Korean stock market. *Finance Research Letters, 45*, 102660.
Liu, L., Wang, E.-Z., & Lee, C.-C. (2020). Impact of the COVID-19 pandemic on the crude oil and stock markets in the US: A time-varying analysis. *Energy Research Letters, 1*(1), 13154.
Naess, A. (1973). The shallow and the deep, long-range ecology movement. A summary. *Inquiry, 16*(1–4), 95–100.
Pham, A. V., Adrian, C., Garg, M., Phang, S.-Y., & Truong, C. (2021). State-level COVID-19 outbreak and stock returns. *Finance Research Letters, 43*, 102002.
Roser, M., Ritchie, H., Ortiz-Ospina, E., & Hasell, J. (2020). *Coronavirus disease (COVID-19)–Statistics and research.* Our world in data. https://ourworldindata.org/covid-cases. Accessed on 20 September 2020.
Russell, S., Milne, M. J., & Dey, C. (2017). Accounts of nature and the nature of accounts. *Accounting, Auditing & Accountability Journal, 30*(7), 1426–1458.
Schwartz, S. H. (1994). Are there universal aspects in the structure and contents of human values? *Journal of Social Issues, 50*(4), 19–45.
Schwartz, S. H. (2003) A proposal for measuring value orientations across nations. *Questionnaire Package of the European Social Survey, 259*(290), 261.
Sun, Y., & Li, Y. (2021). COVID-19 outbreak and financial performance of Chinese listed firms: Evidence from corporate culture and corporate social responsibility. *Frontiers in Public Health, 9.*
Tallis, R. (2020). Philosophy in the time of Plague, Part 2. *Philosophy Now, 139.*
The Guardian. (2017). *Just 100 companies responsible for 71% of global emissions.* https://www.theguardian.com/sustainable-business/2017/jul/10/100-fossil-fuel-companies-investors-responsible-71-global-emissions-cdp-study-climate-change. Accessed on 15 January 2021.
World Bank. (2020). *The worldwide governance indicators.* http://info.worldbank.org/governance/wgi/index.asp. Accessed on 5 November 2022.
World Economic Forum [WEF]. (2020). *How our responses to climate change and the coronavirus are linked.* https://www.weforum.org/agenda/2020/04/climate-change-coronavirus-linked/. Accessed on 9 December 2020.
World Health Organization [WHO]. (2020). *Climate change and human health—Risks and responses summary.* https://www.who.int/globalchange/summary/en/index2.html. Accessed on 7 December 2020.

Wu, X., Nethery, R. C., Sabath, B. M., Braun, D., & Dominici, F. (2020). *Exposure to air pollution and COVID-19 mortality in the United States: A nationwide cross-sectional study*. Harvard University. https://projects.iq.harvard.edu/covid-pm. Accessed on 9 December 2020.

Xu, L., Chen, J., Zhang, X., & Zhao, J. (2021). COVID-19, public attention and the stock market. *Accounting & Finance, 61*(3), 4741–4756.

Zhai, H., Xiao, M., Chan, K. C., & Liu, Q. (2022). Physical proximity, corporate social responsibility, and the impact of negative investor sentiment on stock returns: Evidence from COVID-19 in China. *International Review of Finance, 22*(2), 308–314.

Chapter 4
Exploring the Hybridity Dilemma: The Role of Personal Values

Amira Magdy Mirghani and Raghda El Ebrashi

Abstract In an era where for-profit organizations are not sufficient to deal with the current global challenges, hybrid organizations presented themselves as the light at the end of the tunnel by existing in the blurry line between not-for-profit and for-profit organizations and integrating both social and economic goals. The existence of both goals within the organization forms an internal tension that places hybrids in a dilemma (Battilana and Lee in Academy of Management Annals 8:397–441, 2014). These tensions are manifested in the different set of values that every social entrepreneur (and his/her) team hold, so it seems that values may help us comprehend the motivations or intentions of social entrepreneurs to create hybrid organizations. Accordingly, the aim of this paper is to propose a bundle of different socio-economic values based on Schwartz (Advances in experimental social psychology. Academic Press, New York, 1992) theory of human values to accommodate the different forms of hybrid organizations to better comprehend the value creation vis-à-vis value capture enigma.

Keywords Hybrid organization · Social entrepreneurship · Personal values · Value creation · Value capture · Multiple logics

4.1 Introduction

In a world where modern economies are not sufficient to solve societal problems, Muhammad Yunus, founder of Grameen Bank and Noble prize winner, integrated social entrepreneurship into the equation of economics and strategy to capture the essence of what it is to be human (Santos, 2012, Yunus, 2007). Throughout the literature, different definitions were given to social entrepreneurship. It was defined as the combination of different resources in a process-like form to create social value by Mair and Marti (2006). In addition, Austin et al. (2006) viewed social

A. M. Mirghani (✉) · R. El Ebrashi
The German University in Cairo, New Cairo, Egypt

Management & Organization, German University in Cairo, Cairo, Egypt

D. Crowther and S. Seifi (eds.), *Corporate Social Responsibility in Difficult Times*, Approaches to Global Sustainability, Markets, and Governance,
https://doi.org/10.1007/978-981-99-2591-9_4

entrepreneurship as an entrepreneurial activity coupled with social purpose. Furthermore, Zahra et al. (2009) referred to it as the recognition, formation, evaluation and exploitation of opportunities to create new businesses and models that aim at accomplishing a combined value. Due to the abundance of definitions proposed by scholars across literature, social entrepreneurship became poorly defined and its boundaries with other fields became vague because most of these definitions were driven by practice rather than theory (Santos, 2012). Efforts by Weerakoon et al. (2016) combined social entrepreneurship definitions with respect to business emphasis, entrepreneurial emphasis and institutional emphasis, Santos (2012) derived theory of social entrepreneurship, and El Ebrashi (2013) provided a working definition for social entrepreneurship.

Sulphey and Salim (2020) claim that the lack of unified definition of entrepreneurship is a major obstruction in the advancement of the field. Definitions of social entrepreneurship were viewed from a broad range to a narrow one spanning across a continuum. Broad definitions of social entrepreneurship include the innovative activity with a social intent that exists in for-profit sector such as social-purpose commercial ventures (Dees & Anderson, 2003) and corporate social entrepreneurship (Austin et al., 2004; Saebi et al., 2019) or in the not-for-profits sector (Short et al., 2009) or hybrid organizations (Kadir & Sarif, 2016). For decades, commercial organizations and charitable organizations have been existing on opposing sides of a spectrum; however, recently, the emergence of hybrid organizations blurred the lines that separate them (Battilana & Lee, 2014). Hybrids exist due to the notion that neither traditional-for-profit exclusively addresses social and environmental challenges due to its focus on profit maximization, nor the not-for-profit is sufficient due to its sole focus on philanthropy and negligence of financial sustainability (Haigh & Hoffman, 2011; Santos, 2012). Thus, new organizational forms that aim at doing business coupled with social purpose may fill this gap (Battilana & Lee, 2014; Hossain et al., 2017; Kruse et al., 2019). Hybridity scholars are interested in the definition of hybrid organizations (Cornforth, 2020; Lautermann, 2013; Pestoff, 1998; Shepherd et al., 2019), managing tensions (Cornforth, 2020; Gupta et al., 2015; Jay, 2013), hybrid intensity (Shepherd et al., 2019), governance (Mason et al., 2007) and maintaining legitimacy (Battilana & Lee, 2014; Santos, 2012). The previously mentioned study the requirements and nature of hybrid organizations, how they evolve, and how they are managed. However, one may question the drive that pushes individuals to opt for hybrid organizations over other forms or in other words, the drivers of one's intentions toward hybridity. Across literature, social entrepreneurial intention has been embedded as a corner stone of predicting social entrepreneurship behavior (Hockerts, 2015b; Lacap et al., 2018; Tiwari et al., 2022); however, as we previously mentioned, it was not examined through the hybridity lens.

Understanding one's intention preceding hybrid organizing is interesting to explore due to the assumption that the tension existing between social and economic goals is derived from different beliefs (Fishbein & Ajzen, 2011). These beliefs evolve from different background variables including values which are considered as a main individual factor among others (Fishbein & Ajzen, 2011). Understanding one's individual values is a step closer to understanding how beliefs are shaped (Kotey &

Meredith 1997; Schwartz & Bilsky, 1987) and thus, intentions (Fishbein & Ajzen, 2011; Schwartz 1992). On the same line, Mair and Noboa (2006) and Hockerts (2015b) referred to the importance of values in their theoretical models of explaining social entrepreneurial intentions. However, literature is limited in examining the role of values, especially Schwartz's (1992) theory of personal values in managing tensions and maintaining a sustainable hybrid model. Research examined the role of values in predicting social entrepreneurial intention (Kruse et al., 2019) and not hybridity. Moreover, Jay (2013) stated that the combination of different institutional logics, defined by Tracey et al. (2011) as rules that are enforced through a set of assumptions and values, presents themselves as wise solution to sustain hybridity. Accordingly, Doherty et al. (2014) suggested that future research should explore how hybrid organization can maintain competitive advantage in the midst of conflicting values and tensions to maintain the balance. Thus, the aim of this paper is to understand how the intention toward different forms of hybrid organization is formed through the lens of personal values. In addition, we propose that values are the missing piece in influencing social entrepreneurs' beliefs and thus, attitude, norms and perceived behavioral control to form these intentions that sway between social and economic goals creating hybrid organizations. Moreover, this research proposes set of personal values that exist in the different forms of hybrid organizations, thereby extending the literature that called for understanding values in social entrepreneurship (Battilana & Lee, 2014; Doherty et al., 2014; Gillett et al., 2019).

4.2 The Case of Hybrid Organizations

Due to the current financial instability that led to question morality and sustainability of the economic system as well as current charitable organizations' difficulty in funding, hybrid organizations offer a more rigor alternative as an ethical form of business that serve both social and economic dilemmas (Cornforth, 2020). To understand hybridity, one must start defining the nature of non-hybrid state which includes pure form of social value and economic value prior to blending them into hybridity (Lautermann, 2013). Hybrid organizations are known as the combinations of different aspects of organizational forms as well as mixing different organizational elements that would not normally go together (Shepherd et al., 2019). Different approaches were adopted to determine organizational hybridity. Pestoff (1998) identified hybrid organizations in terms of the space existing between three primary sectors: market, state and community. Alter (2006) defined hybrid organizations spanning across a continuum where social enterprises lie between non-profit and for-profit organizations. Another conceptualization by Cornforth (2020) is based on the theory of institutional logics that states that there are different institutional orders that exist within society and have their own logics that includes normative constructions as well as material practice, values, beliefs and rules; thus, hybrid organization exists due to the combination of different institutional logics, i.e., social and economic logic. The combination of multiple logic is referred to tensions by Battilana and Lee

(2014). Combining different logics can lead to internal instability and conflict within the organization, fearing that one logic can override the others (Cornforth, 2020; Gupta et al., 2015; Jay, 2013). Tracey et al. (2011) highlighted that the existence of multiple logics leads to organizational failure, and hybridity scholars deemed the combination of commercial and social goals as incompatible and a source of conflict within the organization (Mair & Rathert, 2020). Accordingly, an approach to adapt to the pressure of different logics existing in hybrid organizations is compartmentalization, where different parts of the organization contain separate institutional logics and focus on attending different institutional demands. For example, one program would focus on serving beneficiaries, while another program would focus on creating revenue streams from different activities (El Ebrashi, 2013; Alter, 2006). Another approach is to focus on integrating and managing competing or different logics and demands rather than separating them (Cornforth, 2020; Dees, 2012).

Hybrid organizations have different paradigms, value systems and logics (Douglas, 2015). Battilana et al. (2017) recommended that studies examining hybridity should focus on the degree of hybridity and the matter of degree should be imagined across a continuum where economic logic exists on the one end and social logic exists on the other end. Along this continuum, hybridity would be at its greatest in the middle. However, this continuum does not capture the intensity of hybridity where a firm with a moderately weak social and economic logic would be considered the same as a firm with a strong economic and social logic (Shepherd et al., 2019).

In an attempt to capture degree of organizational hybridity, Shepherd et al. (2019) conceptualized hybridity in terms of two components: hybrid relativity and the degree of hybridity. Hybrid relativity refers to the extent of the distribution of different logics within the organization or how the economic logic and social logic are balanced as organizations differ in their emphasis on economic versus social objectives. Degree of hybridity (intensity) is shaped by the entrepreneur, the community, the nature of the opportunity that aims at creating both social and economic values and organizational outcome. Table 4.1 summarizes hybrid relativity and the degree of hybridity with their respective hybrid organizational form.

Table 4.1 shows that corporate social responsibility (CSR) is an example of low relative hybridity as the orientation of most organizations that offer CSR is on economic outcomes. Low relative hybridity can manifest when there is more focus on social logic rather than economic logic (social venture) or more focus on economic logic rather than social logic (economic venture). Hybrid relativity increases when the relative importance of the economic and social logic becomes more balanced. Degree of hybridity or hybrid intensity refers to the strength with which the economic logic is held in the organization and the strength of the social logic held in the organization. Organizations with strong economic and social logic experience high hybrid intensity. Organizations with low social and low economic logic have low hybrid intensity such as small-scale family businesses, lifestyle businesses and other ventures that do not aim to grow substantially. Traditional hybrid venture can accommodate different intensities of the social and economic logic based on the hybrid form of the traditional hybrid ventures (Shepherd et al., 2019).

Table 4.1 Summary of organizational forms with their respective hybrid relativity and intensity (compiled by the researchers)

Organizational form	Hybrid relativity	Degree of hybridity (intensity)
Corporate Social Responsibility	Low hybrid relativity with more focus on ***economic outcomes***	High economic logic intensity
Social venture	Low with more focus on ***social logic***	High social logic intensity
Economic venture	Low with more focus on ***economic logic***	High economic logic intensity
Traditional hybrid venture	High relativity with proportional distribution of economic and social focus	(1) High social and economic logic intensity
	High relativity with proportional distribution of economic and social focus	(2) Moderate social and economic logic intensity
	High relativity with proportional distribution of economic and social focus	(3) Low social and economic logic intensity

Over time, different organizational forms acquire legitimacy and thus, become institutionalized. Combination of organizational forms includes network forms, which are innovative, flexible and interdependent organizations. Hierarchal forms are those organizations that are bureaucratic (Powell, 1990) while governmental ones are those that are present in public organizations (Arellano-Gault et al., 2013). Other forms include commercial and charitable business forms (Battilana & Lee, 2014). A third form of hybridity relies on the combination of different institutional logics. Institutional logics are defined as the beliefs that guide one's behavior in a given activity. In hybrid organizations, multiple logics may co-exist; however, the extent of their existence depends on the importance of the logic to the organization (Battilana & Lee, 2014). Gupta et al. (2015) reaffirmed that the coexistence of both financial and social goals presents some challenges within the hybrid organizations. The need to drive the social impact could be overridden by the desire to increase the finances of the organization, and a further challenge would be the legal structure of the hybrid organization.

Doherty et al. (2014) consider social enterprises as the archetype of hybrid organizations due to the coexistence of different values that arise from different categories, and Battilana and Lee (2014) added that social enterprises' combination of both business and charity forms an ideal type of hybrid organization. Social enterprises adopt approaches that emerge from different sectors such as public, private and non-profit (Doherty et al., 2014; Mair & Rathert, 2020) and adopt different forms as cooperatives (El Ebrashi, 2013) to make sure they maintain their dual goals.

Different views were associated with social enterprises. It was viewed as the creation of a social venture that promotes a social cause (Murphy & Coombes, 2009) or as social ventures that participate in commercial activities to maintain their operations (Hockerts, 2006) or as the exploration of opportunities that leads to social return (Austin et al., 2006). Scholars identified different types of social enterprises across literature. Hockerts (2015a) identified three types of hybrid organizations: first is the work integration social enterprise (WISE) which aids workers that face exclusion, disabilities and discrimination and re-integrate them by employing them and helping them receive their income not from government support but from a productive activities. WISE is one of the most common types of hybrids in developed countries and emerged as a substitute to governmental labor market policies. Second is Base of the Pyramid (BoP), and these organizations provide important products and services to the poor at suitable rates. The final type is the Fair-Trade Hybrid, and their aim is to "manipulate trade relations thus creating income for poor marginalized producers by charging premiums to conscientious consumers in developed countries" (Hockerts, 2015a, p. 90). Bosma and Levie (2010) classified different types of social enterprises, in the Global Entrepreneurship Monitor (GEM) report, based on the earned income strategy and their social and environmental goal proportion in organization. The below spectrum provides a better illustration of the five types.

According to Fig. 4.1, organizations that have social and environmental goals that make up more than 67% and do not have an earned income strategy include: traditional NGOs and not-for-profit social enterprises. The difference between traditional NGOs and innovation-driven NFPs is that the latter focus on attaining social goals in novel approaches. Organizations that include social and environmental goals that make up between 50 and 60% and have an earned income strategy include hybrid social enterprise and for-profit social enterprise. The difference between them lies in the focus on goals whereas hybrid social enterprises focus more on social goals vis-à-vis their economic goals, while for-profit social enterprises focus on the earned income strategy over their social and environmental goals. In the case of hybrid social enterprise, the generated income is sometimes redirected into the sustainability of other projects within the enterprise or re-distributed differently to allow for the growth of the enterprise (Ebrashi & El-Batawy, 2021). Organizations that have social and environmental goals that make up between 1 and 50% are referred to as socially committed business and their social and economic goal composition is far less than their focus on earned incomes (Bosma & Levie, 2010). Thus, one may propose that as you go to the right side of the spectrum, the focus on social and environmental goals, or social relativity and intensity (Shepherd et al. 2019), within the organization decreases while the focus on earned income increases.

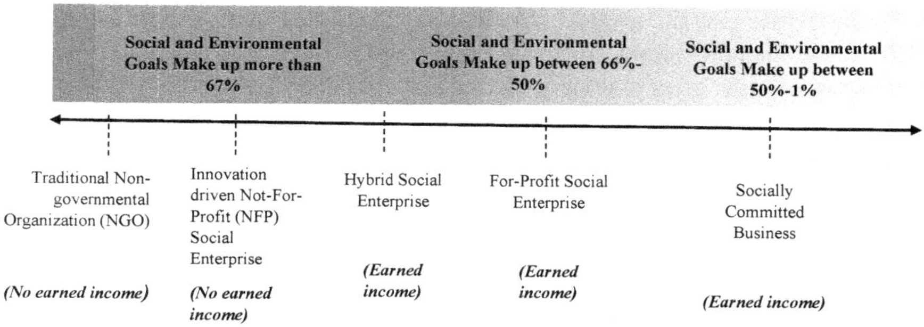

Fig. 4.1 Income versus social and environmental spectrum of social enterprises (developed by the researchers). Adopted from Bosma and Levie (2010)

4.2.1 Sustaining Hybrid Organizations: Value Creation Versus Value Capture

There has been discussion around how social enterprises sustain their social impact (El Ebrashi, 2013; Brown & Murphy, 2003). Some social ventures aim to generate enough financial gains to allow them to carry out their social mission (Mendoza-Abarca & Mellema, 2016). Hybrid social enterprises may choose their financial sustainability from a range of strategies, where some of which are adopted from the non-profit sector such as public funding, private grants, membership fees and contributions, and some others are learned from the for-profit sector such as earned revenue, debt and equity financing (Searing et al., 2021). Questioning the success of social enterprises as hybrids relies on balancing the tensions between their social mission vis-à-vis their commercial performance (Battilana & Lee, 2014). According to Battilana and Lee (2014), sustainability of hybrid organizations does not rely, only, on financial sustainability but also on the sustainability of the whole organization. In other words, Battilana and Lee (2014) suggested that the core organizational activities, workforce composition, organizational design, inter-organizational relationships and organizational culture are important dimensions to be considered when opting for hybrid organizing. Literature suggests that organizations can handle their existing tensions by adopting the dimensions of hybrid organizing proposed by Battilana and Lee (2014) or a sustainable business model by Bocken et al. (2016).

Santos (2012) argued that what distinguishes social entrepreneurship from its commercial counterpart is that social entrepreneurship focuses on value creation while the latter focus on value capture. Value creation from an activity (i.e., more focus on the social mission) occurs when the aggregate utility of members in the society exceeds the opportunity cost of all resources used in that activity (Mendoza-Abarca & Mellema, 2016), while value capture from an activity (i.e., more focus on the commercial performance) occurs when the actor is able to appropriate a part of the value created by the activity after accounting for the cost of resources that they used (Zacharias et al., 2016). Value creation is crucial for a sustainable value capture because activities that allow value capture without value creation will be eventually ousted due to the burden they showcase upon society (Santos, 2012).

Social value creation is a major concept when establishing society-oriented enterprises (Lautermann, 2013). Bargsted et al. (2013) added that there are four ways for social enterprises to create social value. First is to overcome obstacles that hinder individuals' access to proper education and health care. Second is to give voice to minority populations and provide them with better opportunities. Third is to defend people's rights and fourth is to decrease the negative impact of productive sectors. Furthermore, Di Domenico et al. (2010), Mair and Marti (2009) and Zahra et al. (2009) suggested that bricolage, defined as using the resources at hand and improvising based on the context, is a useful approach as it allows social entrepreneurs to combine their limited resources in an innovative way to achieve social value creation.

Because hybridity entails the combination of social and economic logics, one of the challenges that arise is maintaining legitimacy. Even though Santos (2012) urged organizations to be clear whether their main focus is value creation or value capture for the sake of their identity and legitimacy, Douglas (2015) argued that one of the strength points of hybridity is its ability to move freely between economic and social logics. In addition, Battilana and Lee (2014) suggested that hybrid organizations should appeal to both the business and social sectors to maintain legitimacy. Another major challenge facing hybrid organizations is mission drift (Al Taji & Bengo, 2019), where there has to be set of managerial procedure to unravel such mission drift (Żur, 2021). The hybrid organizations' possession of different paradigms, value systems and logics (Gillett et al., 2019) makes it interesting to point out that founders' social values have strong impact on the social versus economic focus of the organization (Bruneel et al. 2016). Gillett et al. (2019) commended the importance of studying values and ethics in managing tensions and called for future research in this area. On that note, Dion (2014) in an earlier study determined that respect, integrity, honesty, responsibility and trust are the main set of values that are considered codes of ethics of social enterprise. However, Shepherd et al. (2019) called on future research to examine entrepreneur's prosocial motivation and entrepreneur's affect as it may provide a basis toward understanding hybridity. Furthermore, Żur (2021) highlighted that the factors that shape social entrepreneur's approach toward handling different tensions are understudied. Accordingly, this study opts for examining the set of personal values that may enable social entrepreneurs to find a balance between social and economic logic.

4.3 Personal Values

Examining entrepreneurs' personal values allows a better understanding for the choice of behavior, plays a vital role in decision-making and appears in an organization's policies and procedures (Tomczyk et al., 2013). Vallaster et al. (2019) consider values held by entrepreneurs as resources because they impact their ethical behavior and the establishment of structures in the entrepreneurial context. Rokeach

(1973) stated that personal values are the cognitive recognition of the suitable way to behave, and Murray et al. (1996) added that values are one of the most important drivers in shaping both intentions and behavior. Personal values are defined as "concepts or beliefs about desirable end states or behaviors that transcend specific situations, guide selection or evaluation of behavior and events, and are ordered by relative importance" (Schwartz and Bilsky, 1987, p. 551). Personal values impact one's judgments, decisions and commitments and differ among individuals (Allport, 1961; Kotey & Meredith, 1997). One of the most renowned theories of values is the theory of human values founded by Schwartz (1992) as continuation to Rokeach's (1973) work. Schwartz (1992) identified ten values based on the underlying motivation of each. The theory states that actions that result from a specific value may either complement or contradict another value. Moreover, the theory established a dynamic relationship between the values depicted in a circular arrangement. Opposing values are in opposing directions from the center while complementary values are adjacent to one another. Furthermore, the closer the values are to each other, the more similar their underlying motivation is. The ten values can be categorized into four higher value domains which constitute two bipolar dimensions: (1) conservation versus openness to change; (2) self-enhancement versus self-transcendence. The conservation versus openness to change entails "values in terms of the extent to which they motivate people to preserve the status quo and the certainty it provides in relationships with close others, institutions and traditions versus following their own emotional and intellectual interests in unpredictable and uncertain directions" (Schwartz, 1992, p. 43). Values that exist in the conservation dimension include *security*, defined as the safety, harmony and stability of society, *conformity*, defined as the restrain of actions that may cause harm to others and disrupt social expectations, and *tradition*, defined as the respect of and acceptance of the ideas that either culture or religion requires. Values that exist in the openness to change dimension include *self-direction*, defined as one's independent thought and actions, *stimulation*, defined as life's challenges and excitement, and *hedonism*, defined as one's sense of gratification and pleasure. The second bipolar dimension: self-enhancement versus self-transcendence posits "values in terms of the extent to which they motivate people to enhance their own personal interests (even at the expense of others) versus to transcend selfish concerns and promote the welfare of others, close and distant, and of nature" (Schwartz, 1992, p. 43). Values that exist in the self-enhancement dimension include *power*, defined as one's control over both people and resources, and *achievement*, defined as one's success by showing the correct competence according to social standards. Values that exist in the self-transcendence dimension include *universalism*, defined as the understanding, appreciation, tolerance and protection of one's welfare, and *benevolence*, defined as the preservation and enhancement of other's welfare with whom one is in frequent contact (Schwartz, 1992).

4.4 Values in Managing the Hybridity Enigma

The ethical dilemma in social entrepreneurship relies in the clash or tension between opposing values of profitability and fostering public welfare (Zahra et al., 2009). Social entrepreneurs are rarely driven by utilitarian values as they aspire to improve social wealth of their communities by resolving pressing social problems (Zahra et al., 2009). However, in the case of Schwartz's circular model, engaging in a certain behavior requires a trade-off. Values that reside on the top (power, achievement, hedonism, stimulation and self-direction) regulate how people deal with their personal interest while values that reside on the bottom (benevolence, universalism, tradition, conformity, security) are concerned with how people socially relate with others. Values that, frequently, impact prosocial behavior are universalism, benevolence, conformity, security and power. Specifically, benevolence encourages action that promotes the welfare of others out of concern for them, while conformity encourages prosocial behavior to avoid negative results for oneself. Security and power values oppose prosocial behavior as security values highlight one's needs over others, while power values justify self-serving behavior which does not conform with prosocial enactment (Schwartz, 2010).

Social entrepreneur's personal values can explain their motivation to establish social enterprises (Sotiropoulou et al., 2021). Research suggests that both empathy and compassion are main motivators in stirring social entrepreneur's intent (Ajzen, 1991) and social entrepreneurship behavior (El Ebrashi, 2013; Hockerts, 2015b; Tucker & Croom, 2021; Urban 2020). Studies show that values of self-enhancement have negative relation with social entrepreneurship behavior because its embedded values of achievement, authority, prestige and personal recognition are prioritized over the social good, while self-transcendent values have shown positive relation (Sastre-Castillo et al., 2015). Kruse et al. (2019) identified not only self-transcendence but openness to change as predictors of social entrepreneurial intention. Another study by Bargsted et al. (2013) found that benevolence, universalism and self-direction were the most related values to social entrepreneurship behavior.

Table 4.2 presents an aggregation of possible values that predicts social entrepreneurial intentions. However, to the best of our knowledge, literature on social entrepreneurship did not study how personal values affect the formation of hybrids. Tan et al. (2020) extensively reviewed social entrepreneurial intention on different levels and categories, and interestingly, the review did not tackle the value system of social entrepreneur prior to establishing their new venture which is a further motivation to the current study. Actually, hybrids, as mentioned before, show clear interaction between social and economic logics, where these logics are entertained from different personal value systems. For example, we may want to ask, what personal values lead to the formation of for-profit social enterprises and hybrid enterprises (Bosma & Levie, 2010)? Will these values follow more "the social part of for-profit social enterprise or the profit part of it"? Will these values be inclined more toward benevolence, universalism, self-direction, stimulation or power, achievement and tradition? Accordingly, this study would propose a bundle of socio-economic

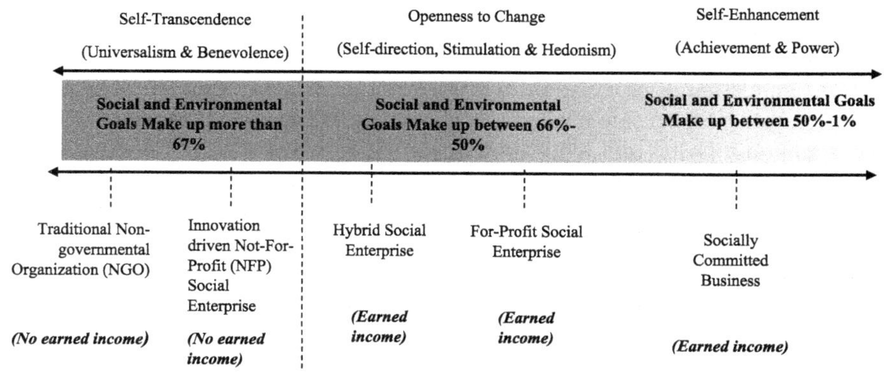

Fig. 4.2 Bundle of socio-economic values' continuum across hybrid forms (developed by the researchers)

Table 4.2 Personal values and social entrepreneurial intention (compiled by the researchers)

Values	Social entrepreneurial intention
Self-Enhancement (Power, achievement and hedonism)	**Negative relation** Sastre-Castillo et al. (2015) and Schwartz (2010)
Openness to change (Self-direction, stimulation and hedonism)	**Positive relation** Kruse et al. (2019) and Bargsted et al. (2013)
Self-Transcendence (Universalism and benevolence)	**Positive relation** Sastre-Castillo et al. (2015), Kruse et al. (2019), Bargsted et al. (2013) and Schwartz (2010)
Conservation (Tradition, conformity and security)	**Negative relation** Schwartz (2010)

values that might be present in the different forms of hybrid organizations that we presented in Fig. 4.1 and based on the categorization of Schwartz's (1992) personal values. Figure 4.2 shows a continuum of socio-economic values across the different hybrid forms to balance between value creation vis-à-vis value capture.

Figure 4.2 demonstrates the combination of different hybrid organizational forms with three pillars of Schwartz's (1992) theory. Self-transcendence values are chosen due to their high relation to prosocial behavior in general and social entrepreneurial intention in specific (Sastre-Castillo et al., 2015; Kruse et al., 2019; Bargsted et al., 2013; Schwartz. 2010), and it is positioned on the left side of the continuum to complement the 67% of social and environment goals within organizations. Thus, this aligns with Schwartz's (1992) assumption that environmental organizations that serve mass populations possess universalism values, as well as with Brulle's (1996) assumption of their relation to benevolent values. As the percentage of social and economic goals decreases as you move to the right of the continuum, one may assume that the intensity of the self-transcendence values decreases and starts to blend with the openness to change values, thus suggesting the circular arrangement of Schwartz

(1992) theory that complementary values are adjacent to one another and the closer the values are to each other, the more similar their underlying motivation is.

The formulation of propositions will focus on the hybrid forms of social enterprises to capture the tension between social value creation and value capture; therefore, traditional NGOs and innovation-driven NFPs will not be considered in the current study due to their nature of having no earned income strategy and depending on funding, private grants, membership fees and contributions (Saebi et al., 2019; Searing et al., 2021). Organizations that have social and environmental goals that make up 66–50% include hybrid social enterprise and for-profit social enterprise. One may argue that hybrid social enterprises include higher percentage of social and environmental goals compared to their for-profit counterpart. The hybrid social enterprise's nature of combining both the social logic and economic logic presents a challenge for its sustainability, and since social enterprises exist in the blurry line between not-for-profit and for-profit organizations (Battilana & Lee, 2014; Searing et al., 2021), therefore, one may propose that sustaining the hybrid model should incorporate a bundle of values to be able to handle this dilemma. Mirghani and El Ebrashi (2022) suggested that social entrepreneurship incorporates both openness to change and self-transcendent values due to the dual nature of social entrepreneurship. Thus, the dual nature of hybrid social enterprises would benefit from a bundle of values in managing their tensions (Gillett et al., 2019). Accordingly, the following proposition states that:

P1. Hybrid social enterprise requires a bundle of high intensity self-transcendence values and moderate intensity of openness to change values.

For-profit social enterprise incorporates lesser social and economic goal percentage make up compared to their focus on earned income. Accordingly, they complement Shepherd et al. (2019) classification of economic venture of having high economic logic intensity. Higher economic logic intensity infers more focus on value capture vis-à-vis value creation (Santos, 2012). Thus, there is more focus on openness to change values, and lesser intensity of self-transcendence, as for-profit-oriented firms are more prone to deal with economic challenges—related to stimulation values—and values of self-direction that entails more independence of thought and actions (Schwartz, 2010) that allow individuals to better capture value. Moreover, and in order for a for-profit social enterprise not to fall into mission drift (Al Taji & Bengo, 2019) by overriding the economic logic and neglecting the social logic along the way, this organizational form requires some level of control over both people and resources—relation to power values—and showing the correct competence—relation to achievement values—which fall in the self-enhancement dimension of Schwartz (1992) theory. Accordingly, the following proposition states that:

P2. For-Profit social enterprise requires lesser intensity of self-transcendence values, high intensity of openness to change values and moderate intensity of self-enhancement values.

Socially committed business includes a composition of 50–1% social and environmental goals, thus highlighting more on the financial gains. Accordingly, one may argue that this organizational form has higher economic logic intensity compared to the for-profit social enterprise. Even though Sastre-Castillo et al. (2015) and Schwartz (2010) found that self-enhancement values negatively influence social entrepreneurial intention, Mirghani and El Ebrashi (2022) assumed that organizations that opt for prosocial economic logic, such as CSR (Shepherd et al., 2019), corporate social innovation (Shan & Ling, 2020) and organization activism for policy change (Becker-Ritterspach et al. 2019), require openness to change and self-enhancement values. However, the current study argues that socially committed businesses should possess a higher intensity of self-enhancement values, such as power, to provide individuals with the needed control over resources and thus, reach profit maximization. In addition, those socially committed businesses should own values of achievement to convey the needed competence in achieving profitability. Again, because there is still "social" commitment, socially responsible businesses may possess some deal of openness to change values, which are related to social entrepreneurship behavior (Bargsted et al., 2013; Kruse et al., 2019). Therefore, the following proposition states that:

P3. Socially committed businesses requires moderate intensity of openness to change values and high intensity of self-enhancement values.

4.5 Conclusion

This paper builds on the literature of tensions and institutional logics in hybrid organizations, by focusing on how personal values intervene in managing those tensions and logics, explaining hybrid organizational behavior. Through the discourse presented around hybridity and highlighting the main gaps, this paper presented a continuum that attempted to capture possible bundles of socio-economic values that may align with various hybrid forms of different social, environmental and economic logics composition. The representation of a continuum and not a typology infers the transcendence and coexistence of values with different intensities in various hybrids. Propositions suggest that hybrid social enterprises entail higher intensity of self-transcendence values with moderate intensity of openness to change; for-profit social enterprises entail lesser intensity of self-transcendence, high intensity of openness to change and moderate intensity of self-enhancement, and socially committed businesses entail moderate intensity of openness to change values and high intensity of self-enhancement values. Future research is recommended to empirically explore these conceptual propositions through the development of a hybrid organizational behavior scale that stems from Schwartz's (1992) theory of human values and build on Ajzen's (1991) theory of planned behavior and Hockerts' (2015b) extension of social entrepreneurial intention model. Empirically exploring the above propositions will be a step closer in understanding the different bundle of values that may be adopted to regulate different forms of hybridity.

References

Ajzen, I. (1991). The theory of planned behavior. *Organizational Behavior and Human Decision Processes, 50*(2), 179–211.

Al Taji, F. N. A., & Bengo, I. (2019). The distinctive managerial challenges of hybrid organizations: Which skills are required. *Journal of Social Entrepreneurship, 10*(3), 328–345.

Allport, G. W. (1961). *Pattern and growth in personality*. Holt, Rinehart and Winston.

Alter, K. (2006). Social enterprise typology. *Virtue Ventures LLC, 12*(1), 1–124.

Arellano-Gault, D., Demortain, D., Rouillard, C., & Thoenig, J.-C. (2013). Bringing public organization and organizing back in. *Organization Studies, 34*, 145–167.

Austin, J., Stevenson, H., & Wei-Skillern, J. (2006). Social and commercial entrepreneurship: Same, different, or both? *Entrepreneurship: Theory & Practice, 30*(1), 1–22.

Austin, J. E., Leonard, H., Reficco, E., & Wei-Skillern, J. (2004). *Corporate social entrepreneurship: A new vision of CSR* (Harvard Business School Working Paper No. 05-021). Boston: Harvard Business School.

Bargsted, M., Picon, M., Salazar, A., & Rojas, Y. (2013). Psychosocial characterization of social entrepreneurs: A comparative study. *Journal of Social Entrepreneurship, 4*(3), 331–346.

Battilana, J., & Lee, M. (2014). Advancing research on hybrid organizing–Insights from the study of social enterprises. *Academy of Management Annals, 8*(1), 397–441.

Battilana, J., Besharov, M., & Mitzinneck, B. (2017). On hybrids and hybrid organizing: A review and roadmap for future research. In *The SAGE handbook of organizational institutionalism* (Vol. 2, pp. 133–169).

Becker-Ritterspach, F., Simbeck, K., & El Ebrashi, R. (2019). MNCs' corporate environmental responsibility in emerging and developing economies: Toward an action research approach. *Critical Perspectives on International Business, 15*(3), 179–200.

Bocken, N. M. P., Fil, A., & Prabhu, J. (2016). Scaling up social businesses in developing markets. *Journal of Cleaner Production, 139*, 295–308.

Bosma, N. S., & Levie, J. (2010). Global entrepreneurship monitor 2009 executive report.

Brown, H., & Murphy, E. (2003). *The financing of social enterprises: A special report by the Bank of England*. Bank of England Domestic Finance Division, London.

Brulle, R. J. (1996). Environmental discourse and social movement organizations: A historical and rhetorical perspective on the development of US environmental organizations. *Sociological Inquiry, 66*(1), 58–83.

Bruneel, J., Moray, N., Stevens, R., & Fassin, Y. (2016). Balancing competing logics in for-profit social enterprises: A need for hybrid governance. *Journal of Social Entrepreneurship, 7*(3), 263–288.

Cornforth, C. (2020). The governance of hybrid organisations. In *Handbook on hybrid organisations*. Edward Elgar Publishing.

Dees, J. G. (2012). A tale of two cultures: Charity, problem solving, and the future of social entrepreneurship. *Journal of Business Ethics, 111*(3), 321–334.

Dees, J. G., & Anderson, B. B. (2003). For-profit social ventures. *International Journal of Entrepreneurship Education (Special Issue on Social Entrepreneurship), 2*, 1–26.

Di Domenico, M., Haugh, H., & Tracey, P. (2010). Social bricolage: Theorizing social value creation in social enterprises. *Entrepreneurship Theory and Practice, 34*(4), 681–703.

Dion, M. (2014). The economic and non-economic dimensions of social entreprises' moral discourse: An issue of axiological and philosophical coherence. *International Entrepreneurship and Management Journal, 10*(2), 385–408.

Doherty, B., Haugh, H., & Lyon, F. (2014). Social enterprises as hybrid organizations: A review and research agenda. *International Journal of Management Reviews, 16*(4), 417–436.

Douglas, H. (2015). Embracing hybridity: A review of social entrepreneurship and enterprise in Australia and New Zealand. *Third Sector Review, 21*(1), 5–30.

El Ebrashi, R. (2013). Social entrepreneurship theory and sustainable social impact. *Social Responsibility Journal, 9*(3), 188–209.

El Ebrashi, R., & El-Batawy, L. (2021). Dependence and resourcefulness: A typology of social impact scaling strategies. *Journal of Social Entrepreneurship*, 1–41.
Fishbein, M., & Ajzen, I. (2011). *Predicting and changing behavior: The reasoned action approach*. Psychology press.
Gillett, A., Loader, K., Doherty, B., & Scott, J. M. (2019). An examination of tensions in a hybrid collaboration: A longitudinal study of an empty homes project. *Journal of Business Ethics, 157*(4), 949–967.
Gupta, S., Beninger, S., & Ganesh, J. (2015). A hybrid approach to innovation by social enterprises: Lessons from Africa. *Social Enterprise Journal, 11*(1), 89–112.
Haigh, N., & Hoffman, A. J. (2011). Hybrid organizations: The next chapter in sustainable business. *Organizational dynamics, 41*(2), 126–134.
Hockerts, K. (2006). Entrepreneurial opportunity in social purpose business ventures. In J. Mair, J. Robinson, & K. Hockerts (Eds.), *Social entrepreneurship* (pp. 142–155). Palgrave Macmillan.
Hockerts, K. (2015a). How hybrid organizations turn antagonistic assets into complementarities. *California Management Review, 57*(3), 83–106.
Hockerts, K. (2015b). The social entrepreneurial antecedents scale (SEAS): A validation study. *Social Enterprise Journal, 11*(3), 260–280.
Hossain, S., Saleh, M. A., & Drennan, J. (2017). A critical appraisal of the social entrepreneurship paradigm in an international setting: A proposed conceptual framework. *International Entrepreneurship and Management Journal, 13*(2), 347–368.
Jay, J. (2013). Navigating paradox as a mechanism of change and innovation in hybrid organizations. *Academy of Management Journal, 56*(1), 137–159.
Kadir, M. A. B. A., & Sarif, S. M. (2016). Social entrepreneurship, social entrepreneur and social enterprise: A review of concepts, definitions and development in Malaysia. *Journal of Emerging Economies and Islamic Research, 4*(2), 51–66.
Kotey, B., & Meredith, G. G. (1997). Relationships among owner/manager personal values, business strategies, and enterprise performance. *Journal of Small Business Management, 35*, 37–64.
Kruse, P., Wach, D., Costa, S., & Moriano, J. A. (2019). Values matter, don't they?—Combining theory of planned behavior and personal values as predictors of social entrepreneurial intention. *Journal of Social Entrepreneurship, 10*(1), 55–83.
Lacap, J. P. G., Mulyaningsih, H. D., & Ramadani, V. (2018). The mediating effects of social entrepreneurial antecedents on the relationship between prior experience and social entrepreneurial intent: The case of Filipino and Indonesian university students. *Journal of Science and Technology Policy Management, 9*(3), 329–346.
Lautermann, C. (2013). The ambiguities of (social) value creation: Towards an extended understanding of entrepreneurial value creation for society. *Social Enterprise Journal, 9*(2), 184–202.
Mair, J., & Noboa, E. (2006). Social entrepreneurship: How intentions to create a social venture are formed. In J. Mair, J. Robinson & K. Hockerts (Eds.), *Social entrepreneurship* (pp. 121–136). Palgrave Macmillan.
Mair, J., & Marti, I. (2006). Social entrepreneurship research: A source of explanation, prediction, and delight. *Journal of World Business, 41*(1), 36-447.
Mair, J., & Marti, I. (2009). Entrepreneurship in and around institutional voids: A case study from Bangladesh. *Journal of Business Venturing, 24*(5), 419–435.
Mair, J., & Rathert, N. (2020). Let's talk about problems: Advancing research on hybrid organizing, social enterprises, and institutional context. *Organizational Hybridity: Perspectives, Processes, Promises, 69*, 189–208.
Mason, C., Kirkbride, J., & Bryde, D. (2007). From stakeholders to institutions: The changing face of social enterprise governance theory. *Management Decision, 45*(2), 284–301.
Mendoza-Abarca, K. I., & Mellema, H. N. (2016). Aligning economic and social value creation through pay-what-you-want pricing. *Journal of Social Entrepreneurship, 7*(1), 101–125.
Mirghani, A. & El Ebrashi, R. (2022). Into the values verse: The epistemic origins of organizational prosocial behavior. In *British Academy of Management Conference 2022*. British Academy of Management (Forthcoming).

Murphy, P., & Coombes, S. (2009). A model of social entrepreneurial discovery. *Journal of Business Ethics, 87*(3), 325–336.
Murray, S. L., Haddock, G., & Zanna, M. P. (1996). On creating value-expressive attitudes: An experimental approach. In C. Seligman, J. M. Olson, & M. P. Zanna (Eds.), *The psychology of values: The Ontario symposium* (Vol. 8, pp. 107–133). Lawrence Erlbaum.
Pestoff, V. (1998). *Beyond the market and state: Civil democracy and social enterprises in a welfare society*. Ashgate. Regulator for Community Interest.
Powell, W. W. (1990). Neither market nor hierarchy. *Research in Organizational Behavior, 12*, 295–336.
Rokeach, M. (1973). *The nature of human values*. Free Press.
Saebi, T., Foss, N. J., & Linder, S. (2019). Social entrepreneurship research: Past achievements and future promises. *Journal of Management, 45*(1), 70–95.
Santos, F. M. (2012). A positive theory of social entrepreneurship. *Journal of Business Ethics, 111*(3), 335–351.
Sastre-Castillo, M. A., Peris-Ortiz, M., & Danvila-Del Valle, I. (2015). What is different about the profile of the social entrepreneur? *Nonprofit Management and Leadership, 25*(4), 349–369.
Schwartz, S. H. (1992). Universals in the content and structure of values: Theory and empirical tests in 20 countries. In M. P. Zanna (Ed.), *Advances in experimental social psychology* (Vol. 25, pp. 1–65). Academic Press.
Schwartz, S. H. (2010). Basic values: How they motivate and inhibit prosocial behavior.
Schwartz, S. H., & Bilsky, W. (1987). Toward a universal psychological structure of human values. *Journal of Personality and Social Psychology, 53*(3), 550.
Searing, E. A., Poledrini, S., Young, D. R., & Nyssens, M. (2021). The hybrid nature of social enterprises how does it affect their revenue sources? *Social Enterprise Journal, 18*(2), 321–343.
Shan, W., & Ling, L. (2020). Corporate social innovation: New integration of social responsibility and innovation. In *The 3rd International Conference on Economy, Management and Entrepreneurship (ICOEME 2020)* (pp. 254–261). Atlantis Press.
Shepherd, D. A., Williams, T. A., & Zhao, E. Y. (2019). A framework for exploring the degree of hybridity in entrepreneurship. *Academy of Management Perspectives, 33*(4), 491–512.
Short, J. C., Moss, T. W., & Lumpkin, G. T. (2009). Research in social entrepreneurship: Past contributions and future opportunities. *Strategic Entrepreneurship Journal, 3*, 161–194.
Sotiropoulou, A., Papadimitriou, D., & Maroudas, L. (2021). Personal values and typologies of social entrepreneurs: The case of Greece. *Journal of Social Entrepreneurship, 12*(1), 1–27.
Sulphey, M. M., & Salim, A. (2020). Development of a tool to measure social entrepreneurial orientation. *Journal of Entrepreneurship in Emerging Economies, 13*(2), 231–253.
Tan, L. P., Le, A. N. H., & Xuan, L. P. (2020). A systematic literature review on social entrepreneurial intention. *Journal of Social Entrepreneurship, 11*(3), 241–256.
Tiwari, P., Bhat, A. K., & Tikoria, J. (2022). Mediating role of prosocial motivation in predicting social entrepreneurial intentions. *Journal of Social Entrepreneurship, 13*(1), 118–141.
Tomczyk, D., Lee, J., & Winslow, E. (2013). Entrepreneurs' personal values, compensation, and high growth firm performance. *Journal of Small Business Management, 51*(1), 66–82.
Tracey, P., Phillips, N., & Jarvis, O. (2011). Bridging institutional entrepreneurship and the creation of new organizational forms: A multilevel model. *Organization science, 22*(1), 60–80.
Tucker, R., & Croom, R. M. (2021). A xenophilic perspective of social entrepreneurship. *Journal of Business Venturing Insights, 15*, 1–7.
Urban, B. (2020). Entrepreneurial alertness, self-efficacy and social entrepreneurship. *Journal of Small Business and Enterprise Development, 27*(3), 489–507.
Vallaster, C., Kraus, S., Lindahl, J. M. M., & Nielsen, A. (2019). Ethics and entrepreneurship: A bibliometric study and literature review. *Journal of Business Research, 99*, 226–237.
Weerakoon, C., McMurray, A., Rametse, N., & Douglas, H. (2016). The nexus between social entrepreneurship and social innovation. In *ACERE Conference, Gold Coast* (pp. 3–5).
Yunus, M. (2007). *Creating a world without poverty: Social business and the future of capitalism*. Public Affairs.

Zacharias, N. A., Nijssen, E. J., & Stock, R. M. (2016). Effective configurations of value creation and capture capabilities: Extending Treacy and Wiersema's value disciplines. *Journal of Business Research, 69*(10), 4121–4131.

Zahra, S. A., Gedajlovic, E., Neubaum, D. O., & Shulman, J. M. (2009). A typology of social entrepreneurs: Motives, search processes and ethical challenges. *Journal of Business Venturing, 24*(5), 519–532.

Żur, A. (2021). Entrepreneurial identity and social-business tensions—The experience of social entrepreneurs. *Journal of Social Entrepreneurship, 12*(3), 438–461.

Part II
Regional Approaches

Chapter 5
Integration Initiatives and Trajectories of Innovative Development of the Financial Market

Natallia V. Maltsevich, Ilya V. Maltsevich, and Tatiana V. Proharava

Abstract The article deals with the integration of the financial market of the Eurasian Economic Union countries. The current situation and barriers to integration, in particular, for the banking sector of the EAEU countries, are investigated. The necessity of implementing banking innovations in the digital economy to transform the format of banking services was substantiated, and prospective directions of digitalization that contribute to the sustainable development of the banking system of the EAEU countries were analyzed. The study applied methods of theoretical generalization to identify approaches to the digital path of sustainable development of the banking sector.

Keywords EAEU financial market · Innovation processes · Digital platform · National banking · Country-subjects · Integration effect · Digital innovations · Sustainable finance · Information technology

Abbreviation

EAEU (EEU) Eurasian Economic Union—economic union of states (Armenia, Belarus, Kazakhstan, Kyrgyzstan, Russian Federation) located in Eurasia

N. V. Maltsevich (✉) · I. V. Maltsevich · T. V. Proharava
Institute of Economics of the National Academy of Sciences of Belarus, Business of School of the Belarusian State University, Minsk, Belarus

D. Crowther and S. Seifi (eds.), *Corporate Social Responsibility in Difficult Times*, Approaches to Global Sustainability, Markets, and Governance,
https://doi.org/10.1007/978-981-99-2591-9_5

5.1 Introduction

The process of strategic development of the national economy, embodying a new stage of socio-economic progress, is not only time-consuming, but also depends on many factors. The leading place among them belongs to financial factors, which allow other factors to reach their full potential. In ensuring the development of the national economy, great attention is paid to the functioning of the banking sector, as it is able to create a powerful financial base with powerful tools to influence these processes (2018). Credit relations and the banking institutions that implement them can play a unifying role in the development of national banking systems of the member states of the Eurasian Economic Union.

In today's world, the problems and prospects of economic integration and financial globalization are perceived ambiguously by different countries, representatives of different social strata and economic schools. Some see integration processes as a panacea for all troubles and misfortunes, a way to stability and prosperity, while others see them as a threat to their national interests, a way to oppression and poverty. The truth, respectively, is in the middle and lies in the need to achieve an optimal balance between positive and negative trends and consequences of integration, on the one hand, and national protectionism, on the other, based on minimizing risks and intensifying the chances formed and realized in the integration processes.

In the context of contemporary challenges, the promotion of regional integration as a determinant of the stability of the member states of integration increases in importance, which strengthens the economic position of the union. For the member states of the union integration of financial markets provide a number of key advantages, which increase profitability of monetary policy, resilience of the economy to external shocks, efficiency and competitiveness in general, as well as the main sectors of the financial services market. The integration component of their development implies the growth of mutual investments in the EAEU, which fully corresponds to the directions of national union member states (2019). Currently, the EAEU is an economic system with enormous economic potential, a significant sphere of geopolitical influence and broad development opportunities for the countries that have joined the EAEU. The decision of the Supreme Eurasian Economic Council "On the main directions of economic development of the Eurasian Economic Union" defines the main directions of development of the union until 2030, which include ensuring macroeconomic stability; creating conditions for innovative development and modernization of the economy; formation of effective financial system; implementation of foreign trade potential; etc. (2015).

This fully applies to national banking systems, organically included in the integration processes. Banks participate in the process of integration into the global community as objects and as instruments or regulators, thereby influencing its pace and effectiveness.

Most of the EEU countries are actively interacting with financial institutions, which is due to the transformation of their infrastructure, the growth of capital, the strengthening of their mutual influence and interdependence. A fundamental factor in the integration of national and local financial markets is the unification of the banking systems of the EEU countries, which is manifested not only in the strengthening of the standardization of their activities, but also in the desire of banks to expand mutually beneficial activities between countries. This is due to the fact that the expansion of integration processes significantly increases the need for banking services. Under these conditions, it becomes relevant to study the level of banking interaction in the EEU countries and identify the existing prerequisites for creating a single market for financial and banking services.

5.2 Prospects and Problems of the Financial Sector in the Context of Digitalization

At this stage, the EAEU is on a more sustainable path of development, movement along which requires deepening financial market liberalization with simultaneous alignment of the regulatory and legal space, coordination of actions to form a consolidated financial market with a high level of security, which is one of priorities of EAEU development (2021).

The viability of the chosen model, the basis of which is the banking sector, largely determines the effective development of this process. This involves the harmonization of the legislation of the union's member states, i.e., the creation of a single financial infrastructure, within which capital flows between the EAEU members states should be carried out. One of the key documents ensuring progress in this direction was the Concept of Forming a Common EEU Financial Market, approved by the decision of the Supreme Eurasian Economic Council No. 20 of October 4, 2018. This fundamental document establishes the aims, tasks, key directions of formation of the financial market with an indication of the stages and measures for their implementation, the legal of its functioning, the order of information interaction and administrative interaction of financial market regulators, goals and authority of the supranational regulatory agency of the EEU common national financial market (2018).

The concept of a general financial sector of the EAEU is the core for the creation of a regulatory framework that will regulate interaction in the banking sector. All this will ensure simplified and non-discriminatory access of EAEU member countries' players to each other's markets. Conditions will be created in the financial market for the realization of the main objectives of the EAEU (2017).

Currently, most EAEU countries are actively interacting with financial institutions, which is due to the transformation of their infrastructure, capital growth, strengthening of their mutual influence and interdependence. A serious moment of market integration is the unification of the banking systems of the EAEU countries, which manifests itself not only in the increased standardization of their activities, but also in the desire of banks to expand mutually beneficial activities between countries. This is due to the fact that the expansion of integration processes significantly increases the need for banking services. Under these conditions, it becomes relevant to study the level of banking interaction in the EAEU countries and identify the existing prerequisites for creating a unified market for banking services (2021). The banking systems of the member countries of the union are not comparable with each other and have a large number of differences in volume and structure (Table 5.1).

The financial industry can be viewed as an object affected by the global unstable environment and at the same time as a subject that creates it. Thus, banks that ineffectively manage risk create instability for the entire economy. In the context of strategic planning at financial institutions, instability is often defined as a given, which must be corrected by mitigating the following risks:

- political (through international business or indirectly through exchange rates);
- economic (financial systems of countries, price volatility, legal regulation);
- social (non-acceptance of innovation, income inequality of the population, insufficient qualification of workers, problems of mentality, which prevents the adoption of creative solutions, to show initiative);
- technological (losses due to reduced efficiency of activities based on the use of outdated technologies, due to improper implementation of new technologies, as well as associated with the capture of market share by competitors using innovative technologies);
- cyber risks (losses due to insufficient data protection. Due to the cloud way of data storage, companies face the problem of creating a security system that meets today's challenges) (2018).

Thus, the trajectory of the financial industry is determined by a combination of external environment factors characterized by increased risks that challenge all financial and credit institutions. Financial institutions face the challenge of implementing breakthrough technologies and innovative management approaches, ensuring their long-term survival in the market (2016).

Current areas of financial markets are informatization and digitalization. Participants in financial markets make decisions based on complex computer modeling, statistical analysis of a large amount of data, the use of mathematical and statistical modeling methods and neural forecasting systems. Digital technologies have revolutionized the financial world and will continue to influence it even more actively. "A new economy, a new world and a new demographic require a new financial system," Bank of England Governor Mark Carney said. Digitalization is changing the structure of the economy and business models of companies, the share of emerging markets in the global economy and finance is growing, and the macroeconomic consequences of population aging are already manifested in lower interest rates and rising asset prices.

Table 5.1 Dynamics of the functioning of the banking sector of the countries-subjects of the EEU

Indicators	2016	2017	2018	2019	2020	2020 in % to 2016	2020 in % to 2019
EEU							
Banks (units)	724	661	578	534	496	68.5	92.9
Branches of banks (units)	2288	2099	1892	1810	1696	74.1	93.7
Banking assets ($billion)	1445	1599	1464	1685	1531	106	90.9
Liabilities of banks ($billion)	1270	1420	1302	1386	1370	108	98.9
Armenia							
Banks, units	19	19	17	17	17	89	100
Share in the EEU (%)	2.6	2.9	2.9	3.2	3.4	0.8	0.8
Branches of banks (units)	523	523	537	551	559	107	101.5
Banking assets ($billion)	8	9	10	12	13	163	105.4
Share in the EEU (%)	0.6	0.6	0.7	0.7	0.8	0.2	0.1
Liabilities of banks ($billion)	7	8	9	10	11	157	106.6
Share in the EEU (%)	0.6	0.6	0.7	0.7	0.8	0.2	0.1
Belarus							
Banks (units)	24	24	24	24	24	100	100
Share in the EEU (%)	3.3	3.6	4.2	4.5	4.8	1.5	0.3
Branches of banks (units)	39	34	27	17	2	5.1	11.8
Banking assets ($billion)	32	35	30	39	35	109	91.1
Share in the EEU (%)	2.2	2.2	2	2.3	2.3	0.1	–
Liabilities of banks ($billion)	28	30	26	33	30	107	91.3
Share in the EEU (%)	2.2	2.1	1.9	2.4	2.2	–	−0.2
Kazakhstan							
Banks (units)	33	32	28	27	26	79	96.3
Share in the EEU (%)	4.6	4.8	4.8	5.1	5.2	0.6	0.1

(continued)

Table 5.1 (continued)

Indicators	2016	2017	2018	2019	2020	2020 in % to 2016	2020 in % to 2019
Branches of banks (units)	343	333	298	301	293	85.4	97.3
Banking assets ($billion)	77	73	66	70	74	96	105.3
Share in the EEU (%)	5.3	4.6	4.5	4.2	4.8	−0.5	0.6
Liabilities of banks ($billion)	68	64	58	61	65	95.6	106.4
Share in the EEU (%)	5.4	4.5	4.5	4.4	4.7	−0.7	0.3
Kyrgyzstan							
Banks (units)	25	25	25	24	23	92	95.8
Share in the EEU (%)	3.5	3.8	4.3	4.5	4.6	1.1	0.1
Branches of banks (units)	324	319	321	323	312	96.3	96.6
Banking assets ($billion)	3	3	3	4	4	133	97.9
Share in the EEU (%)	0.2	0.2	0.2	0.2	0.3	0.1	0.1
Liabilities of banks ($billion)	2	2	3	3	3	99.2	100
Share in the EEU (%)	0.2	1.4	0.2	0.2	0.2	–	–
Russian Federation							
Banks (units)	623	561	484	442	406	65.2	91.9
Share in the EEU (%)	85	86	84	83	82	−4	−1
Branches of banks (units)	1098	890	709	618	530	48.2	85.8
Banking assets ($billion)	1325	1479	1354	1560	1406	106	90.1
Share in the EEU (%)	92	93	92	93	92	0.8	0.8
Liabilities of banks ($billion)	1165	1316	1206	1279	1261	108	98.6
Share in the EEU (%)	92	93	93	92	92	0.8	0.8

Source Compiled by the author (2020)

According to the theory of paradigms, the development of all mankind occurs through the transition from one paradigm to another. At the moment, humanity is entering the era of a global information network, bio quantum society, a characteristic feature of which is information network universalization and globalization. The impetus for the transition to a new paradigm was the fourth industrial revolution, which brought with it the digitalization and cyberfiction of industry, robotics, 3-D design and printing. Digital technologies have become the main driver of economic development (2020).

With the transition to the information society, the nature of data processing has changed significantly, which has affected the nature of the activities of financial and credit institutions. There is an opinion that science was pushed to breakthrough technologies by a huge flow of data, characterized by three main parameters—a significant volume, lightning speed of distribution and a variety of data itself, the sources of which are social networks, information technologies, communication tools, etc. Considering the financial market in the context of information technology, it should be noted that along with the digital reboot of the institutions of the financial industry, not only the restructuring of business processes should take place, but also a change in the outlook of employees, which makes digital transformation also professional transformation. Forbes concludes that companies need to think now about transforming the culture of the organization as a whole and creating a trusting environment that will create a balance between adequate security controls and an acceptable risk of using the latest technologies (2020). The economy in the next decade will change under the influence of technological, demographic and environmental factors, and the financial system will have to change along with the economy (Fig. 5.1).

The modern economy needs markets to bring together borrowers and lenders, buyers and sellers, as well as funds to create capital and manage investments. All this traditionally refers to the functionality of the financial market, where, due to

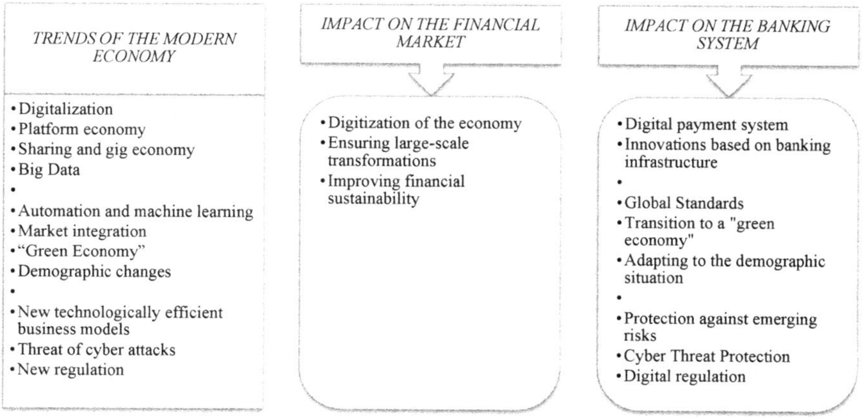

Fig. 5.1 Global digitalization trends and their impact on the banking system. *Source* Compiled by the authors (2021)

increased competition, the banking sector is forced to modify its systems. Digital transformation already requires a new behavior, a new culture and a change in the structure of the company.

It is important to note that if banks cannot keep up with competitors and meet consumer expectations for fast, affordable and personalized financial services, tech companies may completely squeeze them out of the high-margin direct customer interaction segment. In this case, the role of banks risks being reduced to the mere provision of infrastructure. In addition to technology giants, the fintech sector of companies poses a threat to the banking sector. These companies are focused on providing solutions that reduce the cost of finding suitable parties to a transaction and ensure the efficient use of large amounts of data and cheaper and more secure information transfer. The reason why fintech is generating so much hype and research interest right now is that it is competitively outperforming traditional banks in providing financial services.

5.3 Banking Sector Transformation Options

It is becoming clear that financial market players such as large technology companies, as well as fintech and neo-banking companies, can leave the traditional banking industry on the sidelines. The digital format allows you to determine the place of the banking sector in the structure of the financial market and schematically present it in three versions (Fig. 5.2).

Fintech companies are expanding the market, redistributing part of the users from banks to themselves. However, due to narrow specialization, now this is not a very tangible amount. People who have not previously invested in art, did not keep advanced records of personal finances, did not invest in projects that they see as promising (crowdfunding), will find out that now this can be done. However, banks have advantages over fintech companies such as access to a lot of data and capital, not to mention the advantages provided by the factor of government regulation.

Experts in the EY report "Unleashing the Potential of Fintech in Banking" emphasized that cooperation with fintech companies, instead of competition, can provide

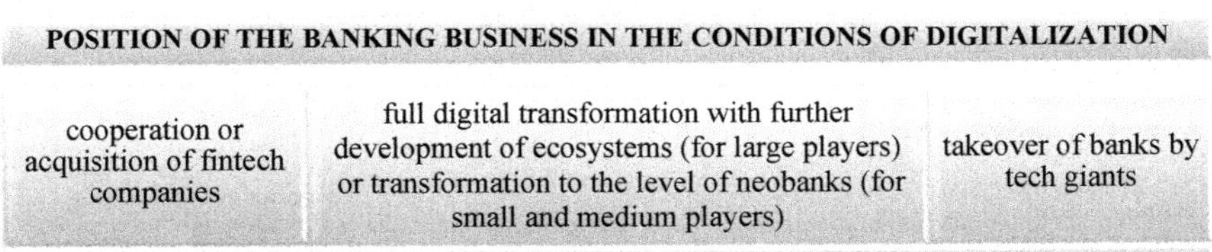

Fig. 5.2 Place of the banking business in the structure of the finance sector. *Source* Compiled by the authors (2021)

banks with fresh technology solutions. The presence of shared services and knowledge allows the distribution of the product offering through data analysis tools such as predictive analytics, which will provide deeper interaction with customers (2019). There are four main areas here:

1. improvement of the client interface,
2. digitalization of processes,
3. advanced analytics and
4. expansion of the product offer.

Amid the pandemic crisis, banks and fintechs must finally trust that such a partnership benefits both parties and leads to win-win scenarios. However, survey data in 2020 show something completely different, and more than two-thirds of banking top managers say they do not see the positive results of such cooperation. The strategic priorities and KPIs of the two partners do not coincide and are not consistent, as a result, both partners usually suffer. Analysts at Capgemini and Efma believe that the reason for most failed partnerships between banks and fintech is that their cooperation is poorly structured. This leads to the fact that banks and fintechs do not use each other's strengths, and the goals of the partnership are not achieved. And in the current environment, spending resources and time on partnerships that do not bring results is unacceptable (2021).

The second scenario (full digital transformation of banks) assumes that classic banks with "legacy" are characterized by a landscape based on monolithic or modular core banking systems (hereinafter referred to as CBS) from large vendors that solve accounting tasks, accounting for interest, covenants under contracts, calculating tariffs, setting up and accounting for product properties, generating various types of reporting (managerial, mandatory reporting by the Central Bank, etc.) and monitoring credit debt.

The current problem for CBS is universality. At one time it was a trend in the market, which has led to an increase in non-core functionality and the collection of non-core data, often incomplete and incorrect. In most banks, CBS serves as the primary source of data for corporate centralized or distributed data warehouses, an information system with multiple integrations with other banking systems and, in some cases, the reporting system. This results in the system becoming difficult to tune, performance and resiliency issues are identified, the system becomes complex and time-consuming to test, and investment in maintenance is steadily increasing. All this can become a serious barrier to the digitalization of the bank. Although the solution to the problem lies on the surface, it is not so easy to implement. If there is no question of switching to a fundamentally new system or architecture, then it is necessary to rid the CBS of non-core functions and data, if possible, split it into weakly dependent modules and modernize the integration tools.

A distinctive feature of a modern bank is the Internet and mobile banks, personal accounts, websites and other services for various categories of customers. Banks direct an impressive part of their investments to improve customer experience in digital channels, expand the range of relevant services and functions, adapt interfaces, ensure reliability, cybersecurity and onboarding and speed up online services. Today, a mobile app is becoming a key channel, with users accessing it multiple times a day to check card balances, track transactions, secure transfers and pay for services, and to get or repay a loan, place deposits or buy insurance. A banking mobile application is already a part of everyday life, and banks are trying to interest customers with additional features—interesting information, life hacks, information about where it is better to pay with a bankcard for additional benefits and others. Obviously, in the near future, mobile banking will be an important part of the business model of any bank that works with a mass client (2019). This means that although traditional banks have advantages now, after a while it may completely disappear. That is why digital transformation is very important for banks.

The third option (transformation of a traditional bank, up to neo-banking) suggests that the key to the bank's business model is the use of technologies from fintech companies. The banking business is completely moving into a digital format, access to services be carried out through online tools in the absence of offices, which significantly reduces the bank's costs.

One of the key ideas for organizing an ecosystem is the integration of all services into a single IT space with a single end-to-end user ID. Each service must know everything (or almost everything) that happens to the user in other services, and exchange information. For example, for individual entrepreneurs, this is a current account + cloud accounting + Internet acquiring + electronic document management (EDS) with external counterparties + marketplace (an online platform for selling products and services). For individuals, this is a current account + online purchases + mobile communications + taxi, etc. It is possible to create so-called super-applications that combine all "personal accounts" and data.

However, big tech companies have one thing in common: they don't want to be regulated like banks. Instead of crowding out banks, the strategy of big tech companies is to stealthily take over customer relationship management by offering digital financial services. This gives the bankers a choice: fight against competitors or join forces. Increasing access to financial services is a fundamental benefit for global policymakers and has a special place in the United Nations Sustainable Development Goals. According to most politicians, banks have not made enough progress on their own; for example, according to the World Bank, 1.7 billion adults do not have a bank account or use a mobile phone, and do not have a credit history or access to a regular bank branch. Under these conditions, a large technology company can provide banking services to these citizens. China's recent progress in expanding financial inclusion offers supporting evidence.

Thus, the three options for expanding the capabilities of the banking industry in the conditions of active development of technologies have both advantages and limitations, which implies the search for opportunities for further productive development of the banking business. There is no easy way to say how banks can hold their own in the face of rapid innovation. If financial institutions are to remain competitive, they must become more customer-focused, flexible and innovative, which will require changes in corporate culture, business plans and prospects for cooperation with non-traditional financial institutions.

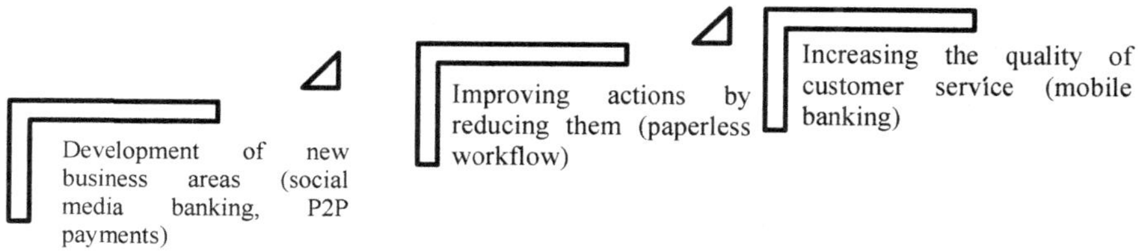

Fig. 5.3 Directions of innovative development of the banking sector. A source (2019)

And while bankers are still talking about the problems of legacy systems hindering enterprise-grade capabilities, it's not technology complexity. There are all the necessary tools to overcome backwardness: software, ERP, enterprise data warehouses and modular service-oriented architectures (Service-Oriented Architecture, SOA). The problem lies with the bank itself. If the bank does not have a unified approach to the client at the corporate level, it will not be able to work effectively and interact with clients.

Most banks are already actively using new services and improving channels to improve interaction with customers. However, there needs to be a way to conduct banking business that allows customers to have the level of service they are used to in other areas of everyday life. Banking relationships with a single multi-channel approach and a "human face" are needed. In the near future, banks should focus on innovation in three main areas (Fig. 5.3).

Thus, innovation today is a way of onboarding to an environment that is changing at an increasingly rapid pace. The digital revolution has led to the formation of a new direction of social relations; if consumers are changing, the banking business must find a model to serve them and interact with them (Table 5.2).

By making technology a central component of strategic planning, banks can differentiate their product and service offerings and dynamically respond to new market opportunities and demands. To be successful, the bank of the future will need to embrace emerging technologies, remain flexible to embrace evolving business models and put customers at the center of every strategy.

5.4 The Trajectory of Digitalization of the Banking Sector of the EAEU

In the context of globalization, the integration development of the national banking systems of the EAEU member states does not occur in isolation, but as an integral part of the economic, political, demographic, socio-cultural integration of the country into the world community. At the same time, credit relations and the banking institutions that implement them can play a unifying role, which is determined by the broad relationships of credit entrepreneurship. Integration processes in the modern world, problems and prospects of economic integration and financial globalization

Table 5.2 Banking sector development models and their economic effects

Development models economic effects	Development models economic effects
Consolidation and globalization of the banking market	International banking groups take over medium and small banks, as well as specialized financial institutions
Formation of ecosystems of universal banks and narrow-industry financial institutions	Large financial institutions generate high returns on the economies of scale; narrow financial institutions sell programs and offer products and services that can address individual customer needs
The client determines the conditions for the development of the banking business:	Expansion of knowledge on the offered banking services allows customers to put forward requirements for the quality of products and the transparency of banking procedures
Investing in building consolidated enterprise data warehouses	Requirements for the confidentiality of client information, the security of information infrastructure and its protection from potential risks activate banks to apply measures aimed at bringing them to compliance with regulatory standards
Formation of the banking infrastructure, including requirements for the development and transformation of banking business processes, the use of analytical systems and Business Intelligence	Application of more flexible approaches to managing the efficiency and payback of the banking business through the involvement of specialists working at the junction of information technology and the front office, capable of coordinating the interaction of banking departments and integrating the tasks they implement
Expansion of banking IT infrastructure	Information technologies help to improve the efficiency of banking activities and allow banks to increase the functionality of legacy infrastructure systems and IT solutions

Source Compiled by the author (2017)

are perceived ambiguously by different countries, representatives of various social strata and economic schools. Some see integration processes as a panacea for all troubles and misfortunes, a path to stability and prosperity, while others see integration as a threat to their national interests and a path to oppression and poverty. The truth, respectively, lies in the middle and consists in the need to achieve an optimal ratio of positive and negative trends and consequences of integration, on the one hand, and national protectionism, on the other, on the basis of minimizing risks and intensifying the chances formed and implemented in integration processes.

This also applies in full measure to national banking systems organically included in integration processes. Banks participate in the integration process as objects and as regulators, thus influencing its pace and efficiency (2018).

The main reasons that caused changes in the banking activities of the member countries of the union, including Belarus, in the era of globalization are as follows:

1. The development and increase in the need for adequate banking services and appearance of new banking products and services.
2. The unfinancial sector of the economy and the financial and banking systems of national economies are becoming increasingly unified, which leads to the convergence of rules governing domestic and foreign economic transactions.
3. National banking systems, which are designed to accumulate and redistribute financial resources within the national economic system, are increasingly dependent on the international capital market, which in the era of globalization has become an autonomous factor in the evolution of the global economy.
4. The growing expansion of corporations, banks, and other financial institutions in the global capital market, including in the sector of direct investment, is increasingly affecting the national monetary policy.

The growing instability of the global economy is especially evident in the banking sector, which is most sensitive to external factors (Table 5.3).

In the context of the interconnection of economies, the development of international economic organizations and associations, no country can remain on the sidelines. Improvement of the banking sector and its development, taking into account the experience of the union member states, is relevant for Belarus. Thus, it is necessary to create conditions for the formation of an integral, liquid, transparent and efficient Belarusian banking sector as part of the process of optimizing national legislations of the member states.

The financial sector in Belarus and also other countries of the union is represented by a neo-continental financial market model, which is characterized by the predominance of the banking sector, a low level of financial depth and corporate governance with a high level of volatility. Due to the prevalence of the banking segment of the financial market, the rest of its segments are not sufficiently developed to carry out the convergence of the national financial markets of the EAEU countries in order to form a financial market.

Particular attention at the current stage of integration policy is paid to the digital economy, the creation of regulative dispute resolution in the financial market, maintaining and protecting the interests of service consumers and investors in a single economic space (Fig. 5.4).

The digital agenda is one of the key areas for the development of the EAEU, digitalization, as a change in traditional economic models, directly affects the macro-stability of the region and integration, and especially, the formation of a common financial market by 2025, therefore, requires the close attention of the EAEU authorities.

The banking sector's digital evolution in the EAEU member countries is already well underway. In particular, it can be noted that over the five-year period there has been a decrease in the number of banks and their branches, respectively, by 31.5% and by 25.9% in the whole Economic Union. A similar trend is observed in the banking system of the participating countries. But at the same time, there is a steady growth in

Table 5.3 Prospects and problems of credit institutions in the innovative economy

Prospects for the problem	Prospects for the problem
Stimulating innovation as the most important condition for achieving a competitive advantage	Low competitiveness of national banks compared to international players
Removal of restrictions for non-residents to enter national markets	Termination of activities of small banks and microfinance organizations
Reorganization and cooperation of banks between themselves and non-bank financial institutions, the growth of banking alliances	Forced competition with other financial institutions: insurance and investment funds, financial companies, etc.
Predominance of syndicated lending	Inevitable regular increase in the bank's expenses for the introduction of new information and telecommunications technologies
Expanding the customer base by improving quality, increasing the availability of credit funds and reducing the value of financial services. Increased volume of transactions	Opening up of national economies (for weak economies this has a very adverse effect, while strong economies benefit)
Sustainability of the functioning of credit institutions in the long term	The trend of leveling the diversity of monetary institutions makes only large transnational banking businesses highly profitable
Exchange of the best management skills, the most efficient procedures and the latest information systems	Organizational and personnel changes (reduction of employment, number of departments, retraining of specialists, etc.)
Innovative development of national banks through the participation of foreign banks in their capital	A crisis, even in the most backward country, can cause a powerful response in the entire global banking system
Online banking as an alternative to the traditional system	The need to improve the information security system and increase information security in credit institutions
Reducing the volume of manual labor with the help of information systems	Development of proposals for opening new jobs
Spread of electronic banking through the introduction of technologies for remote banking services	Dependence on various service providers in the framework of electronic banking may lead to a decrease in the possibility of direct control over them by the management of a credit institution
Access to information about the course of trading in real time, thus reducing risks, speeding up settlements	Underdevelopment of the legal environment to regulate the activities of brokerage firms in developing countries
Increasing the degree of market transparency, accessibility of customer information	Non-observance of the confidentiality of information about customers can lead to a loss of confidence in the banking system
Specialization of banking institutions	Limited opportunities for the development of specialized banks in an unstable economic situation

Source Compiled by the author (2021)

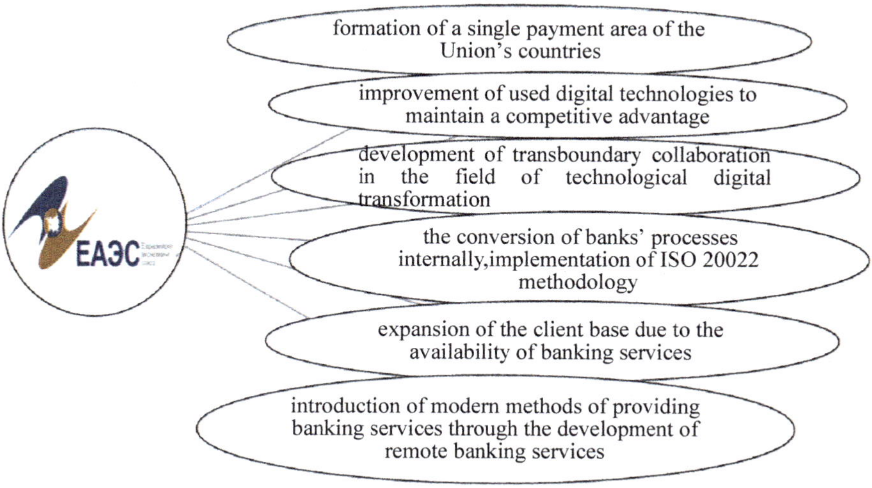

Fig. 5.4 Directions of regulation and integration of financial markets of EAEU countries in light of digital transformation. *Source* Compiled by the author (2012)

the volume of assets and liabilities of banks in the EAEU member countries. This fact shows that as a result of the banking information technology, it became possible to qualitatively expand the market for products and services, cover a larger market share through the use of ATMs, electronic settlement systems, Internet technologies and prompt customer access to information. All this will facilitate the active introduction into banking practice of the most recent achievements in the sphere of computer technology, network and information technology, methods of information protection and data processing.

The union's digital transformation project has been launched; it is time to form a Eurasian digital infrastructure that will determine the competitiveness of the financial system and traditional business. In October 2019, the decision of the Supreme Eurasian Economic Council approved the Concept of Forming a Common Financial Market of the Union, which became a key event in this area. By the same decision, the governments and national (central) banks of the EAEU countries were instructed to ensure the realization of the concept. In January 2020, the Central Bank of the Russian Federation took on the function of coordinating the development of the agreement on the standardized license and the National Bank of Kazakhstan—the agreement on the supranational body regulating the EAEU general finance market. The implementation of the strategy will create the conditions and tools for the digital transformation of the union, ensuring the comprehensive introduction of electronic technologies in economic processes, increasing the effectiveness of the union's supranational bodies, expanding the scope of economic collaboration between EAEU member states and taking responsibility for the implementation of a coordinated policy to create transparency in the financial market.

To improve the Belarusian financial market in the context of the establishment of a unified financial space of the EAEU member states, it is necessary to carry out its qualitative transformation, to eliminate the main imbalances associated with the predominance of the banking sector, the high level of dollarization, directed lending and concentration of assets and capital. The result of the implementation of the planned measures to improve the financial market of Belarus will be to ensure its balanced structure against the background of the accelerated development of the non-banking sector, improvement of the efficiency of allocation of credit resources and introduction of instruments of the long-term financing, which will allow it to function effectively in the system of harmonization processes within the EAEU (2012).

In the short term, the effectiveness of the EAEU will largely depend on whether the leaders of the member states are able to avoid a situation where economic problems and disagreements on certain points escalate into a crisis of confidence. In the case of the EAEU, the consequences of such a development will be even more severe, and for all of its participants, since their economies are very closely linked. The consequences of breaking these ties will be extremely difficult to overcome. To date, the EAEU member countries have the potential to overcome existing difficulties and disagreements. Therefore, the main obstacle that the EAEU has to overcome today is possible short-sightedness and sacrificing the medium- and long-term prospects to short-term interests.

5.5 Conclusions

As a result of the study, modern approaches to creating favorable conditions for the stable development of the banking sector of Belarus, increasing the sustainability and efficiency of its functioning have been formulated. The advancement of banking operations on the basis of the practical implementation of innovations in the context of the developing digital economy makes it possible to change the technology of banking operations, and the structure of existing business processes and the banking strategy in the implementation of specific projects is accompanied by changes in requirements to the bank. Implementation of banking innovations in the digital economy predetermines the necessity of developing theoretical and methodological foundations for creating an adaptive banking infrastructure to reduce new banking risks in the digital economy.

The identified pattern in the application of innovative technologies by banks allows a quick and accurate assessment of the risks of their customers. A more transparent banking system will also have a positive impact on investment attractiveness and can significantly expand financing opportunities for most economic agents and increase the sustainability of the banking industry. Digitalization positively affects the "inclusiveness of the banking sector," i.e., provides a high degree of access to banking services, and greater access to banking services means increased demand for them, which serves as a driver for further growth of the banking sector in a sustainable manner.

In addition, the consistent development of the banking system in the direction of innovation will provide the banking products and services competitiveness compared to non-banks and fintech products, taking into consideration the reasonable areas of development, management and adoption of banking innovations in the digital economics. In addition, the above factors contribute to the predictability and stability of the EAEU supranational economic space, strengthening its competitive position at the international level. The success of the integration association as a global player will be shared by five, bringing economic and political dividends to its participants.

References

Alekseenkova, E. S. (2017). EAEU by 2025: Priorities and expectations of member states. In I. S. Ivanov (Ed.), *EAEU development prospects up to 2025: Working paper: Special issue* (pp. 6–39). NPMP RIAC, Moscow.

Andreeva, A. V., Guseva, O. G., & Ragovik, L. V. (2012). Peculiarities of integration of Russian banking system in global financial economy. *Terra Economicus, 10*(1–3), 233–238.

Auge-Dickhut, S., Koye, B., & Liebertrau, A. (2016). *Customer value generation in banking: The Zurich model of customer-centricity*. Springer International Publishing.

Blokhina, T., Gladkaya, A., & Kostina, A. (2018). The Eurasian economic UNION' banking sector integration: problems and the development directions. *Vestnik Universiteta, 10*, 130–135. https://doi.org/10.26425/1816-4277-2018-10-130-135

Boston Consulting Group. (2021). *The CEO's guide to cybersecurity*. https://media-publications.bcg.com/BCG-Executive-Perspectives-CEO-Guideto-Cybersecurity.pdf. Accessed 24 September 2021.

Carney, M. (2018). *New economy, new finance, new bank*. Bank of England. https://www.bankofengland.co.uk/-/media/boe/files/speech/2018/new-economynew-finance-new-bank-speech-by-mark-carney.pdf. Accessed 10 September 2021.

Cornell, A. (2020). *What if banks disappeared and nobody noticed?* https://bluenotes.anz.com/posts/2020/08/andrew-cornell-column-bigtechbanking-technology. Accessed 29 April 2021.

Eurasian Economic Commission. (2020). Eurasian Economic Union in figures: A brief statistical compendium. Moscow.

Eurasian Economic Commission. (2021). Financial statistics of the Eurasian Economic Union: Operational data for 2020: statistical compendium. Moscow 8.

Eurasian Economic Council. (2015). *The main directions for the development of the EAEU until 2030*. Moscow. https://eec.eaeunion.org/upload/medialibrary/923/broshyura_ONER-_final-05.05.2016_pdf. Accessed 10 September 2021.

Eurasian Economic Union. (2018). *Declaration on further development of integration processes within the framework of the Eurasian Economic Union*. https://docs.eaeunion.org/docs/en-us/01122031/ms_10122018_doc.pdf. Accessed 11 August 2021.

Eurasian Economic Union. (2021). *On the results and prospects of the socioeconomic development of the member states of the Eurasian Economic Union and the measures taken by the member states in the field of macroeconomic policy: Annual report for 2020*. Eurasian Economic Union. https://eec.eaeunion.org/upload/medialibrary/0ce/Annual-report-2020.pdf. Accessed 15 September 2021.

Indicators of Financial Structure, Development, and Soundness. (2005). *Financial sector assessment: A handbook* (pp. 15–33). World Bank. https://doi.org/10.1596/978-0-8213-6432-1

Murphy, D. (2019). *Big tech's invasion of banking*. Milken Institute Review. https://www.milkenreview.org/articles/big-techs-invasion-of-banking. Accessed 23 July 2021.

National Legal Internet Portal of the Republic of Belarus. (2021). About the state program "Digital Development of Belarus" for 2021–2025: Resolution of the Council of Ministers of the Republic of Belarus, February 2, 2021 no. 66. https://pravo.by/document/?guid=12551&p0=C22100066&p1=1. Accessed 11 September 2021.

Petralia, K., Philippon, T., Rice, T., & Véron, N. (2019). *Banking disrupted? Financial intermediation in an era of transformational technology*. International Center for Monetary and Banking Studies CEPR.

PwC. (2019). *Global FinTech Report 2019*. https://www.pwc.com/gx/en/industries/financial-services/fintech-survey.html. Accessed 17 July 2021.

Savitsky, P. N. (2021). *Eurasianism*. http://www.gumiLevica.kuLichki.net/SPN/spn09.htm. Accessed 7 June 2021.

Streeter, B. (2021). *Gen Z says they're eager to use big techs for banking—But will they?* The Financial Brand. https://thefinancialbrand.com/102357/gen-zsays-they-would-bank-with-amazon-google-or-walmart-branch/?internal-link. Accessed 20 July 2021.

Supreme Eurasian Economic Council. (2019). *Decision on the concept for the formation of a common financial market of the Eurasian Economic Union dated 01.10.2019 no. 20*. https://www.nbrb.by/today/internationalcooperation/eeu/acts/decision20-2019.pdf. Accessed 12 September 2021.

The Financial Times. (2020). *When the banks closed in Wuhan, nobody cared*. https://www.ft.com/content/76291c8f-0ad0-472b-ac1e-bff1646bfb1a. Accessed 29 April 2021.

Vinokurova, E. Y. (Ed.). (2017). *Eurasian Economic Union*. Center for Integration Studies, St. Petersburg.

UK Finance. (2019). *UK payment markets*. Summary 2019. https://www.ukfinance.org.uk/sites/default/files/uploads/pdf/UK-Finance-UKPayment-Markets-Report-2019-SUMMARY.pdf. Accessed 10 October 2021.

Chapter 6
A Training Evaluation Context of Corporate Social Responsibility Education Case: Université Des Mascareignes

Nirmal Kumar Betchoo

Abstract Corporate Social Responsibility (CSR) currently occupies an important place in the training programmes of organisations and empowers universities and training institutions to focus on this prospective area. Businesses need to be community-oriented and through CSR, they recognise some of the insights of this discipline which is heavily influenced by Carroll's CSR dimensions. At UdM, a public university in Mauritius, there was a need to integrate CSR into the learning curriculum and a first course was undertaken through the provision of a 25-h programme. With regard to the length of the course and the mode in which it was delivered, the CSR course was assessed in two stages: pre- and post-assessment. These were based on the CIRO and the Kirkpatrick model. The results showed that the context and contribution of the CSR training programme were important in ensuring that the course was relevant to the learning needs of the students. At the same time, students achieved satisfaction in the form of positive feedback such as relevance and engagement, including learning outcomes that were more focused on the philanthropic and ethical content of the course compared to the economic and legal content. The main recommendation following the evaluation of CSR was to extend it to future programmes of the university and to improve its content so that CSR is positioned as a valuable future training component in a university curriculum. There is also the question of aligning the programme with the constant evolution of CSR so that the trends from the outside can be matched with training resources from the inside.

Keywords Corporate social responsibility · CSR training · Pre- and post-evaluation · University · Outcomes · Training models · Training context · Education

---

N. K. Betchoo (✉)
Université des Mascareignes, Pamplemousses, Mauritius

D. Crowther and S. Seifi (eds.), *Corporate Social Responsibility in Difficult Times*, Approaches to Global Sustainability, Markets, and Governance,
https://doi.org/10.1007/978-981-99-2591-9_6

6.1 Introduction

Corporate social responsibility (CSR) has gained prominence in the higher education curriculum as it impacts student learning. University graduates leave university to take up employment either in the public or private sector, but are essentially equipped with specific academic learning related to their field of study. To some extent, training and education in participatory approaches is considered an effective method to generate the development of the required soft skills (Tang, 2016). Soft skills are gradually gaining ground in education by allowing the student to acquire additional skills through their learning programme. At the Université des Mascareignes (UdM), a public university in Mauritius, soft skills are imparted through communication courses aimed at improving the oral or verbal skills of students. Given the importance of CSR in today's contemporary context, it is seen that such a course could be included in communication curricula and add to the soft skills that need to be developed in university students. Today, employers need to understand soft skills and higher education institutions need to understand what employers expect from their graduates (Kruger, 2015). Basically, this new course can apply to all types of students, but as a precaution, the CSR module seems to be more appropriate in the first place for business students who have some prior knowledge of the concept. The CSR course was introduced from January 2022 and its impact on student learning needs to be assessed to see if the course fits into the university curriculum and how this could be improved later.

6.2 The Rationale for a CSR Course

First of all, the university curricula must be constantly reviewed. New curricula and learning objectives should be established during curriculum development. In the recent past, most UdM courses integrated themes related to the digitisation and dissemination of Information and Communication Technologies in various spheres of learning, whether business or information technology. A little later, a programme on "Work Ethics" was included in the programme due to a request from a local anti-corruption institution; the Independent Commission Against Corruption (ICAC). It is understood that new courses are incorporated into the learning curriculum as an urgent need or current requirement. Mauritius, for example, aspires to be a digitally well-connected and anti-corruption nation. To this end, the two courses have been added to the university's apprenticeship programme.

Regarding CSR, there is an imminent demand for Mauritian organisations to be more involved in community issues. This can be ensured by programmes directed to the benefit of society, sponsorship, contribution to charitable institutions as well as greater involvement in future problems such as sedentary diseases, stress, family problems, etc. The concept of CSR has this pervasive impact as it can have a direct or indirect influence on most of the social issues that have been described. Beyond that, it is a community engagement that partly liberates organisation from being stereotyped on being profit-oriented and non-compliant with social issues that are also linked to the state of being of a country. Deigh et al. (2016) comment that social investments through community programmes are potentially cost-effective ways to grow enterprise and improve competitiveness.

6.3 CSR in Higher Education

Corporate social responsibility (CSR) is defined by the ethical relationship and transparency of the company with all its stakeholders who maintain a relationship as well as by the establishment of corporate objectives compatible with the sustainable development of society, the preservation of environmental and cultural resources for future generations, respecting diversity and promoting the reduction of social problems (Filho et al., 2010). If CSR indicates a way for companies to contribute to the well-being of society, it also gives the opportunity to create a real competitive advantage and a positive reputation for the business world (Porter & Kramer, 2006).

Cloke and Brown (2009) argue that the idea of CSR may have emerged with the work of scholars such as Bowen (1953—cited as the "father" of CSR) and followed by the work of Davis (1973), Jones (1983) and more recently Carroll (1991, 1999). The idea really took off, however, in the post-Earth Summit period of 1992, when CSR became a full-fledged industry with its own "practitioner review conferences" and related discussions.

According to Kantanen (2004), a university should strive to provide benefits to society, as institutions of higher education (HEI) contribute greatly to the knowledge economy and social progress. Vasilescu et al. (2010) comment that universities are one of the main components of society and that it should be considered that they can develop the social responsibility of companies, communities and stakeholders if they adopt CSR practices.

The growth in CSR education has been quantitative, in the sense that the number of training courses offered by HEIs has increased, but also qualitatively, with a wider range of topics covered, addressing a wide variety of topics, the relationship between business and society to ethics and sustainability globalisation, including the environment and corporate governance (Cowton & Cummins, 2003; Van Liedekerke & Demuijnck, 2011).

Regarding CSR in higher education. Atakan and Eker (2007) point out that most universities tend to focus only on teaching social responsibility in terms of CSR initiatives and do not go beyond trying to improve their communities. Nevertheless, to be competitive in the changing education industry and also to fulfil their mission in an ever-changing world, HEIs must recognise that their own actions must reflect the values and standards they claim to embody. Dahan and Senol (2012) claim the deepening of HEIs in the commitment to CSR at the operational level as well as at the academic level, mainly through curricular activities. This will not only be beneficial for the institution itself, but also for society in general.

Dima et al. (2013) approach university competitiveness as the ability of such an institution to create and maintain competitive advantages over other universities nationally and internationally. The university develops the ability to maintain its long-term performance better than its competitors, as evidenced by teaching, income, research output and employability of graduates. Universities continue to educate the modern generation and provide community service (Dima et al., 2013).

In a nutshell, Galvão et al. (2019) summarise that higher education institutions have a duty to foster ethical, responsible and sustainable behaviours among students. To achieve this, curricula must emphasise teaching methods that enhance CSR and provide a comprehensive understanding of the dimensions of CSR. Such a goal can be achieved through CSR courses and volunteer activities that allow students not only to develop personal skills, but also to acquire a stronger orientation towards philanthropic responsibility (Galvão et al., 2019).

6.4 Carroll's CSR Model

The relevance of the implementation of CSR in the learning programme of UdM comes from the fact that CSR is encouraged by the Mauritian government, in particular the Ministry of Finance, for companies to ensure that they are socially responsible and involved. To this end, the leadership of professional organisations as well as public institutions must be involved in building capacity to effectively address the issue of CSR. From a preliminary point of view, it might appear like a public relations exercise with a minimal grip on social responsibility while the scope of CSR is quite broad as it involves the four key paradigms according to the model of Carroll (1991) namely philanthropic, ethical, legal and economic perspectives. All of these must be considered when a course is created and ultimately developed as an instructional programme.

According to Carroll (2016), each of the four components of accountability caters to different stakeholders in terms of varying priorities in which stakeholders might be affected. The pyramid is seen as a sustainable stakeholder framework.

Ethical responsibilities affect all stakeholder groups. Shareholder demands are becoming increasingly important. When a review of the ethical issues facing businesses today is measured, they naturally involve employees, customers and the environment in particular. Legal liabilities are important for owners, but in today's uncertain society, the threat of litigation against businesses most often comes from employees and consumers. Economic responsibilities have a greater impact on shareholders and employees, because if the company is not financially viable, these two groups will be significantly affected. Finally, philanthropic responsibilities most affect the community and non-profit organisations, but also employees, as some research has concluded that a company's philanthropic commitment is significantly related to the morale and commitment of its employees (Carroll, 2016).

In the conceptual framework proposed by Carroll (1991), CSR is divided into four dimensions of responsibility: economic, legal, ethical and philanthropic. A Mauritian perspective of CSR in the Carroll model is described below.

6.5 A Mauritian Perspective of the CSR Model

Economic responsibility requires effective management to maximise profits for owners or shareholders by providing goods and services that match market demand. The case for economic responsibility is to ensure that activities are viable for the organisation. There are risks that profits will be reduced by the involvement of CSR. These could compromise the original perspective. Sometimes one would expect companies to engage in social responsibility only when they have generated significant profits. Nevertheless, this situation constitutes the preliminary basis for the CSR commitment. In the Mauritian context, CSR has been given greater prominence since the new millennium, long after the Ministry of Finance considered local organisations to become more involved in CSR, prior to which non-compliance would lead to corporate taxation by 2%. In a sense, engagement became a desirable ambition for local businesses, knowing that they could justify such engagement after initially making a profit.

Legal responsibility includes the CSR commitment in accordance with the legal framework in force. It could be related to activities and practices that are permitted and cannot be subject to legal scrutiny for injustice and doubt. All Mauritius companies largely adhere to the legal aspect on being registered and tax-compliant with the government authority, the Mauritius Revenue Authority regarding taxation, the Registrar of Companies regarding permission to operate legally, etc. The question is whether there is a legal obligation to engage in CSR. This argument could be aligned with the type of engagement that Mauritian companies might have to prove. For example, all CSR activities must be legally acceptable. Using CSR as a pretence to build reputation or community involvement to create publicity, coupled with activities where the exploitation of resources could be compromised, could all be considered illegal. Another critical area for CSR could be compliance with financial regulations ensuring that the CSR commitment is not aimed at money laundering.

In terms of ethical responsibility, companies must act with justice, equity and impartiality and always respect social standards. Mauritian companies might have looked closely at the issue of ethical CSR, as those that do not adhere to ethical practices could face legal action. Religious activities in a multicultural Mauritius could be an important area to address. What about an organisation that funds a community on a religious basis? How could this social commitment be perceived by different communities in Mauritius?

On the other hand, the ethical concept is also broad as it can cover activities that can be confused with the legal aspect such as tax evasion, circumventing legally acceptable activities. Ethical responsibility should imply that Mauritian companies do not underestimate the risk of engaging in practices that could undermine their

CSR commitment. The case of a local lottery company claiming that CSR is central to its core values has raised concerns about the ethical principle underlying CSR. The argument raised was the rationale for the focus on CSR when the key business was the lottery business which was more of a gambling business than a philanthropic business.

Finally, philanthropic responsibilities must be purely voluntary (Carroll, 1991; Ibrahim et al., 2008). This affirmation remains important in the Mauritian context because it is presented as the most essential commitment within CSR. This level raises the profile of companies in terms of social commitment. An underlying philosophy could be the extent to which a local organisation is interested in social engagement after starting a business and making profit over the years. Areas that are gaining in appeal are education, social and cultural. To some extent, the philanthropic approach in Mauritius could be a motive to claim that inequalities and injustice towards low-income groups and the poor are partly addressed.

From an egalitarian point of view, this form of engagement aims to obtain positive feedback from the media and society in general. Continued commitment to philanthropy is welcomed while the image of the sponsoring organisation is enhanced. This form of engagement has also broadened its perspective recently by addressing social events. A recent sponsorship of the Maiden Cup 2022 edition by a local conglomerate has enabled all stakeholders to preserve horse racing in Mauritius as a national sport enjoyed as a heritage event for over two centuries.

From this standpoint, it is clear that the commitment of Mauritian companies becomes a desirable standpoint for educational institutions to accept that CSR is important in Mauritius today and is no longer considered an ancillary activity. Viewed earlier with reluctance to spend money on a social cause, CSR is today seen as a valuable commitment that might earn public recognition. This is where UdM duly considered integrating a CSR course that could be quite acceptable as part of its teaching and learning curriculum.

6.6 Planning a CSR Course at UdM

Introducing a CSR course into a university curriculum may not be an easy issue to define given that students have not been exposed to it, although an introductory course to "Ethics in the workplace" can give them insight into the importance of ethical business practice. CSR engages additional components as mentioned earlier. Consultations could have been made with existing university curricula offered locally or internationally, but they appear to be quite elaborate and demanding in terms of depth and scope of learning required.

Regarding the integration of CSR in a university curriculum, Stonkuté et al (2018) argue that the public sector plays an important role in the development of social responsibility, of which universities are an essential part because they play an irreplaceable role in society, where they participate in the creation and increase of human capital. The social responsibility of universities is seen as part of the so-called "third role" of universities, perceived as the sense of the impact of the activities of universities on society in the broadest sense (Stonkuté et al., 2018).

To integrate CSR into a course already developed at UdM, it was deemed useful to develop the concept in a soft skills programme that would be covered in 25 h spread over approximately eight weeks. The introductory approach for students could have the nomenclature of a training programme based on a combination of theoretical and practical aspects.

6.7 CSR Course Development

After being successively debated at the university's departmental meeting, the curriculum development committee and the academic council, the CSR course was accepted as a soft skills programme that would be originally offered to business students. With a shorter duration compared to the main taught modules which are around 45 h per semester, the CSR course would form part of the communication component of the university curriculum.

The CSR course covers among others: (a) an understanding of the concept of CSR, (b) an analysis of the importance and impact of CSR on business, (c) the use of the Carroll Pyramid of CSR, (d) an analysis of the importance of sustainability in business and (e) the key factors for the implementation of CSR. It is at the basic level and is positioned in the first years of undergraduate university programmes in the field of business management.

The objectives are based on a basic coverage of the concept of CSR while the course aims to inspire students to discuss the concept of CSR in a simple and effective way. However, the test case is to see how students assimilate CSR education and grasp if there could be wider application, for example, in a thesis or in-depth context as a core module later. At present, the programme is linked to the development of soft skills with the prospect that it may be extended to other areas of learning in the near future.

6.8 Implementation of the CSR Course

The CSR course was set up from March 2022 and is in its very first edition. It was provided by a resource person and was offered over eight weeks. There is a taught component of the programme that lasts up to an hour where CSR concepts and theories are explained. The rest includes student participation in discussion forums that allow them to better understand and apply the components of CSR.

The course was assessed by means of a short report prepared by the students accompanied by a presentation where the students had explained how well they could apply the learning objectives to a practical situation. With respect to Bloom's taxonomy of learning, the CSR curriculum was focused on knowledge and application or better understanding and application within the expanded taxonomy (Anderson & Sosniak, 1994).

In terms of knowledge, the implementation of CSR teaching at UdM was first considered as a training course whose objective is to refine knowledge and skills. Although the course looked practical from an initial point of view, thought was given to imparting knowledge and skills related to the course. The knowledge aspect related to key areas of CSR modelled on Carroll's perspective on CSR, which also included various contributions from other researchers. In today's rapidly changing world, more publications related to CSR are available and these can be used as the basis of knowledge creation for the CSR course.

The second aspect was the application of this knowledge. The practical nature of the training should ensure appropriate application of the learning in practice. For an introductory course, it might not be possible to seek out applications in a wide range of fields but, at least, students from diverse work environments should look for opportunities to apply their learning in their own work environment. The argument could be to see to what extent CSR is understood and applied to work and how there could be a more critical appreciation of this concept.

6.9 Need for Course Evaluation

Course evaluation is an essential requirement for any programme offered by an institution and this applies to UdM in its end-of-term evaluation. This activity includes an online assessment completed by students taking any course and covering all major areas of assessment, namely course facilities, access to learning facilities, communication issues, evaluation of the course facilitator and any gaps encountered during the training. Bohms (2011) points out that to put students at the heart of higher education, universities must begin to review and improve the course evaluation process. Given the level of investment that students are asked to make in their future, it is not unreasonable to allow them to have a say in how they are taught and to tell them what impacts their feedback.

The current form of assessment is primarily academic but does not adhere to a standardised assessment. It is hereby assumed that the 15-h CSR course could be more aligned with a training course since it is offered as a beginner's course.

For the purposes of the research, a questionnaire was provided to the students with the aim that the evaluation would not only focus on their personal appreciation of the programme but, that it would be more aligned with the objectives of the research which rather involve an assessment through a type of evaluation that fits into two classic models that are described in the following paragraph.

6.10 Using Training Evaluation Templates

Training evaluation is explained as the systematic process of collecting information that is used to improve training. Evaluation provides feedback to help determine if the training has achieved the intended results and helps in making decisions about future training. A CSR course offered by UdM could have been evaluated simply using the standard evaluation form. Given the importance of such a programme, it was deemed useful to consider evaluation using established training evaluation models or templates.

There are a variety of training evaluation models among which the Kirkpatrick model (2016) and the CIRO model (1970) might be the most popular and widely accepted evaluation techniques. There might be criticisms of the overall simplicity and outcome expectations of both models, but these are useful for making summative assessments based on what makes the training an effective exercise.

6.11 The Kirkpatrick Model

The Kirkpatrick model that identifies four levels of training evaluation, is a key tool for evaluating the efficacy of training within an organisation. Developed in 1959 and reviewed subsequently over the years, this model is globally recognised as one of the most effective evaluations of training (Kirkpatrick, 1996; Kirkpatrick & Kirkpatrick, 2016).

Level 1: Reaction–The degree to which participants find the training favourable, engaging and relevant to their jobs.

Level 2: Learning–The degree to which participants acquire the intended knowledge, skills, attitude, confidence and commitment based on their participation in the training.

Level 3: Behaviour–The degree to which participants apply what they learned during training when they are back on the job.

Level 4: Results–The degree to which targeted outcomes occur as a result of the training and the support and accountability package.

6.12 CIRO Model

The CIRO model developed by Warr et al. (1970) in their book "Evaluation of Management Training" is another useful training evaluation model. The acronym CIRO stands for Context, Input, Reaction and Output. The key difference in CIRO and Kirkpatrick's models is that CIRO focuses on measurements taken before and after the training has been carried out. This model is better positioned as an evaluation for the CSR programme.

Context: The ultimate objective is needed to eliminate organisational deficiency. The intermediate objectives are required to change work behaviour. The immediate objectives are needed to bring new knowledge and skills.

Input: Training inputs in terms of their design, planning, management and delivery. It also includes evaluating the organisational resources and how these can be best used to achieve the desired objectives.

Reactions: Analysing the reactions of the students to the training in order to make improvements. Evaluation needs to be collected in a systematic and objective way.

Output: Outcomes are measured at the following four levels, namely, the learner level, the workplace level, the team or department level and the business level.

Compared to the theoretical frameworks briefly described above, an adaptation of the models has been undertaken. It was a precautionary measure to adapt the model to the context of the UdM which offers a course to students and does not ideally represent a training organisation where it requires substantial managerial input. The current context is more related to the faculty offering the programme, the resource person or lecturer involved in designing and delivering the course and the students participating in it. Such a condition has less to do with organisational performance and profits and requires making adjustments to the models used.

6.13 Methodology

The methodology used the two aforementioned models to analyse CSR training at UdM. A single model could have been perceived as subjective given that there are several that have been developed. For CSR assessment purposes, the Kirkpatrick and CIRO models were used. The use of the two models made it possible to provide a more balanced assessment and to verify whether there was convergence in such training.

The full sample of 25 students participating in the CSR training as well as those who did not take it but who were interested in such training were interviewed. An online survey methodology was used, including additional questions that were posed directly to respondents. A total of 90 respondents completed the survey. The initial low number of students enrolled in the course could be a barrier to a useful evaluation and for this reason the size was expanded to approximately 100. This included the next group of students who would take the course and a stratified sample of business students from fields like marketing, human resource management and banking who were likely to take the module and who have already taken a work ethics course that aligns with the same philosophy of new additions to current learning.

The questionnaire consisted of 10 questions that covered the main research questions formulated. The response rate was low at first, but a class survey prompted students to be more responsive. Similarly, for students less eager to answer the questions, the questionnaire was handed out at the end of the course. The methodology was aligned with a pre- and post-evaluation of the CSR training.

6.14 Key Research Questions

The survey identified some key questions that respondents needed to answer that could effectively address the rationale for offering such a programme. A questionnaire survey was undertaken using a Likert scale which addressed the two theoretical concepts, namely the CIRO and the Kirkpatrick model. The main arguments are set out below:

- What is the importance of a CSR course at UdM?
- What are the results of the pre-evaluation of a CSR course at UdM?
- What are the post-evaluation results of a CSR course at UdM?
- What findings have been drawn from CSR training at UdM?
- What are the lessons learned from the implementation of a CSR course at UdM?

The research results were linked to the main research questions that were identified. They focused on the importance of the CSR course, the pre- and post-evaluation of the training, the observations made during the course and the main lessons learned after a first edition of such a course. The results are shown in the next section.

6.15 Importance of a CSR Course at UdM

The importance of a CSR course was first felt at the university level. Given the interest in developing new programmes in the Faculty of Business and Management, the programmes on Ethics and CSR have caught the attention of all stakeholders, including course providers from the UdM.

Students who responded to the survey identified the following reasons:

The increasing importance of CSR as an organisational strategy, the possibility of being engaged in CSR activities in an organisation (0.72), the practicality of CSR in today's workplace (0.75), the philanthropic perspective of CSR and the resulting organisational image (0.83) and the attractiveness of a CSR approach for an organisation (0.80). Figure 6.1 provides a graphical interpretation.

The popularity of philanthropy has arisen from the fact that such a perspective encompasses the voluntary actions that companies undertake in response to societal expectations, either in the form of financial support or in-kind donations of products and services to organisations in non-profit and community service organisations (Rangan et al., 2012).

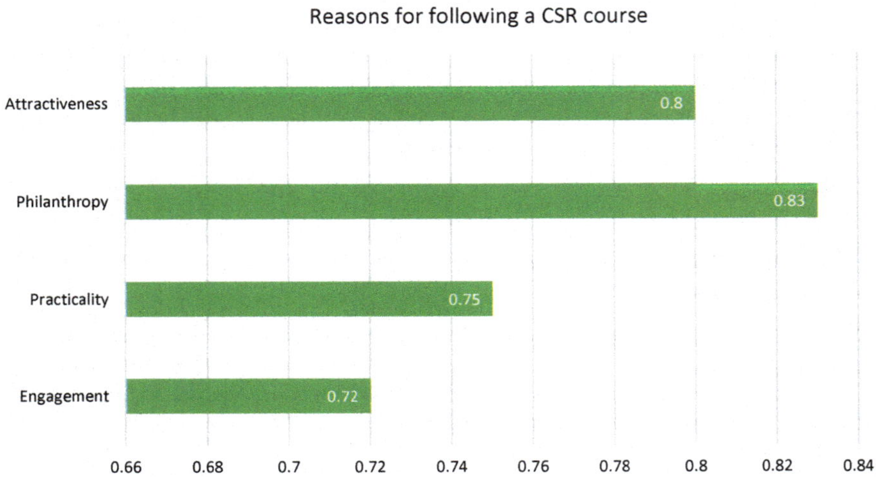

Fig. 6.1 Students' opinion of the reasons for following a CSR course

Regarding the high attractiveness score of the CSR course, the result aligns with the opinion of Story and Castanheira (2016) that CSR practices, whether internal or external, influence perceptions of organisational attractiveness.

6.16 Pre- and Post-assessment of CSR Training

The pre-assessment of the CSR course could be linked to the CIRO model which allows both forms of assessment. The purpose of the pre-assessment is to see how the training programme could be most appropriately applied and how any initial difficulties that might arise from the training could be overcome. It also prepares the trainer to see what gaps in the training might be and what adjustments could be made.

6.17 Pre-assessment of the CSR-Context Course

The context of the training was first assessed in the training evaluation. It was at the pre-evaluation level since the CIRO level offers the possibility of a pre-evaluation of a training.

It can be seen from Table 6.1 that the training context was completely adequate and adapted to the needs of the students. Although it targeted a relatively small number of students, it appears that the context was appropriate and suited the purpose of the course implementation. Rehmani (2020) confirms this point by stating that contextual

Table 6.1 Context of training evaluation

Mean values regarding training context evaluation	Mean	Variance	SD
The CSR training is relevant for my learning needs	3.11	0.86	0.92
The CSR training addresses the level of students	2.88	0.61	0.78
The CSR training has an adequate timeframe	2.22	0.94	0.97
The CSR training has adequate learning objectives	2.28	0.61	0.78
The CSR course fits in the learning programme	2.78	0.44	0.66

training is the most effective and efficient strategy to ensure continuous learning. In addition, the Praed Foundation (2021) states that contextualisation is an opportunity for the trainer to clearly inform the audience of the purpose of the training and acts as an opportunity to motivate and encourage buy-in from training participants.

6.18 Pre-assessment of the CSR-Input Course

The second pre-evaluation of the CSR training programme came from the training contribution. These inputs concerned: the training facilitator or lecturer, the course material, the necessary classrooms, the financial resources, including the preparation of the course.

From a first observation, the desire to embark on a CSR programme had to be feasible. A correlation matrix was used and course material and preparation were found to matter most in such a setting with high positive regression values seen in Table 6.2. Constraints stemmed from financial resources related to course materials, including course materials and course preparation. A question arose namely: Are there standard books on CSR that could be used for the programme or have resources been taken from Internet sources to organise the course? Although all correlations are positive, there could be questions regarding the physical facility needed for a CSR course. Could it just be provided in a regular classroom or was a room specially designed for presentation and discussion needed?

The issue of preparing for a CSR module was important as this would allow the course to be delivered in the most efficient way. It should be noted that the present research has focused on assessments made in a first cycle of courses and that the values could be revisited in other offerings of the programme. Otara and Niyirora (2016) explain that there should be a focus on improving the quality of teaching and learning dynamics of teacher training and processes as a critical input. Researchers further add that more effort should be devoted to aspects such as curriculum design, pedagogical assessment of learners' performance and progress (Otara & Niyirora, 2016).

Table 6.2 Correlation matrix of CSR course input

Correlation matrix	Facilitator/ lecturer	Course material	Classroom facilities	Financial resources	Course preparation
Facilitator/ lecturer	1.00				
Course material	0.85	1.00			
Classroom facilities	0.65	0.45	1.00		
Financial resources	0.50	0.33	0.62	1.00	
Course preparation	0.72	0.40	0.20	0.63	1.00

6.19 Post-assessment of the CSR Course

At the post-assessment level, the CIRO and Kirkpatrick models were used. They were mixed because a missing element in one model could be mixed in another. For example, behavioural outcomes, ultimate value and learning-focused assessment were part of Kirkpatrick's model.

6.20 Evaluation Centred on the Reaction of the CSR Course

The reaction of trainees was an important variable in the CSR course offered by UdM. For a first round, it can be said that most of the reactions were very well noted. Students found the programme both locally focused and engaging (90%), interesting (86%), followed by relevant (82%) and supportive (80%), respectively. Figure 6.2 provides a comparative representation of the evaluations.

Respondents viewed that a CSR course should be locally focused. This argument aligns with NI Business (2022) which states that for most businesses, it makes sense to get involved in community CSR that is related to a company's product or service. This allows individuals to use their expertise at the local level and show the human face of their business at the same time.

Regarding the need for engagement, Hunnes and Olsen (2018) argue that the primary motivator for institutions is to engage students in critical reflection on ethical dilemmas in business. Additionally, there is a need to shift students' attention from memorising basic theory in ethics and CSR, to understanding through the application of theories. To do this, students can be involved in case discussions in groups and seminars.

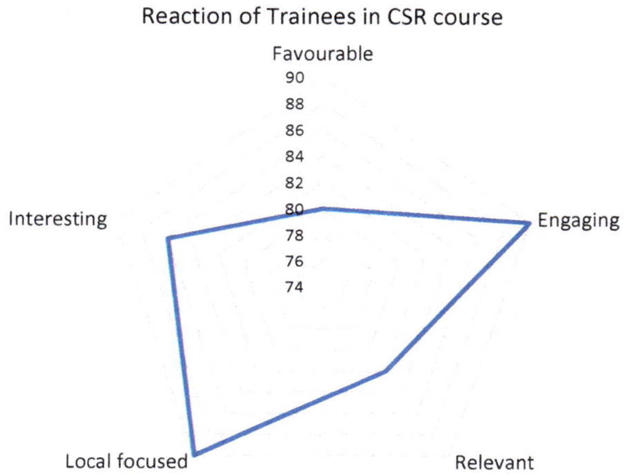

Fig. 6.2 Reaction of Trainees in CSR course

Regarding favourable outcomes for students in a CSR course, Stobierski (2022) comments that the concept of corporate social responsibility has been around for decades, but goodwill has started to take on greater importance in recent years, as consumers have become more informed about the issues such as climate change and economic inequality, among other issues of concern. As such, current and future business leaders would do well to develop a solid understanding of CSR and its impact not only on their day-to-day role and responsibilities, but also on their long-term career path.

6.21 Learning-Centred Evaluation of CSR Course

Learning-centred evaluation was linked the 4 key variables of Carroll's CSR namely economical, legal, ethical and philanthropic perspective.

Table 6.3 identifies selected responses in relation to the key learning outcomes of the CSR course and its evaluation. They address each perspective through selected responses that are synthesised.

The pyramid is a sustainable stakeholder framework and has served as a basis for analysing the students' perspective on their learning within the 4 key CSR responsibilities. According to Carroll (2016), the CSR pyramid was intended to be seen from the perspective of stakeholders in a holistic view. The CSR pyramid holds that companies should engage in decisions, actions, policies and practices that fulfil all four components simultaneously. This is also where the learning outcomes of the CSR course have also been focused.

The pyramid model of CSR ensures that companies are expected to fulfil all of their responsibilities simultaneously. The positioning or ordering of the four categories of responsibility strives to represent the fundamental or basic nature of these

Table 6.3 Learning-centred feedback evaluation of CSR

Learning perspectives	Feedback of key learning outcomes
Economic	There must be an engagement that does not affect an enterprises' profitability CSR activities must be efficient for the organisation CSR involvement must not be overbearing in order to affect a company's corporate profits CSR engagement must be value for money
Legal	CSR practice must align with legal requirements Mauritian companies must engage around 2% of their profit for CSR activities CSR activities must not engage in affecting the natural environment
Ethical	CSR must not be a means of boosting a company's image Societal issues must not be exploited to build a company's reputation CSR activities must not be carried out to improve company's profits Businesses must not expect to take advantage of CSR to boost their image while they are profit-oriented
Philanthropic	This level was positioned as the most important perspective The relevance of philanthropy for local organisations was an important issue The engagement of local enterprises in philanthropy was important The benefit gained from philanthropic engagement was essential both from the financial and the non-financial aspects

four categories to the existence of business in society. Carroll (2016) comments that economic and legal responsibilities are necessary; ethical and philanthropic responsibilities are expected and desired. These positions are clearly highlighted from the results described in Table 6.3.

Companies that choose to implement a CSR approach should note that it will involve a dynamic learning process. Regarding a CSR course, learners must acquire "the critical thinking, technical and leadership skills necessary to rethink, innovate and shape the sustainable businesses and inclusive economies of tomorrow", according to HEC's Paris CSR course (Greenly Earth, 2022).

6.22 Lessons Learned from a First CSR Course

This research paper analysed the need for evaluation of the training of a CSR course newly implemented at UdM. According to a first evaluation, it can be seen that the course has been applied with great success. Since CSR training is offered in 25 h and in the form of a communication or soft skills module, it was useful to evaluate it as training.

The mixture of two classic evaluation models, namely the CIRO and the Kirkpatrick model, was effective because they allowed a pre- and post-evaluation of the CSR course. Not all components of both models were used. They were rather adapted to the current situation in the offer of the CSR course.

The main lessons learned from the CSR assessment at the pre-assessment stage were: (a) the context that determined what type of CSR course should be delivered and what were the main expected objectives of it, (b) course inputs which included course facilities and logistics, i.e. trainers and lecturers, as well as basic logistics to run the programme effectively.

The main outcomes of a post-assessment were: (a) achievement of learning outcomes that promote learning across Carroll's four key perspectives: philanthropic, ethical, legal and economic. This allowed UdM staff to see which areas were priorities for students in the course and how they could be supported. In addition, learning feedback was significant, as CSR trainees were found to praise training that was locally oriented, engaging and relevant to their needs in the near future. Such a reaction could also influence the adjustments of the next CSR programme that would be executed.

6.23 Recommendations

Through a first launch of a CSR course, some recommendations emerge. They include in particular: the need to extend this training to part-time and full-time students, the possibility of integrating CSR into certain Master's programmes offered by the university, the possibility of developing a longer and more committed course in the future and the need to review the resources with a view to making the CSR course more adaptable to the learning programme. These points are developed below.

6.23.1 The Need to Extend CSR Training to Part-Time and Full-Time Students

Originally designed as a part-time module, one of the first recommendations might be to extend the course to full-time students. Currently, the course has just launched and student feedback has shown that there is potential to develop and improve the programme. Certainly, by successive reviews, the CSR course will be mastered and will be able to better meet the needs of the students. In line with "Workplace Ethics" as a new course, a CSR course should be better acclaimed by a wider group of students and full-time courses will allow more students to be trained in CSR. At the same time, soft skills will be enhanced through this new training opportunity. If students learn about CSR in universities, they are more likely to become employees and employers who use socially responsible business practices. Universities help to create better companies and better business people (Giva UK, 2016).

6.23.2 The Possibility of Integrating CSR into Certain master's Programmes Offered by the University

Master's programmes offered at UdM's Faculty of Business and Management could afford to have components of a CSR programme. The Master programmes currently address Sustainable Development, E-Learning and Digital Humanities. With such new courses emerging at post-graduate level, the integration of CSR could be commendable but could obviously be at the basic level of learning experienced at UdM Teaching Unit 1 (UE1). It fits quite well within the parameters of a modern management course that favours a more human view of society. A Masters in Corporate Social Responsibility might enable students to identify, analyse and assess a range of business-related issues. They can develop appropriate responses to these problems and be able to select the most appropriate course of action (MTOC, 2022).

6.23.3 The Possibility of Developing a Longer and More Committed Course in the Future

The development of an elaborate and more engaged programme at UdM could be considered in the longer term once the concept is well-established as part of the learning requirements. This could involve qualified and specialised staff to provide training at an advanced level. It is also necessary to have people from industry to provide elaborate training, including resource people to build capacity to provide CSR training. Rangan et al. (2015) argue that there is growing pressure to dress up CSR as a business discipline and demand that every initiative delivers business results. Specialised courses exist in CSR in international university curricula and these could be used as models to develop a Mauritian CSR course. Tilt (2016) comments that research of this type must be transdisciplinary because perspectives from fields such as political science, philosophy and economics are essential. It is only with a thorough and contextualised understanding that improvements in the nature of CSR activity can be implemented.

6.23.4 The Need to Leverage the Resources in Order to Make the CSR Course More Adaptable to the Learning Programme

Existing resources are quite limited and rare with regard to the CSR course. Textbooks, journals and specialised periodicals are an essential requirement to ensure that the CSR course meets current and future student expectations. Given the very nature of CSR as an independent field that can be easily integrated with other management and business fields, it is important to see how CSR adapts to changes in the business environment and how new areas need to be understood and included to move forward. Doh and Tashman (2014) state that nowadays, business schools and universities have demonstrated a range in terms of propensity and approaches to integrate CSR into their curricula, influenced by numerous factors, such as ranking, size, funding, recruitment policy, training capacity, religious affiliation and cultural framework. This is also a requirement that the UdM might be called to reflect upon in the future.

6.24 Insight into the Current CSR Programme at the UdM

From a broad perspective, it is seen that globalisation has triggered a desire for inclusive development. Entrepreneurs argue that to achieve long-term success, sustainability and emerge as resilient competitors, social and ethical responsibilities must be integrated into corporate governance. They understand that building the image of a CSR-focused business will help them to achieve substantial long-term growth, thereby creating product preference and loyalty among customers (Sharma, 2015). This is a point where the UdM academics mounting the CSR course must reflect on how it can evolve with long-term business expectations.

A recent publication of Carroll (2021) states that CSR has continued to grow in support, adaptation and applications by business and academia. Corporate acceptance of CSR, recently referred to as purpose or sustainability, has been a major driver of CSR growth. Social activism by business leaders has increased. Global growth, and in particular developments in developing economies, was another driving force.

Munro (2020) went further by explaining that the key principles and themes of CSR 4.0 would include the "purpose" as an essential priority; innovation, inclusion and collaboration with all partners; identification, engagement and co-creation with all stakeholders; shared and embedded value at a deeper level; profound transformation and networking in a new ecosystem; and measurable Sustainable Development Goals (SDGs) with continuous review and renewal. The alignment of CSR with SDGs is already in force in Mauritius but the new paradigm is not currently closely monitored.

The present challenge is to know how to integrate the abovementioned business issues into the teaching programme of UdM. Currently, it is presented as a short course aimed at developing soft skills that address the basic understanding of the CSR model. There is a need to see how the local Mauritian environment should now adapt to the changing form of CSR and how this might enable academics and stakeholders support such a programme which could respond more openly to the needs of future students. Needless to say, constant adaptation to a changing business environment compels UdM to offer a course that meets the needs of its target audience.

6.25 Conclusion

It is concluded that the success of the CSR programme based on a first run of the course laid the foundation for the long-term viability of the programme. This aligned with the university's current strategy of developing student skills and being community-focused. UdM, as a new university, has strived to be innovative and industry-oriented in the courses it offers. The CSR course comes at a time when innovations like a green campus concept, artificial intelligence and sustainability are constantly being discussed as part of the university's strategy. The challenge of introducing CSR to the university curriculum is welcome because it is a platform to highlight the concern and involvement of UdM in terms of social commitment. Universities today are required to respect the environment and to be attentive to the needs of society which is incidentally an important player in this aspect. Certainly, the course cannot stay in the same format for long since there is the potential to enrich it and better integrate it into the long-term perspective of teaching and learning at UdM. Particular attention is to see the evolution of CSR 4.0 as a new concept and how it aligns with innovation, sustainability and inclusive growth in modern society. The success of the feedback obtained calls for greater attention to improving the course content in the future and integrating CSR as part of a teaching and learning course in a modern university that the UdM ambitions to be.

References

Anderson, L., & Sosniak, L. (1994). *Bloom's taxonomy: A forty-year retrospective.* Ninety-third yearbook of the National Society for the Study of Education, Pt.2. University of Chicago Press.

Bohms, E. (2011). Higher education standards: Improving course evaluation. *The Guardian.*

Bowen, R. (1953). *Social responsibilities of the businessman.* Harper & Row.

Carroll, A. (1991, July/August) The pyramid of corporate social responsibility: Towards the moral management of organizational stakeholders. *Business Horizons, 34*, 39–48.

Carroll, A. (2016). Carroll's pyramid of CSR: Taking another look. *International Journal of Corporate Social Responsibility, 1*, 3. https://doi.org/10.1186/s40991-016-0004-6

Carroll, A. (2021) Corporate social responsibility: Perspectives on development and the future of CSR construction. *Business and Society, 60*(6), https://doi.org/10.1177/00076503211001765

Cloke, J., & Brown, E. (2009). (2009) CSR in higher education. *An International E-Journal for Critical Geographies, 8*(3), 474–483.

Cowton, J., & Cummings, J. (2003). Teaching business ethics in UK higher education: Progress and prospects. *Teaching Business Ethics, 7*, 37–54.

Dahan, G., & Senol, I. (2012, March). Corporate social responsibility in higher education institutions: Istanbul Bilgi University case. *American International Journal of Contemporary Research, 2*(3).

Davis, K. (1973). The case for and against business assumption of social responsibilities. *Academy of Management Journal, 16*, 312–322.

Deigh, L., Farquhar, J., Palazzo, M., & Siano, A. (2016). Corporate social responsibility: Engaging the community. *Qualitative Market Research: An International Journal, 19*(2), 225–240. https://doi.org/10.1108/QMR-02-2016-0010

Dima, M., Vasilache, S., Ghinea, V., & SAgoston, A. (2013). A model of academic social responsibility. *Transylvanian Review of Administrative Science, 9*(38), 23–43.

Doh, J., & Tashman, P. (2014). Half a world away: The integration and assimilation of Corporate Social responsibility, and Sustainable development in business school curricula. *Corporate Social Responsibility and Environmental Management, 21*(3), 131–142.

Filho, M. de S., Wanderley, L., Gomez, C., & Farache, F. (2010). Strategic corporate social responsibility management for competitive advantage. *BAR—Brazilian Administration Review, 7*(3), 294–309.

Galvão, A., Mendes, L., Marques, C., & Mascarenhas, C. (2019). Factors influencing students' corporate social responsibility orientation in higher education. *Journal of Cleaner Production.* https://doi.org/10.1016/j.jclepro.2019.01.059

Giva UK. (2016). *The rise of CSR in UK universities.* https://www.giva.uk.com

Greenly Earth. (2022). *What CSR training will your employee need?* https://www.greenly.earth/blog-en/what-csr-training-will-your-employees-need

Hunnes, A., & Olsen, T. (2018). How to engage students in ethics and CSR? Evidence from blended learning. https://doi.org/10.21125/inted.2018.0954

Ibrahim, N., Howard, D., & Angelidis, J. (2008). The relationship between religiousness and corporate social responsibility orientation: Are there differences between business managers and students? *Journal of Business Ethics, 78*(1), 165–174.

Jones, T. (1983). An integrating framework for research in business and society: A step toward the elusive paradigm. *Academy of Management Review, 8*(4), 559–565.

Kantanen, H. (2004). *Civic mission and social responsibility: New challenges for the practice of public relations in higher education.* Presented at the 11th International Public Relations Research Symposium, Lake Bled, Slovenia.

Kirkpatrick, D. (1996). *Evaluating training programs: The four levels* (p. 229). Berrett-Koehler Publishers.

Kirkpatrick, J., & Kirkpatrick, W. (2016). *Kirkpatrick's four levels of training evaluation.* Association for Talent Development.

Kruger, K. (2015). *US universities should follow UK in promoting students' 'soft skills'.* https://www.timeshighereducation.com/

Munro, V. (2020). *CSR for purpose, shared value and deep transformation.* Emerald.

MTOC. (2022). *Corporate social responsibility.* https://www.mastersavenue.com/disciplines/corporate-social-responsibility

NI Business. (2022). *Corporate social responsibility: Local community.* https://www.nibusinessinfo.co.uk/content/corporate-social-responsibility-local-community

Otara, A., & Niyirora, A. (2016). Educational inputs: A defining factor in planning for quality secondary education in Rwanda. *International Journal of Development and Sustainability, 5*(3), 120–136.

Porter, M., & Kramer, M. (2006, December). Strategy and society: The link between competitive advantage and corporate social responsibility. *Harvard Business Review, R0612D*, 1–15.

Praed Foundation. (2021). *Characteristics of a good training: Setting the context.* https://praedfoundation.org

Rangan, K., Chase, L., & Karim, S. (2012). *Why every company needs a CSR strategy and how to build it* (Working Paper No. 12-088, pp. 1–31). Harvard Business School.

Rangan, K., Chase, L., & Karim, S. (2015). The truth about CSR. *Harvard Business Review.*

Rehmani. (2020). *Using contextual microlearning to train employees in the "New Normal".* https://trainingindustry.com/

Sharma, S. (2015). *The evolution of CSR.* https://www.lexquest.in/

Stonkuté, E., Vveinhardt, J., & Srok, W. (2018). Training the CSR sensitive mind-set: The integration of CSR into the training of business administration professionals. *Sustainability Journal, 10*, 754. https://doi.org/10.3390/su10030754

Story, J., & Castanheira, P. (2016). Corporate social responsibility and organizational attractiveness: Implications for talent management. *Social Responsibility Journal, 12*(3), 484–505. https://doi.org/10.1108/SRJ-07-2015-0095

Stobierski, T. (2022). The benefits of corporate social responsibility training. *Harvard Business Review*.

Tang, K. (2016). Beyond employability: Embedding soft skills in higher education. *The Turkish Online Journal of Educational Technology—April 2019, 18*(2), 1–9.

Tilt, C. (2016) Corporate social responsibility research: The importance of context. *International Journal of corporate Social Responsibility*. Springer Open.

Van Liedekerke, L., & Demuijnck, G. (2011). Business ethics s a field of training, teaching and research in Europe. *Journal of Business Ethics, 104*, 29–41.

Vasilescu, R., Barna, C., Epure, M., & Baicu, C. (2010). Developing university social responsibility: A model for the challenges of the new civil society. *Procedia-Social Behaviour. Science, 2*(2), 4177–4182. https://doi.org/10.1016/j.sbspro.2010.03.660

Warr, P., Bird, M., & Rackham, N. (1970). *Evaluation of management training* (p. 112). Gower Press.

Chapter 7
Evaluating Extents of Assistance of Telecommuting in Businesses During the COVID-19 Pandemic

Shameera Lauthan, Mahejabeen Peermamode-Mohaboob, Mohammad Kaleem Galamali, and Muhammad Hishaam Ibn Afzal Lauthan

Abstract Since the Coronavirus-2019 or COVID-19 outbreak caused the worldwide lockdown, the business world is overall regressing. Nearly every worker/consumer had to stay at home for more than a month and some even lost their jobs. The coronavirus is also causing global concern and economic hardship for consumers, businesses, and communities. Businesses and their employees were compelled to intensify working from home. Information and Communication Technologies (ICTs) were critical in allowing economic activities to seemingly continue and a major section of the population to continue generating income by supporting teleworking from home. Most companies have already decided on business continuity plans, but these plans are not prepared to face the fast-moving process and yet unknown facets of the pandemic. For businesses to stay afloat, many turned to digital technologies, using tools like videoconferencing, cloud services, virtual private networks, Emails, and File Servers among others. Businesses that had pre-existing telework capabilities or quickly adapted, were best positioned for seamless transitions to working from home while maintaining laudable output levels. However, telecommunication was not the hero during the pandemic. Small businesses closed. To survive, businessmen even tried to adapt and devise strategies to modify their business methods but many failed. Eventually, remote working engendered some downsides like the fading gaps between family and job, personal and work time, distraction by pets, children, chores, television, and even neighbourhood activities. The study investigates the impact of COVID-19 on Small and Medium Enterprises (SMEs) in Mauritius. The current research assists in gaining a deeper understanding of the current lived realities of individuals afflicted by the pandemic. Two major obstacles to research and development in the COVID-19 context, namely "time limits" and "physical distancing", are addressed. These findings may contribute towards the formulation of key policies

S. Lauthan (✉)
Department of Software Engineering, Université des Mascareignes, Beau Plan, Mauritius

M. Peermamode-Mohaboob · M. K. Galamali
Université des Mascareignes, Beau Plan, Mauritius

M. H. I. A. Lauthan
Rabindranath Tagore Secondary School, Ilot, Mauritius

D. Crowther and S. Seifi (eds.), *Corporate Social Responsibility in Difficult Times*, Approaches to Global Sustainability, Markets, and Governance,
https://doi.org/10.1007/978-981-99-2591-9_7

and best practices that will define the pandemic's responses henceforth. This research highlights the role of corporations in promoting CSR among SMEs in Mauritius, as well as in specific sectors using telecommuting to counteract unemployment. It also focuses on the importance and the role of CSR in the achievement of the United Nation's Sustainable Development Goals (SDGs).

Keywords Telecommuting · ICT—Information and Communication Technology · COVID-19 · SME—Small and Medium Enterprise · OECD—Organisation for Economic Co-operation and Development · WFH—Work from Home · CSR—Corporate Social Responsibility · NGO—Non-Governmental Organisation · MSMEs—Micro · Small · And Medium-sized companies

7.1 Introduction

7.1.1 Understanding Small and Medium Enterprises (SMEs)

Despite being small, SMEs are crucial to the economy. They are far more numerous than big businesses, employ a substantial workforce, and are often entrepreneurial in nature, generating innovation. As mentioned by Liberto, D. (2022), small to medium businesses can be found in practically every sector although, they are more likely to be found in those that have lower labour costs and lower up-front investment requirements. Legal services providers, dentists' offices, cafés, and restaurants are examples of typical SMEs. Because they function fundamentally differently from huge, multinational corporations, SMEs are separated from them. Large, complicated businesses may need sophisticated ERP systems, communication between locations throughout the world, or more complex organisational structures. SMEs, on the contrary hand, can have more modest upward potential but also more simple activities (Small and Mid-size Enterprise (SME) Defined: Types Around the World, n.d.).

7.1.1.1 Small and Medium Enterprises (SMEs) in Canada

According to Statistics of Canada (Analysis on small businesses in Canada, first quarter of 2022, 2022), around 98% of all Canadian employer enterprises were small businesses in 2021. Moreover, 10 million people were employed by small enterprises, which is more than three times the number of people employed by medium firms. According to the Canadian government's interpretation of Canadian Industry Statistics, the type of a company is determined by the number of workers. It takes 1–4 people to run a micro business. Employers in small firms range from 5 to 99. 100–499 people work for medium-sized enterprises. 500 + workers are employed by large companies.

7.1.1.2 SMEs in the European Union

The European Union (EU) provides definitions of what constitutes and does not constitute a small business. A medium-sized firm is defined as having fewer than 250 people, whereas a small-sized enterprise has fewer than 50 employees. There are micro-companies in addition to small and medium-sized businesses, and they have up to 10 employees.

SMEs make up 99% of all enterprises in the European Union, as is the case in other nations. SMEs are thought to be responsible for 100 million jobs and more than half of the nation's Gross Domestic Product (GDP) (*SMEs*, n.d.).

7.1.1.3 SMEs in China

In China companies are often classified based on their operational revenue, the number of workers, or the total assets of the organisation. For instance, if a Chinese retail company has more than 10 people but less than 50 and an annual operating income of at least $1 million, it is considered modest. Chinese entrepreneurs are considered modest if their total assets are more than $20 million but less than $50 million and their yearly operational revenue is more than $1 million but less than $10 million. If a Chinese agriculture company's yearly operating revenue is more than $0.5 million but less than $5 million, it is considered modest (Roopchund, 2020).

7.1.1.4 SMEs in Developing Nations—Kenya–India

Small and medium-sized businesses are referred to as MSMEs or Micro, Small, and Medium-sized companies, in developing nations like Kenya. MSMED or Micro, Small, and Medium Enterprise Development is the terminology used in India. Despite naming variations, all nations classify firms based on their size or organisational structure. Many individuals in developing nations work for small and medium-sized businesses. The Organisation for Economic Co-operation and Development estimates that SMEs provide around 50% of total employment and 40% of GDP in these nations (OECD).

7.1.1.5 SME in Mauritius

The importance of SMEs in driving economic expansion and raising the quality of life is now well acknowledged. According to statistics from the Continuous Multi-Purpose Household Survey and the previous two Censuses of Economic Activities (CEA), small and medium-sized businesses are creating more employment than large ones (CMPHS). The value added produced by SMEs is also increasing (Small & Medium Enterprises, 2013). According to the SMEDA Act of 2017 in Mauritius (Small and Medium Enterprises Act 2017 (No. 16 of 2017). | InforMEA), a company or firm qualifies as a small or medium enterprise if it meets any of the following criteria:

1. An enterprise with a turnover of under 10 million MUR per year is considered a small business (250,000 USD).
2. An organisation with a yearly turnover of more than 10 million MUR but less than 50 million MUR is referred to as a medium firm (1,250,000 USD).

The Mauritian economy is significantly impacted by SMEs, and their share of total economic activity has been rising. Around 99% of the businesses operating in various economic sectors in 2020 were SMEs (Statistics Mauritius, 2020).

7.1.2 Brief on Teleworking

Telecommuting, often known as 'telework', 'remote work', or 'work from home', is a work arrangement that permits workers to work away from the company's premises (Betchoo, 2015). Some employees work from home full-time, while others have the option to work from home on certain days of the week or special occasions (e.g., during pregnancy, health issues, pandemics among others). As stated by the OECD Policy Responses to Coronavirus (The Organisation for Economic Co-operation and Development (OECD), 2021), telework is growing increasingly popular as the bulk of materials and tools required to execute everyday job tasks are now available online for many occupations. Telecommuters communicate with their co-workers using online platforms and visit their offices when necessary.

The term "telecommuting", which refers to working remotely from an office, primarily through telephone contact, as a substitute for actual travel, was coined in the 1970s, stimulating the initial broad interest in teleworking (Lamond et al., 1997). In the 1980s, Grant et al. (1985) classified teleworking as "one kind of remote working, or doing typical work activities while away from one's normal workplace". The definition of remote work is enlarged to encompass elements of the procedures needed to organise work outside the typical organisational limitations of geography and time when computer and communications technology is taken into account (Lamond et al., 1997b). Kelly in 1985 pointed out teleworking has drawn increasing interest from employees, businesses, transportation planners, communities, the telecommunications sector, and others (Kelly, 1985). By the 1980s, it was being referred to as the "next workplace revolution" (Handy & Mokhtarian, 1996). Recently, the term "virtual organization", has been introduced where work is widely spread over time and location thanks to telecommunications technology (Handy, 1995). Employers' and employees' willingness to allow telework to take advantage of it will determine the future of teleworking. A shared understanding of telework is consequently necessary so that employers and employees may decide for themselves and their organisations how valuable telework is.

According to statistical evidence, telework was more common before the pandemic in industries reliant on information and communication technologies and knowledge workers in general, however there were significant various changes within the EU ('Telework before the COVID-19 pandemic', 2021). Moshe Beauford in 2022 analysed that the number of people working remotely has surged by 140% since 2005 (The State of Video Conferencing, 2022). As mentioned by Santo Milasi et al. (2021), teleworking has known significant increase some 10 years before the pandemic outbreak. In1996, the International Labour Organization (ILO) defined work from home as a type of work organisation in which the employee is dispersed from the company's headquarters or production facilities and unable to interact personally with co-workers (Türkeș & Vuță, 2022). In fact, major players in video conferencing like Zoom, Cisco WebEx, and Skype for Business have seen some of their greatest user metrics in years as a result of the demand for capabilities like file/screen sharing, real-time file editing among others. One of the most downloaded programs is Zoom, a video conferencing tool that enables users to speak with up to 99 other people at once. Video conferencing software is expected to continue to grow dramatically (Zoom Boom), as it already had before the COVID-19 outbreak. Businesses are adopting this technology as they see the advantages of having a mobile workforce on a local, national, and international level (The Rise of Video Conferencing—Latest News—Office Reality, n.d.).

As the world prepares for the possible spread of the COVID-19 pandemic, companies have begun to evaluate their level of assistance to their employees who choose to telecommute to keep all employees healthy and productive. Many companies offer their employees financial incentives to keep their offices as close to the facility as possible, while some have even offered their employees paid time off to ensure that their employees are as healthy as possible during the pandemic. Both responses are indicative of the extent to which companies are prepared for the potential pandemic.

During the pandemic, many businesses around the world closed their doors or reduced their operations to help their employees cope with the COVID-19 pandemic which has been one of the deadliest, most widespread and most intense pandemic events in human history. As many nations struggle with the re-opening and, in some cases, re-closing of their borders because of the COVID-19 epidemic, the notion of remote work or Work from Home (WFH) is gaining traction among businesses (BBC, 2021). Telecommuting has become an increasingly common way for employees to work during the COVID-19 pandemic. During the COVID-19 pandemic, many businesses have had to adjust their operations to continue their business activities. One such adjustment that many businesses have had to make is the telecommuting of their employees, such as the ability to work from home or the use of web-based communication platforms. The use of telecommuting platforms has enabled employees to work from locations that are protected from the COVID-19 pandemic, allowing them to continue to work without having to leave their families.

Faced with the new reality, employees and entrepreneurs alike are turning to WFH or telecommuting to get through the year 2021 and beyond. Based on a survey done by Global Workplace Analytics (GWA), a research-based consulting firm that helps employers optimise hybrid-remote and flexible workplace strategies, stated that among 3000 employees who worked remotely during the pandemic, 73% find it a success to work from home, while 86% stated that they are fully productive working from their home and 76% want to keep on working from home at least for 2.5 days per week (The Organisation for Economic Co-operation and Development (OECD), 2021). As mentioned by Organisation for Economic Co-operation and Development (OECD), it was found that in Australia, France, and the United Kingdom, 47% of employees teleworked during lockdowns in 2020.

In Japan, where there was no countrywide lockdown, the teleworking rate climbed from 10 to 28% between December 2019 and May 2020. However, while telecommuting has allowed certain businesses to avoid closing their doors, it has also forced others to shut down their doors for good. This has had a significant impact on the economy of Mauritius, which was heavily reliant on the tourism industry. As far as Corporate Social Responsibility (CSR) is concerned, COVID-19 has put sustainability under the corporate spotlight. Companies are leading providers of sustainable construction products and services and have been recognised for their achievements in the field. One of the many ways they have done this is through their partnership with the United Nations (UN). Companies have been working with the UN's sustainable infrastructure initiative, UN-Habitat, to improve the lives of people in areas they work in, by providing them with improved stormwater drainage and other infrastructure.

7.1.3 History of Corporate Social Responsibility (CSR)

The history of CSR is long. There are several theories most notably, the development of social responsibility, corporate social responsibility and corporate citizenship. It is an important concept to understand, as a corporate social responsibility policy is not complete if it is not understood from the start. Corporate Social Responsibility (CSR) is an approach to business that focuses on the social and environmental impact of how a company operates. There are a variety of ways that a company can incorporate CSR into its operations, such as by supporting community development projects and engaging with customers. From the inception of the CSR movement in the early twentieth century to the year 2000, companies aimed to reduce their negative social, environmental, and economic impact and improve their corporate reputation.

From its beginning, CSR has been a major driver for ethical business practices and responsible citizenship. In this section, the history of CSR and the ethical considerations that have shaped its development since the inception of the movement is explored. As per management historian Daniel A. Wren, there were complaints about the developing industrial system in the United Kingdom, mainly regarding the employment of women and children, and the same difficulties also happened in America (Carroll, 2009). Carroll (2009) mentioned that the industrial system was seen by reformers in both nations as the root of many other social issues, including strikes, poverty, slum areas, and child and women work. According to management historian, Daniel A. Wren, the early industrial benefit of the community as a multitude of altruism, generosity, and financial expertise. Wren (2005) mentioned entrepreneurs such as John H. Patterson, an employee at National Cash Register, as one executive who helped to shape the industrial welfare movement. The plans of this welfare movement aimed at preventing labour difficulties and increasing performance by adopting steps that were both corporate and social in nature. Wren also mentioned that hospital clinics, bathhouses, lunchrooms, profit sharing, leisure facilities, and other similar activities are all examples of welfare schemes. Was it more acceptable to think of the establishment of these programs to enhance employees' circumstances as economic or social decisions? Did they show businesses taking responsibility for their employees that went above what was required by law? Carroll even noted that it was hard to give definitive answers to these inquiries, even though both intentions appeared to be obvious (Global-Insight, 2018).

According to Global Insight (2018), CSR has recently become more prominent. However, evidence of corporations' concern for society can be traced back to actions dating back to the Industrial Revolution. Industrialists were more concerned with worker's well-being and productivity in the mid-to-late 1800s (Carroll, 2009). At that time, industrial improvement and welfare initiatives were seen as a mix of social justice and financial savvy. As Carroll (2009) noted, back in the 1900s well-known industrialist Andrew Carnegie, who acquired his income in the steel business, was known for contributing significant sums of money to educational and scientific research causes. Carroll also pointed out that some 9 years later oil industry entrepreneur John D. Rockefeller contributed almost half a billion dollars to religious, educational, and scientific institutions (Carroll, 2009).

7.1.4 Objectives of CSR

CSR is based on the idea that businesses should seek additional pro-social goals in addition to achieving profits. Minimising environmental and social costs, fostering volunteerism among firm employees, and contributing to charity are examples of popular CSR aims. This managerial concept, as known today, is mostly a twentieth-century product, having emerged in the early 1950s (Latapí Agudelo et al., 2019). The first corporate social responsibility (CSR) initiative in the corporate world was launched by Procter & Gamble in 1956 when it set out to improve working and living conditions for people in the developing world. The corporate social responsibility (CSR) movement emerged in the 1960s to respond to a crisis. It sought to create a set of practices that corporations could follow to bring about social and environmental good. The movement spread beyond the business world, becoming deeply ingrained in the social practices of society at large. In recent years, the CSR movement has taken on new dimensions as a subsidiary of corporate social responsibility (CSR). However, over the past decades, many companies have followed suit, adopting CSR policies to increase sales, boost employee morale, and make the brand more socially responsible.

CSR, on the other hand, did not take off until the 1970s (A Brief History of Corporate Social Responsibility (CSR), 2019). According to Staff (2019), the Committee for Economic Development established the notion of a "social contract" between corporations and society in 1971 ('A Brief History of Corporate Social Responsibility (CSR)', n.d.b). This contract promoted the concept that businesses function and exist because of public consent, and those businesses have a responsibility to contribute to society's needs. By the 1980s, early CSR had progressed as more businesses began to incorporate social concerns into their operations while being more responsive to stakeholders (Latapí Agudelo et al., 2019b). Businesses have used Corporate Social Responsibility (CSR) for decades to contribute to society while enhancing their brand reputation. CSR began to gain wider popularity in the 1990s. Donna J. Wood, a University of Pittsburgh professor, released Corporate Social Performance Revisited in 1991, which expanded and developed on early CSR models by proposing a framework for evaluating CSR programs' impacts and outcomes (Latapí Agudelo et al., 2019b). Nazami et al. (2022) explain that CSR has become an appropriate approach for many firms by the early 2000s, with multibillion-dollar businesses like Wells Fargo, Coca-Cola, Walt Disney, and Pfizer implementing the concept of CSR into their operations. CSR is a major topic in today's business, administration, and governance, especially since the United Nations Global Compact (UNGC) was developed in 2000 to urge corporations throughout the world to implement sustainable and socially responsible practices and report back to them (Nazami et al., 2022). CSR is a concept in which businesses incorporate social and environmental issues into their company operations, voluntary and mandated activities. The concept of corporate social responsibility offers everyone in an entire company the opportunity to make contributions to the community, the environment, the nation, and other areas. Many people perceive that people are living for themselves, but it can be argued that accomplishing anything or living for someone else is a very different experience. In addition to giving a sense of inner satisfaction, pride, and happiness, making people happy is simply because an organisation is committed to educating the underprivileged children of a specific town and bringing a smile to their faces. The values of society and the environment in daily lives should never be underestimated. There is an urge to consider those who are less fortunate and affluent than those in the immediate surroundings. CSR works towards allowing working for the advancement of society and to make it a better place to live.

CSR plays a significant role in spreading positive information about the company. Contributing to society, stakeholders, and consumers will not only elevate the company but also guarantee its long-term success and growth. Corporate social responsibility is essential to building brand recognition among the target audience, which includes the media, other organisations, and most crucially, direct consumers. People form a favourable opinion of a company when it takes the effort to educate underprivileged children, plant more trees for a greener environment, supply energy to a community, hire people, and do other similar actions. The cost of CSR initiatives is rather low. Engage in CSR initiatives because of care about the cause, not just to get attention. Numerous companies reach out to isolated areas; some of them are even unheard of as a corporate social responsibility effort. Additionally, CSR makes employees feel happy. The workers claim to take satisfaction in teaching those in need or kids whose families are unable to send them to normal schools and acquire a real education (The Organisation for Economic Co-operation and Development

(OECD), 2021). CSR initiatives improve relationships among colleagues. People get into the practice of cooperating to assist others. They start to value their time spent working together and eventually develop constructive friendships. Additionally, they grow a sense of faithfulness and commitment to their company, which at most has a social responsibility as a priority.

7.1.5 CSR Around the World

In several nations, including Sweden, Norway, the Netherlands, Denmark, France, India, Malaysia, and Australia, CSR reporting is already required by law. The Indian government is thinking about making CSR efforts mandatory, which is a significant step beyond that.

The concept of CSR, or corporate social responsibility, has developed from its foundations as a motto that some corporations adopted to the current challenges of the twenty-first century, where being socially responsible is no longer only fashionable but rather a corporate necessity (Corporate Social Responsibility—Meaning, Need and its Evolution, n.d.). Clean development, human capital, contextualisation, corruption, cooperation, and communication are just a few of the CSR challenges that Corporate South Africa faces (Key challenges of CSR in South Africa.pdf | Course Hero, 2019). CSR in Nigeria is philanthropic in nature and has culture of charity as companies and wealthy individuals contribute to charitable causes and use these contributions to reap positive publicity (David, 1970). In Tanzania, Corporate Social Responsibility (CSR) is widely understood as philanthropy (doing well with part of the profit) and thus refers to charitable community support projects in most cases ('Corporate Social Responsibility in Tanzania', 2021). The Rwanda Social Security Fund is the country's national social security fund (commonly known as Caisse Social du Rwanda or CSR). All salaried employees in Rwanda, both natives and foreigners, are required to pay into the plan (*Rwanda—Individual—Other taxes*, 2022).

Ghanaian businesses refer to their charitable giving to the unprivileged, hospitals, and even unsuccessful state agencies as CSR (Joy Business, 2021). Some build schools and other social amenities for people in rural communities, others emblazon their brand logos and paint buildings among other things and describe them as CSR activities (Sarpong, 2017). CSR evolves too rapidly—in 5 years' time there will be the need for a re-situation of the meaning of CSR. It can be noticed that there has neither been a true standardisation of CSR around the world nor a multinational policy. Hence the need to explore the type of CSR prevailing around different parts of the world. It is desirable to harmonise the best practices of CSR at least over ICT tools including telecommunicating amenities (*The Practice of CSR around the World*, 2015).

7.1.5.1 CSR Orientation in Europe and US

If the focus is on the geographical development of the ideology, or the adoption and application of the concept by businesses in various areas of the world, neither the chronology nor the agreed-upon definition of CSR is shared by all firms globally. For example, even though the US was responsible for its early introduction into business literature, CSR as a concept has grown rapidly more in Europe than in the US. The "green movement" and "green awareness" gained significant advances in Europe, which meant that businesses and corporations on the continent were more receptive to CSR than their counterparts in the US. However, there has been a "rebalancing off" in recent years as the US body politic acknowledges the necessity for firms to be held accountable and sheds the prolonged reluctance that surrounded them during the period when Europe was making quick progress in adopting CSR (The Practice of CSR around the World, 2015).

7.1.5.2 Progress of CSR in the West and Asia

The concept of CSR has become more widely accepted as a result, and in the West, it is seen to be just as important for business as caring for employees. Many businesses often incorporate their commitment to CSR and their support of the necessity of social responsibility in the policies and initiatives that they have introduced. Although corporations have a social obligation, other areas like Asia and Latin America have drifted behind for a very long time. The fact that many companies and businesses in these regions practised a particular form of capitalism that was specific to those countries, and which included a certain inbuilt social conscience may make it seem primitive or Realist to say that businesses need to have no responsibility towards society (The Practice of CSR around the World, 2015). Consequently, it cannot be stated that these nations and areas completely lagged, but the idea as it is understood in the West was not applied here. Similar to the criticisms levelled at early adopters in the US and Europe, many observers in these nations first criticised the concept of CSR as an imperialist invention and a luxury. But in recent years, nations like India and Brazil have taken the lead in pressuring firms to adopt socially responsible, environmentally conscious, humane in their treatment of people, and resource-conserving practices. With its promotion of the "Global Compact", to which several nations have signed, the United Nations has contributed significantly to the notion of CSR becoming universally accepted. This international agreement binds the signatories to generally recognised standards of social responsibility, which firms in those nations are expected to uphold and whose implementation is monitored.

7.1.5.3 CSR in Malaysia

In recent times, Malaysia has paid a lot of attention to corporate social responsibility, or CSR. CSR was incorporated into the Malaysian Prime Minister's budget adjustments. The Malaysian stock exchange, Bursa Malaysia, has also established a comprehensive framework for listed companies in Malaysia to take CSR more seriously. Companies involved in strategic CSR have developed policies and programs in various sectors such as employee relationships, marketplace, environmental, and community development. The annual report of these companies also reflects the information about how CSR is being implemented in the corporate world. Companies can join a CSR index such as the Dow Jones Sustainability Index. Investors now have access to information on companies with strong CSR, thus enabling them to make a wise choice in terms of investment. Malaysia is truly experiencing a positive CSR activity. Good CSR practices allow businesses to become more sustainable and add value to their capital markets and bring goodwill to them. Recent studies and newspaper articles indicate that there may be more CSR in Malaysia than is often believed (Aaijaz & Ibrahim, 2012).

7.1.5.4 CSR in Singapore

Limits in the context of command and control have been arbitrarily set by the Singaporean government. Moreover, according to the government, developing standards and values is the only way to put CSR into practice. The nation's code of corporate governance urges domestic businesses to adhere to high standards of governance in this respect ('"The State of Play of CSR in Singapore" by Eugene K B Tan', n.d.). Additionally, in 2011, Eugene K B Tan mentioned that CSR is marketed in Singapore as a method of doing business that is supportive rather than a substitute. The environment is of vital importance in the context of sustainable business operations, as demonstrated by the rising trend of sustainability reporting by Singaporean enterprises and CSR in the mainstream. Additionally, Singapore has not established any requirements for the implementation and management of CSR. Additionally, Singaporean businesses have been making efforts in every area to uphold their social responsibilities. Hoven Lovells is interacting with other businesses to support the expansion of social enterprises. Additionally, businesses like Comfort Delgro have developed wheelchair-accessible buses and offer free emergency taxi services for students with disabilities (An Analysis of Corporate Social Responsibility Expenditure in India: | Economic and Political Weekly, 2014).

7.1.5.5 CSR in the Netherlands

There are two different CSR policies in place in the Netherlands. The national policy establishes a framework for enterprises along which the legislation establishes specific requirements. For companies that operate in countries with ineffective legal enforcement, international CSR policy is useful. Together with the government, NGOs and labour unions work to find solutions to the world's challenges. The Dutch government is crucial in educating firms about CSR practices. It also raises other countries' awareness of their duties. Graafland et al. (2003) stated that companies must also submit CSR reports if they have more than 250 workers and net revenue of at least EUR 35 million (Firdouse R A H M A N Khan—Academia.edu, 2019). 500 Dutch corporations are ranked by the Ministry of Economic Affairs based on how transparent their business operations and CSR programs are. In addition, the Netherlands has created a fresh set of international regulations that control business activity abroad as well. Few businesses in the Netherlands have implemented CSR programs since NGOs take on most of the responsibility. Among these select few corporations, Royal Friesland Campina has taken significant steps towards sustainable development.

7.1.5.6 CSR in India

India is the first nation in the world to formally mandate CSR on April 1, 2014. For businesses with a specified turnover and profitability, Section 135 of the Indian Companies Act mandates that they devote 2% of their average net profit over the previous three years to CSR. Moreover, still according to Section 135(1) of the Act, any business with the required net worth, revenue, or net profits must set up a CSR committee. Therefore, when a section 8 company reaches the required net worth, turnover, or net profits, it must also create a CSR committee and adhere to CSR regulations (Corporate Social Responsibility Under Section 135 of Companies Act 2013, 2022).

7.1.5.7 CSR in Australia

In Australia, CSR has been regulated primarily through "soft" law initiatives. Several driving factors increase the rates of CSR adoption in Australia, especially over the past two decades. This includes the desire to improve corporate reputation and brand management. A variety of high-profile clues that assess corporate citizenship performance; pressure on companies from NGOs, particularly concerning environmental and human rights issues; wider audience sophistication and awareness of corporate social responsibility; socially responsible or ethical investment funds; new governance structures have put more emphasis on cross-sectoral partnerships between governments and NGOs and businesses; the need for companies to improve relationships with stakeholders; and the desire to continue improving government relations to avoid long-term regulation. Positive effects of CSR inside companies are derived from motivation, commitment, retention, training, recruitment, and staff turnover (improving employee morale is often cited as a driver of CSR activities) (Bird et al., 2012).

7.1.5.8 CSR in Mauritius

In Mauritius, CSR guidelines were eliminated in 2015, and companies were set free to use their funds allocated for CSR following their framework (Government of Mauritius, 2016) ('The New Corporate Social Responsibility (CSR) Framework Background', 2016). As stated by Bissoon in 2018, Profit-making businesses in Mauritius are required by law to provide 2% of their net income to CSR initiatives (Bissoon, 2018). A registered NGO, a special purpose company, or any business partner may carry out these activities. Bissoon also mentioned that the creation of a National CSR foundation is mandated under the new CSR framework outlined in the budget for 2016–2017. The foundation would implement initiatives for the underprivileged groups' social welfare. The CSR funding will also be distributed to the organisations. Additionally, several studies showed the connection between participating in CSR activities and a nation's businesses having a competitive edge (Deloitte, 2008). This demonstrates how seriously CSR is taken in Mauritius (Choudhury, 2019). Many businesses in Mauritius have embraced groundbreaking programs for environmental sustainability and education as part of their CSR operations. Air Mauritius and the Mauritian Wildlife Foundation (MWF) have developed the "One Take Off, One Tree" project for the aviation sector. Initiative MWF plants a tree because of each take-off. Alteo is also assisting neighbourhood education efforts in the hotel industry. Additionally, the business donates money to help poor kids ('The New Corporate Social Responsibility (CSR) Framework Background', 2016).

Although the idea was established in the Income Tax Act in 2009 ('CSRGuide', 2021), there is still no specific statutory definition of CSR in Mauritius. Meanwhile, the new code of corporate governance 2016 (the Code) (the-national-code-of-corporate-governance-for-mauritius, 2016), which was released in February 2017 and took effect in July 2017, defines CSR as a concept in which businesses act to balance their economic success with the country's long-term social and environmental development as an integrated approach. The code goes on to say that a firm that does well in CSR, goes above and beyond legal compliance to actively pursue good benefits for local people and the environment (Beebeejaun, 2020).

Beebeejaun (2020) also mentioned that too frequently, businesses see CSR as just another source of pressure, and as a result, they take a box-ticking strategy rather than truly tackling issues that CSR contributions are intended to address. In light of the above, according to Beebeejaun (2020) Mauritius created CSR legislation in 2016 that included several key areas of intervention for which CSR funding will be used. CSR's origins in Mauritius would be traced back to the concept of corporate philanthropic activities. Beebeejaun (2020) describes this concept with casual actions that lead to the promotion of social and community-related activities which are complementary to company strategies and processes. However, global macroeconomic crises such as the Great Recession of 2008 (Segal, 2022), as well as company failures such as Enron from the Maxwell Publishing Empire, and WorldCom, have triggered government interferences in business operations throughout the world. Likewise, in Mauritius, to raise knowledge and awareness of economic activities on the environment and society, the government amended the Income Tax Act of 2005 in 2011 to make it mandatory for corporations, incorporated or registered, in Mauritius to set up or finance a CSR Fund equivalent to 2% of their book profits to set up or finance programs that contribute to the social and environmental development of the country (Beebeejaun, 2020).

7.2 Mauritian Work Culture and CSR

The private sector in Mauritius has a long history of CSR, specifically in the areas of voluntary social participation in the areas where they function and in the larger community. They have contributed significantly to the country's social and environmental development throughout the years (Bissoon, 2018). According to previous Mauritius Employers' Federation (MEF) survey results of the years 2006 and 2008, most Mauritian firms feel that their role in society extends beyond wealth development and that seeking corporate interests must be coupled with social and environmental responsibilities ('Survey Report On The Practical Implementation of CSR under The New Legislation', 2011). Internal CSR initiatives, undertaken for the benefit of employees, along with external CSR initiatives, developing or supporting social and community-related activities, have been undertaken by Mauritian enterprises, driven primarily by:

- ethical considerations,
- employee motivation,
- brand positioning, and
- company reputation.

According to the MEF Surveys, CSR has taken a charitable approach, with ad hoc efforts that are independent of company performance and profitability ('Survey report on the practical implementation of CSR under the new legislation', 2011). As such, companies in Mauritius have been legally required to donate 2% of their profit after tax to CSR practices in the following recognised areas of engagement since July 2009:

- Socio-economic development (including Gender and Human Rights),
- Health,
- Education and Training,
- Leisure and Sports,
- Environment, and
- Catastrophic Interventions and Support.

A legal change passed in December 2010 mandates that half of all CSR payments go to three programs that support state housing, the well-being of children in affected populations, and the elimination of deep poverty (Bissoon, 2018). The government examined the use of CSR money in 2010, intending to emphasise the major challenges to optimising social benefits and guaranteeing connectivity. Companies were then committed to donating half of their CSR funds to three national programs. Conversely, in 2015, the law was changed to remove all CSR guidelines, allowing corporates to use their CSR funds as they deemed worthy. Bissoon (2018) mentioned that this was in response to criticisms that the new policy limited business enterprises' ability to use their CSR funds appropriately, as well as concerns raised by NGOs about accessing funds through corporate CSR programs. Private companies have special sub-committees for CSR programs. They work from home, they approve budget and offer training ('prg-series-no-3-april-2018.pdf', 2018).

The creation of the "CSR framework" was left entirely to the discretion of the boards of directors of the concerned firms, and any NGO with a minimal charitable objective could readily acquire CSR funding. If a corporation does not develop a CSR program, the equivalent of 2% of net profits must be transferred to the MRA as income tax, which will then direct the funds to a contingency fund controlled by the government for financial assistance to non-governmental entities. Tasks are carried out through:

- the company's approved programs,
- approved national programs, and
- approved NGOs.

Indeed, Mauritian government has treated CSR as a tax measure which can be deducted from private companies' annual budget as a boost for the private companies and same time to help society. It is a win–win situation and a socially responsible measure (Ramdhony, 2018). Old Sugar factories—VIVEA and Terra—have transformed their sites into smart business parks which in turn inhabit private companies conducting CSR activities closer to socially vulnerable neighbourhood (About ENL foundation—Citizenship—ENL Foundation—ENL Group Mauritius, 2018).

7.3 Approach and Methodology for This Research

For the current study, it would be too time-consuming to prepare research on a nationwide scale. It was deemed that limiting the target audience within the scope of the study and targeting people within a specific niche would be more relevant. Based on the research questions, a range of response items were developed so that the SMEs could rank the options using multiple-choice questions, Likert Scale, Matrix questions, and ranking questions to express their preferences. There were also open-ended questions that were synthesised to bring about a suitable response to a few questions. The owners of the business' confidentiality were respected where names and particulars would not be recorded but the gender was used and recorded for research purposes only. Random sampling was implemented through which people from Mauritian villages were considered. A sample of 50 entrepreneurs from both genders were selected, among which 48 responded positively to the survey. The industries were varied at large—from inland SMEs like retail trade, construction, food facilities services, garages, handicraft and manufacturing to offshore SMEs like farming and fishing.

7.3.1 Key Research Questions

Telecommuting has brought about many positive changes to the work culture of entrepreneurs.

The COVID-19 outbreak has caused an increase in telecommuting, which has changed the nature of work for many people literally instantly. To better understand the idea of working remotely, four research questions were asked to determine the feeling of the entrepreneurs on this new normal.

1. What changes telecommuting has brought to your work culture?
2. What tools have you used for the betterment of your enterprise during the COVID-19 period?
3. Has your company implemented a work-from-home policy in response to COVID-19?
4. What, in your opinion, are the major opportunities that COVID-19 has brought, is providing, or is going to offer to your company and/or other SMEs?

7.3.2 *Research Findings and Discussion*

The study findings derived from the survey that was conducted are analysed and discussed in the following section. The fact that there were more replies from men than from women indicates that men are more interested in teleworking than women are. The results concern the teleworking environment, employee perceptions, benefits, and drawbacks, as well as the sustainability of the idea during the new normal.

7.3.2.1 The Entrepreneurs and Their Operations

The survey shows that 20 entrepreneurs (men and women) were registered as SMEs while the remaining were not yet approved SMEs, and this effectively represented the sample size. Figure 7.1 depicts 10 of the SMEs (50%) that were in business between 1 to 5 years while some 15% were already working as registered entrepreneurs from 5 to 10 years and more than 10 years. Some 20% had been in business for less than a year.

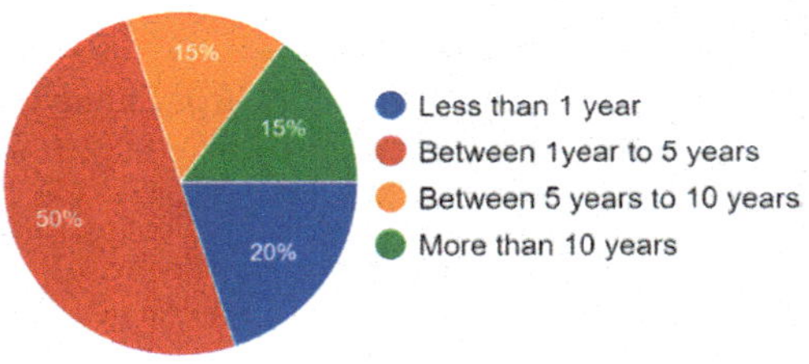

Fig. 7.1 Running business

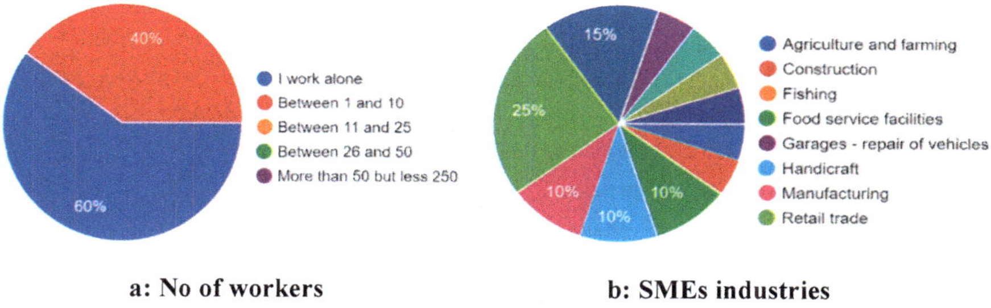

Fig. 7.2 Number of workers and the related SME Industries

7.3.2.2 Effect of COVID-19 on the Entrepreneurs and the Related Industries (Fig. 7.2)

A majority of 60% of the SMEs work alone while 40% have at most 10 workers. COVID-19 made already difficult situations worse by obstructing access to crucial markets like retail traders, wholesale trade, manufacturing, agriculture, and farming among others. Mr. Paul Baker, CEO of International Economics analysed that the increasing cost of manufacturing, distribution and reducing output and productivity have impacted SMEs since workers were unable to reach manufacturing sites due to a lockdown.

7.3.2.3 SMEs Help from Private Sectors and Their Survival (Fig. 7.3)

As Mauritius tried to adjust to the situation, 80% of the entrepreneurs were affected by COVID-19 in different industries—Retail, Agriculture and Farming, Handicraft, manufacturing, and Foodservice among others. It was noticed that with the strong involvement of the private sector, 75% were still in business during the pandemic and a sizeable number (70%) were still in operation.

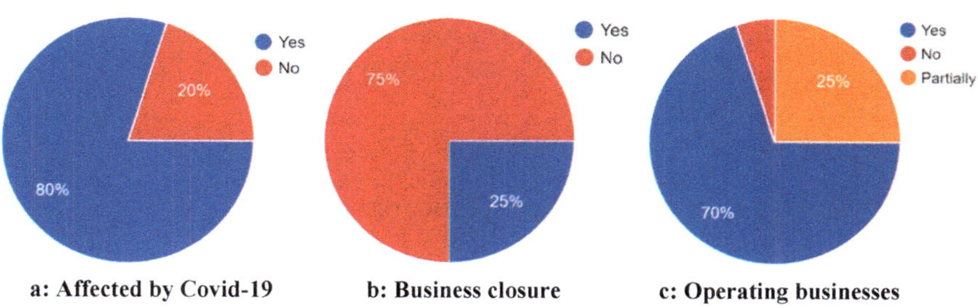

Fig. 7.3 Private sector help and survival of SMEs

Table 7.1 Challenges encountered during COVID-19

	No. of entrepreneurs affected	
Difficulties entrepreneurs faced	The year 2020	The year 2021
Insufficient funds	10	8
Sickness	7	12
Shortage or costly raw materials	11	13
Low clients' demand	10	13
Inability to increase business	9	11

7.3.2.4 Perceived Challenges Encountered During COVID-19

Many SMEs being affected by the COVID-19 pandemic faced huge challenges in the year 2020 and 2021 lockdown periods.

Another research question that analyses the difficulties faced during the pandemic showed that entrepreneurs were highly affected. The findings are presented in Table 7.1 in the form of a multiple-choice table for the year 2020 and the year 2021 COVID-19 periods respectively. Five challenges were proposed to the respondents who had the choice of selecting the same difficulties yearly.

The biggest difficulty was the shortage of costly raw materials. This was a huge problem for most Mauritian entrepreneurs claiming that raw materials costs had been on the rise since the onset of COVID-19 about two years back. The survey also reveals that entrepreneurs experienced (1) Low client demand in different industries, (2) Insufficient funds, and (3) inability to increase business. The pandemic caused an almost immediate consumption shock, resulting in a 67% decline in demand for goods and services in various industries. Business Mauritius and Statistics Mauritius acknowledged the efforts of the United Nations System to support the socio-economic response and recovery efforts in Mauritius. Moreover, sickness and the high incidence of non-communicable illnesses in Mauritius affected the COVID-19 mortality rate, with 8 out of 10 fatalities being due to comorbid cardiovascular diseases and other ailments. This led to either employee missing work or due to government instructions, a strict nationwide curfew was implemented to stop the spread of COVID-19 and enable employees to recover safely.

7.3.2.5 Effects of COVID-19 on Entrepreneurs

Sales, profit of the companies, Net cash flow, and Production costs were equally moderately and severely affected by the pandemic in 2020 but in Jan 2020, the impact was less. However, the level of interest in the goods and services, production capacity, and paying employees' wages remained moderately affected. Many fear a probability of 42.1% of temporary closure while some 15.8% still trusted the after COVID-19 era. Meanwhile, COVID-19 has also created other avenues and opportunities for entrepreneurs—shift to online sales and different markets thus leading to an increase in sales.

7.3.2.6 Effects of COVID-19 on Productivity

Economically speaking, the pandemic has caused a drop in investment, a loss of human capital owing to unemployment, and a downturn in international trade and supply chains. Additionally, it can be linked to a limitation on countries' capacity to boost incomes over the long term and a decline in productivity (Pauline Ramos & Tri Prasetyo, 2020). When considering the reduction in labour force (people made redundant, sick, or on leave), tightening of financial circumstances, and disruption of supply chains in the short term, the negative effects of the pandemic are most obvious (Ahumada et al., 2022). Productivity has decreased for workers in sectors and professions that are less suited to remote work, such those in the food industry (Bloom et al., 2021). This was also seen in low-income individuals, those who worked for themselves, and women, especially those who had children (Etheridge et al., 2020).

7.3.2.7 Solutions Brought to Entrepreneurs During and Post-COVID-19

Those entrepreneurs fully registered as SMEs profited fully from the CSR program. They received financial help, training, and sponsorship and hence have been able to keep their businesses active. Moreover, they have intelligently rethought their businesses as shown in Fig. 7.6 (Figs. 7.4).

The reinvention of their enterprises as seen in Fig. 7.6 brought them to think differently. 76.9% of the SMEs had a common drive force to "*Put the client first and ask the right questions to them to know their needs and wants*". Eight (61.5%) chose to add new products and services and deliver them differently while six out of thirteen (46.2%) among the surveyed SMEs decided to redesign their workshops and offer training programs to foster online interaction and keep people engaged in a virtual environment.

Fig. 7.4 Business active

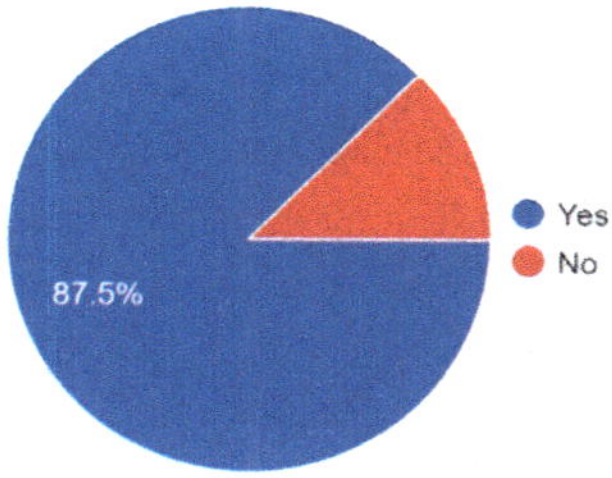

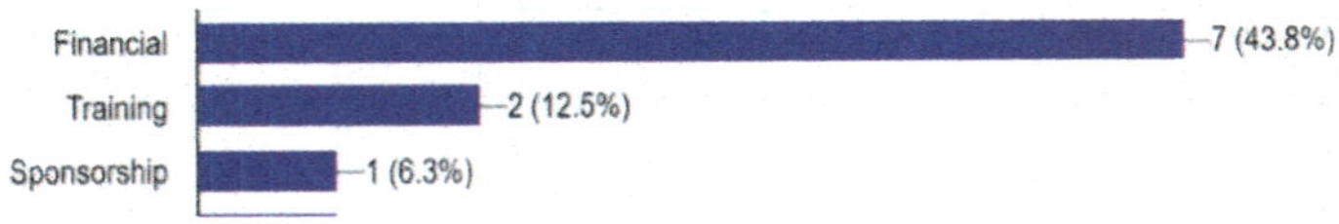

Fig. 7.5 Type of CSR help

There has also been a "psychological understanding" that the changes also mean acceptance of a drop in income and a conversion of investment strategies. Fortunately, lowering the managerial level and the help of Information Technology have brought a sign of relief and a breath of fresh air to the entrepreneurs. These analyses can be seen in Fig. 7.7. The commitment to keep their businesses ongoing was strong. Entrepreneurs trained their staff on new processes and protocols with regard to work in a safe environment and sustained new digital work for those willing to work remotely were the main reasons for their success (Figs. 7.5 and 7.6).

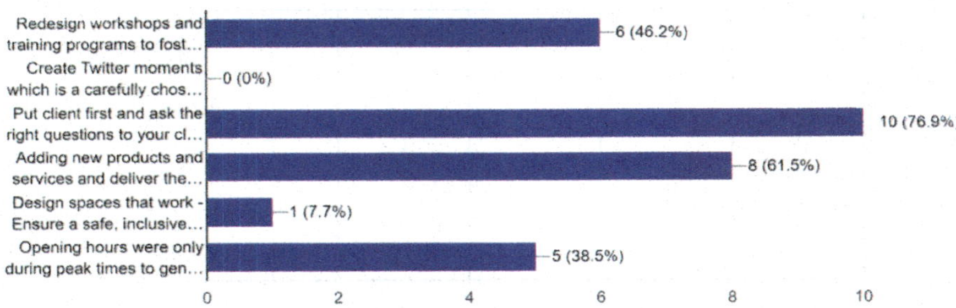

Fig. 7.6 Reinvent the business + profitable

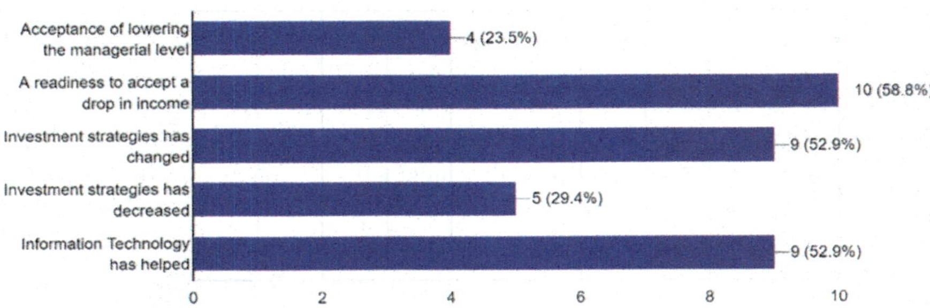

Fig. 7.7 Management of business during COVID-19 with a resilience of acceptance

7.3.2.8 Work Culture and Telecommuting

Even COVID-19 was at its peak and lockdown hit severely, staff at large trusted the entrepreneurs since they brought about positive changes to the work culture. Staff members had been working in more flexible and independent ways hence bringing in job satisfaction. Mauritius Telecom allowed to enhance internet connectivity much higher than normal to 20 Mbps to allow businesses to telecommute and work effectively and efficiently from home. Several media and TV channels were accessible to anyone for ethical entertainment to prevent burn out and resiliency. It has been noticed through the survey that most entrepreneurs were already digitally knowledgeable since some 94.7% were using the WhatsApp application to communicate with their staff and customers while 63.2% were acquainted to social media like Facebook and 42.1% were exchanging mails.

7.3.2.9 Recovery from COVID-19

With the proper digitally enabled environment and assistance of government towards SMEs, many entrepreneurs had been able to recover from COVID-19. DBM provided loan scheme and the Wage Support Scheme for Export Oriented Enterprise to help many affected entrepreneurs due to COVID-19. Other schemes such as Business loan, Agro Industry and loans to women entrepreneurs were also offered by the DBM. Entrepreneurs placed caring at the core of their businesses and communicated with their staff with compassion and confidence. This has helped to have sustainable staff development.

7.4 Evaluation of Research

This research depicts that most registered SMEs (41.7%) are from the retail and trade businesses; a male-dominated area and the minority range from marketing, textile, bakery, agriculture and farming, fishing, handicraft, and construction. Some 50% of the businesses who are still active were hit by the pandemic and 20% have been affected after the pandemic. Some 5% have not been able to surface out of the water during the pandemic. The situation created by the global pandemic is no doubt reshaping the socio-economic environment in which businesses operate and are conducted. The difficulties faced by the businesses are decrease in business activities due to less raw materials to work with. Import and export facilities were largely reduced due to mobility restrictions and thus international trade being affected. The influx of customers was extremely low due to restrictions imposed by the local authority, or many people got sick with the virus. The whole nation was taken aback with the rapid rise of COVID-19 cases daily and had to comply with the sanitary protocols in place. The net income and turnover of businesses drop drastically.

On the other side, to overcome the difficulties and effects of the pandemic, telecommuting coupled with CSR has reshaped and given a new birth to several businesses. Restructuration of business models is needed to adapt to the new normal and to the retraining of employees to enhance productivity and service delivery. Many businesses moved online and made massive use of the online platforms such as Facebook to advertise their products and reach out to customers by offering a home delivery service. They did their best to satisfy their customers. Employers also provided several equipment such as phones, tablets with internet connectivity and facilities such as working from home, flexible working hours to keep their businesses active. Online trainings were given to employees to join the new trend and to keep people engaged in their businesses. Applications such as WhatsApp has been widely used for local and international trade in sharing of files, videos, sales receipts among various others. Phone calls remain the second best in terms of direct interaction for a quick and immediate response. This brought an overall change in the work culture and increased flexibility among employers and employees. Also, CSR played a major role in assisting SMEs in providing government grants, supportive loans, and wage assistance schemes to the registered businesses. This inevitably created new avenues of development and a sense of relief for all these businesses to remain active. The eligible businesses welcomed the government aids as a blessing.

The little portion who did not re-invent their businesses were either not registered as an SME and could not benefit from CSR facilities or were not strong-willed enough to take risks in taking supporting loans. Also, some businesses due to the different nature of their activities could not telecommute or benefit from financial aids. They only relied on the bare facilities that were at their disposal.

The paradox remains that although most SMEs have benefited from government aids, their online sales have increased by only 40% and they predict the future as still uncertain and dark as it is tough to predict whether there will be a rise in demand in the coming future. The study shows that 55% of the population appreciate that the government has provided sufficient measures to help the SMEs and that if the grants are removed, another next best measure to help the SMEs is to defer the TAX payment to alleviate the burden of the SMEs and help them to sustain.

7.5 Telecommuting—A Catalyser for SMEs Post-COVID-19 with the Help of CSR.

There have been many opinions regarding the role of corporate social responsibility during the pandemic, and much of it has been strongly debated.

The place of CSR within the current pandemic and exploration of the impact of CSR on Mauritius' businesses and society during the pandemic has been discussed.

In Mauritius during the lockdown period, 77% of the manufacturing sector was not operational while 57% of the Professional, Scientific, and Technical services and 63% of the Information and Communication Sector maintained their operations

(Report on Impact of COVID-19 on Businesses in Mauritius) (Khan Jaffur et al., 2022).

Since then, most companies have already decided on business continuity plans, but those plans are not prepared to face the fast-moving process and unknown features of the COVID-19 pandemic (Guide to Business Continuity and Pandemic Planning, 2021). Usually, business continuity plans are more appropriate for events like natural calamities, cyber incidents, and power failures, among others (E-guide What is BCDR? Business Continuity and Disaster Recovery Guide, n.d.). They do not usually account for widespread quarantines, extended school closures, or additional travel restrictions that may be imposed in the event of a health emergency. The Global Workplace Analytics (GWA), a research-based consulting firm that helps employers optimise hybrid-remote and flexible workplace strategies, states that before the pandemic, 56% of the US workforce held a job compatible with remote work and only 3.6% of the employee workforce worked at home half-time or more (Lister, 2021).

The Mauritian government has implemented many assistance measures in response to the worldwide COVID-19 epidemic to assist companies and save jobs. The State Investment Corporation Limited (SIC), Investment Support Programme Limited (ISP), SME Equity Fund Ltd (SEF), and Development Bank of Mauritius Ltd. introduced the COVID-19 "Plan de Soutien" Cell (DBM) (Government Business Support Measures—Business Mauritius, 2020).

7.6 Conclusion

This analysis has aimed to broaden views on some of the key challenges of telecommuting assistance to businesses during and after the COVID-19 pandemic. The crisis caused by COVID-19 made us rethink our whole perception of life. Businesses also had to adopt new behaviour to transfer their activities in an online environment and devised new ways of work. In adopting a new normal and seizing several opportunities available such as government grants, supporting loans and wage assistance schemes, businesses have been able to remain active and are striving to sustain in the long run. The rapid evolution of work culture using information and communication technology tools have contributed largely to enable most companies to commute during the pandemic. Due to their nature of activities, unwillingness to accept change and lack of motivation to take risks, certain companies have not been able to work remotely or telecommute. Companies and businesses are strongly encouraged to reinvent themselves to keep pace with the rapidly changing world in order to evolve, grow, and attain greater heights.

Appendix: Questionnaire

Questions

1. Do you have a "Small and Medium Enterprise" (SME)? *

- Yes
- No

Profile of your enterprise

2. Which industry does your company operate in? *

- Agriculture and farming
- Construction
- Fishing
- Food service facilities
- Garages - repair of vehicles
- Handicraft
- Manufacturing
- Retail trade
- Transportation and warehouse
- Wholesale trade
- Other: ______

3. Approximately how long has your business been running? *

- Less than 1 year
- Between 1year to 5 years
- Between 5 years to 10 years
- More than 10 years

4. Were you forced to close your business due to covid? *

- Yes
- No

5. Are you still operating your business today? *

- Yes
- No
- Partially

6. Number of workers *

- I work alone
- Between 1 and 10
- Between 11 and 25
- Between 26 and 50

7. Gender of enterprise owner *

- Male
- Female

8. Are you registered with SME Mauritius *

- Yes
- No

9. Have your business been affected by COVID-19? *

- Yes
- No

Not affected

10. In what way(s) your business has not been affected. *

Affected by Covid-19

11. What are the biggest difficulties your company has encountered in light of COVID-19? You may select more than one challenge.

	2020	2021
The amount of money needed to keep the workers and the firm running was insufficient		
Due to sickness or government instructions, employees missed work		
Operations were slowed because there was a shortage of raw materials or because they were highly costly		
Due to affected customers/clients, demand was lower than usual		
Being unable to increase business or make any anticipated		

12. What effects has the pandemic had on your business since the first Covid-19 case in Mauritius? *

	Severe compression	Moderate compression
The level of interest in the company's goods and services		
Sales (Revenue)		
Profit		
Production capacity of the Company (output produced)		
Paying employees' wages and other operational costs		
Net Cash Flow		
Production costs		

13. How much, in your opinion, has COVID-19 impacted the overall performance of your company compared to the same time in 2019?

	Severe compression	Moderate compression
Jan 2020 to Dec 2020	☐	☐
Jan 2021 to Dec 2021	☐	☐
Jan 2022 to July 2022	☐	☐

Type of help

14. Did you get assistance from any Corporate Social Responsibility (CSR) fund? *

- Yes
- No

15. What type of help did you get? *

- ☐ Financial
- ☐ Training
- ☐ Sponsorship
- ☐ Other: ____

16. Have you been able to keep your business active? *

- Yes
- No

Managing active business post COVID-19

17. According to you, how do you feel you have managed your business during Covid-19? *

- ☐ Acceptance of lowering the managerial level
- ☐ A readiness to accept a drop in income
- ☐ Investment strategies has changed
- ☐ Investment strategies has decreased
- ☐ Information Technology has helped
- ☐ Other: ____

Re-Invent

18. Did you re-invent or re-engineer your business? *

- Yes
- No

19. Explain how you reinvent your business to keep it ongoing and profitable(customer oriented point of view) *

- ☐ Redesign workshops and training programs to foster online interaction and keep people engaged in a virtual environment
- ☐ Create Twitter moments which is a carefully chosen story that is shared with masses through tweets
- ☐ Put client first and ask the right questions to your clients to know what they want and need
- ☐ Adding new products and services and deliver them differently
- ☐ Design spaces that work - Ensure a safe, inclusive working environment
- ☐ Opening hours were only during peak times to generate most significant revenue

20. Explain how you commit to keep your business strong (point of view of your staff)

- Place caring at the core - Communicate with your staff with compassion and confidence
- Sustain new digital workers - for those willing to work remotely
- Train staff on new processes and protocols and how to use personal protective equipment properly
- Use financial as well as calendar targets to monitor early warning signs of outbreaks and be ready to act
- Solve in phases
- Physical/virtual workplace enablement
- Other: ____________

No re-invention

21. Explain why you did not reinvent your business.

- Too risky and uncertain
- Too expensive
- Difficult to adjust to new ways of thinking and doing.
- Stubbornness - Lack of willingness to innovate
- Other: ____________

Work Culture

22. How do you feel the public has trusted your company during Covid-19? *

	1	2	3	4	5	
Lowest trust						Highest trust

23. What changes telecommuting has brought to your work culture? *

- More independence
- No commute
- Increase in flexibility
- Increased in productivity
- Job Satisfaction
- Risk of over working
- Increased isolation
- Decrease in productivity
- Increased home office costs
- Less face time
- Other:

24. What tools have you used for betterment of your enterprise during Covid-19 period. *

- Emails
- Phone
- Whatsapp - for individual calls and group calls
- Zoom - for meeting - group calling
- Facebook
- Twitter
- Instagram
- Tik Tok
- Google Drive
- Google Meet
- Ms Teams
- Other:

Work Policy

25. Which of the following best describes your actual work policies? *

- Most (or all) staff are at the workplace.
- Not (or all) staff have chosen the work from home strategy.
- Staff have chosen both alternatives - work from home and on site.
- I work on my own and do have any staff.

26. According to you, which measures would help your SME recover from COVID-19. You may select more than one answer. *

- Government grant
- Supportive loans
- Wage Assistance Schemes
- Delaying payments of utility bills (telephone, electricity and water bills)
- Deferment of VAT payment
- DBM moratorium for all borrowings, interests, facilities for a 1 year period
- Other:

27. Do you fear there is now a threat to the survival of your company? *

- Yes, there is a possibility of a brief shutdown
- Yes, a potential permanent shutdown exists
- No threat of closure exist
- Not sure

28. By how many employees was COVID-19 responsible for layoffs? *

- Between 1 and 5
- Between 6 and 10
- More than 10
- None
- I didn't have any employees before COVID-19

29. Has your company implemented a work from home policy in response to COVID-19? *

- Yes
- No
- For the kind of business activity, remote work is not possible

30. Which of the following best sums up how you currently organize your work? *

- The majority of staff are on site
- The majority of the staff are working remotely
- Staff are able to work both on-site and from home
- I do not employ anyone

31. What effect do you anticipate COVID-19 will have on your company's demand for 2022 compared to 2019? (Prior to COVID-19's breakout)

- Drop of over 50%
- Drop between 25% -50 %
- Drop up to 25%
- Rise up to 25%
- Rise between 25% -50%
- Rise over 50%
- It's tough to predict/I'm not sure

32. How much do you believe Covid-19 will affect the overall success of your company as compared to actual performance? *

	Severe compression	Moderate compression
Next 3 months		
Next 6 months		
Next 12 months		

33. Do you fear your company will eventually experience a closure due to COVID-19? *

- Yes, there is a probability of a temporary shutdown soon.
- Yes, there is a probability of a permanent shutdown soon.
- No threat of closure exists
- Not sure

34. What, in your opinion, are the major opportunities that Covid-19 has brought, is providing, or is going to offer to your company and/or other SMEs?

- Economic growth
- Sales increase
- Increased revenue
- Online sales
- Shift to different markets
- No opportunities
- Other:

35. How well do you think the government is assisting SMEs in their fight against COVID-19? *

	1	2	3	4	5	
Least assistance						Highest assistance

36. Have you requested government assistance for your business? *

- I applied since my business qualified
- My business qualified, but I chose not to apply
- My business was not qualified for any incentives

37. How successful was government assistance if you applied for it and received it? *

	1	2	3	4	5	
Least successful						Most successful

38. Which of the following strategies would, in your opinion, assist your business and/or other SMEs recover from the pandemic? Choose all that apply *

- Government grants
- Supportive loan
- Tax reduction
- New set of economic policies (decrease in taxes and payroll contributions)
- Wage Assistance Schemes
- Postponing utility payments (telephone, electricity and water bills)
- Other:

References

Aaijaz, N., & Ibrahim, M. (2012). CSR inflections: An overview on CSR Global Strategies adopted by companies in Malaysia and other Asian countries. *The Journal of Southeast Asian Research*, 1–16. https://doi.org/10.5171/2012.266824

About ENL Foundation—Citizenship—ENL Foundation—ENL Group Mauritius. (n.d.). https://www.enl.mu/en/citizenship/enl-foundation/about-enl-foundation. Accessed December 6, 2022.

Access Information on Multilateral Environmental Agreements. (n.d.). *InforMEA*. https://www.informea.org/en/legislation/small-and-medium-enterprises-act-2017-no-16-2017

Ahumada, H., et al. (2022). Sectoral productivity growth, covid-19 shocks, and infrastructure. *Economics of Disasters and Climate Change, 6*(1), 1–28. https://doi.org/10.1007/s41885-021-00098-z

Al Salmi, H., & Khan, F. R. (2019). A comparative case study on accountability of Corporate Social Responsibility (CSR) practices in Oman LNG and OMIFCO at Sur City in Oman. *Humanities & Social Sciences Reviews, 7*(5), 490–502. https://doi.org/10.18510/hssr.2019.7556

Article—The Rise of Video Conferencing. (n.d.). *Office reality*. https://www.officereality.co.uk/cat/articles/article-the-rise-of-video-conferencing. Accessed December 7, 2022.

Beebeejaun, A. (2020). Piercing the corporate veil for environmental torts in mauritius: A comparative study. *Journal of Financial Crime, 28*(4), 1259–1274. https://doi.org/10.1108/jfc-09-2020-0184

Betchoo, N. K. (2015). Research for all, an initiative to promote research in the Mauritian society. *International Letters of Social and Humanistic Sciences, 64*, 73–80. https://doi.org/10.18052/www.scipress.com/ilshs.64.73

Bird, R., Momenté, F., & Reggiani, F. (2012). The market acceptance of corporate social responsibility: A comparison across six countries/regions. *Australian Journal of Management, 37*(2), 153–168. https://doi.org/10.1177/0312896211416136

Bissoon, O. (2018). Corporate Social Responsibility in Mauritius: An analysis of annual reports of Multinational Hotel Groups. *Asian Journal of Sustainability and Social Responsibility, 3*(1). https://doi.org/10.1186/s41180-017-0017-4

Bloom, N., Davis, S. J., & Zhestkova, Y. (2021). Covid-19 shifted patent applications toward technologies that support working from home. *AEA Papers and Proceedings, 111*, 263–266. https://doi.org/10.1257/pandp.20211057

Carroll, A. B. (2009). A history of corporate social responsibility. In *The Oxford handbook of corporate social responsibility* (pp. 19–46). https://doi.org/10.1093/oxfordhb/9780199211593.003.0002

Choudhury, S. B. R. (2019). *An overview of CSR policies in Mauritius, Singapore, Netherlands and India, Knowledge Tank*. https://www.projectguru.in/csr-policies-mauritius-singapore-netherlands-india

ClearTax. (2013). *Corporate Social Responsibility under Section 135 of Companies Act 2013*. ClearTax. https://cleartax.in/s/corporate-social-responsibility

Corporate Institutions Urged to Align CSR to Government Development Agenda. (2021). MyJoyOnline.com. https://www.myjoyonline.com/corporate-institutions-urged-to-align-csr-to-government-development-agenda

Corporate Social Responsibility in Tanzania. (2021). *Art in Tanzania Blog*. https://volunteer-africa-blog.org/2021/03/11/corporate-social-responsibility-in-tanzania

David, O. (1970). *An assessment of the impact of Corporate Social Responsibility on Nigerian Society: The examples of banking and communication industries: Semantic scholar, undefined*. https://www.semanticscholar.org/paper/An-assessment-of-the-impact-of-corporate-social-onDavid/24392adcf31fc3c3034b5a7563d396827d2ed4bb

Defining Telework: What Is It Exactly?—Researchgate. (n.d.). https://www.researchgate.net/publication/236111508_Defining_Telework_What_is_it_Exactly

Eugene, K. B. T. (2011). *The state of play of CSR in Singapore*. Ink.library.smu.edu.sg. https://ink.library.smu.edu.sg/lien_reports/2/

Fscmauritius.org. (2016). *Financial Services Commission, Mauritius*. https://www.fscmauritius.org/en

Gittlen, S. (2021). *Guide to Business Continuity and pandemic planning: TechTarget, Disaster Recovery*. TechTarget. https://www.techtarget.com/searchdisasterrecovery/The-impact-of-coronavirus-on-business-continuity-planning

Government Business Support Measures. (2020). *Business Mauritius*. https://www.businessmauritius.org/latest-news/bm-covid-19-support-measures/

Guide on Corporate Social Responsibility (CSR). (n.d.). https://www.mra.mu/download/CSRGuide.pdf

Handy, S. L., & Mokhtarian, P. L. (1996). The future of telecommuting. *Futures, 28*(3), 227–240. https://doi.org/10.1016/0016-3287(96)00003-1

Heyward, C. (2022). Council post: The growing importance of social responsibility in business, Forbes. *Forbes Magazine*. https://www.forbes.com/sites/forbesbusinesscouncil/2020/11/18/the-growing-importance-of-social-responsibility-in-business/?sh=2cd0f1f92283

Josh Seddon. (2003). *Article—The rise of video conferencing—Latest news, Office Reality*. https://www.officereality.co.uk/blog/article-the-rise-of-video-conferencing

Kelly, M. M. (1985). *Next workplace revolution: Telecommuting*. AGRIS. https://agris.fao.org/agris-search/search.do?recordID=US201301410575

Key Challenges of CSR in South Africa.pdf. (n.d.). https://www.coursehero.com/file/46137528/Key-challenges-of-CSR-in-South-Africapdf

Khan Jaffur, Z., et al. (2022). The impact of covid-19 outbreak on the Mauritian Export Trade: A disaggregated analysis. *International Trade, Politics and Development, 6*(1), 14–44. https://doi.org/10.1108/itpd-06-2021-0007

Latapí Agudelo, M. A., Jóhannsdóttir, L., & Davídsdóttir, B. (2019). A literature review of the history and evolution of Corporate Social Responsibility. *International Journal of Corporate Social Responsibility, 4*(1). https://doi.org/10.1186/s40991-018-0039-y

Liberto, D. (2022). *Small and mid-size Enterprise (SME) defined: Types around the world, Investopedia*. Investopedia. https://www.investopedia.com/terms/s/smallandmidsizeenterprises.asp

Lister, K. (2021). *Work-at-home after covid-19—Our forecast*. Global Workplace Analytics. https://globalworkplaceanalytics.com/work-at-home-after-covid-19-our-forecast

Maloney, G., et al. (2022). *Analysis on small businesses in Canada, first quarter of 2022*. Government of Canada, Statistics Canada. https://www150.statcan.gc.ca/n1/pub/11-621-m/11-621-m2022004-eng

Milasi, S., González-Vázquez, I., & Fernández-Macías, E. (2021). *Telework before the COVID-19 pandemic, OECD iLibrary*. OECD. https://www.oecd-ilibrary.org/economics/telework-before-the-covid-19-pandemic_d5e42dd1-en

Nazami, M., Nezami, I. M., & Zargar, Z. H. (2022). The journey from Corporate Social Responsibility to corporate social innovation: The WHYS and the hows. *Technium Business and Management, 2*(2), 27–39. https://doi.org/10.47577/business.v2i2.6539

Panneer, S., & Mathur, S. (2016). *Corporate Social Responsibility in healthcare service delivery in India—A review*. https://www.researchgate.net/publication/365423196_Corporate_Social_Responsibility_in_Healthcare_Service_Delivery_in_India_-_a_review

Pauline Ramos, J., & Tri Prasetyo, Y. (2020). The impact of work-home arrangement on the productivity of employees during COVID-19 pandemic in the Philippines: A structural equation modelling approach. *The 6th International Conference on Industrial and Business Engineerin* [Preprint]. https://doi.org/10.1145/3429551.3429568

Prachi Juneja. (2015). *Corporate Social Responsibility—Meaning, need and its evolution*. https://www.managementstudyguide.com/corporate-social-responsibility.htm

Ramdhony, D. (2018). The implications of mandatory corporate social responsibility—A literature review perspective. *Theoretical Economics Letters, 08*(03), 432–447. https://doi.org/10.4236/tel.2018.83031

Roopchund, R. (2020). SMEs in Mauritius: Economic growth, employment and entrepreneurial culture. *International Journal of Entrepreneurship and Small Business, 39*(4), 585. https://doi.org/10.1504/ijesb.2020.10028265

Rwanda. (2022). *Individual—Other taxes*. https://taxsummaries.pwc.com/rwanda/individual/other

Sarpong, S. (2017). Corporate Social Responsibility in Ghana: Issues and concerns. *CSR, Sustainability, Ethics & Governance*, pp. 191–205. https://doi.org/10.1007/978-3-319-52839-7_10

Segal, T. (2022). *Enron scandal: The fall of a wall street darling, Investopedia*. Investopedia. https://www.investopedia.com/updates/enron-scandal-summary/

Small and Medium Enterprises. (2013). *Index*. https://statsmauritius.govmu.org/Pages/Statistics/By_Subject/SME/SB_SME.aspx

SMEs. (2022). *Internal market, industry, entrepreneurship and SMEs*. https://single-market-economy.ec.europa.eu/smes_en

Staff Writer. (2019). *A brief history of corporate social responsibility (CSR)*. https://www.thomasnet.com/insights/history-of-corporate-social-responsibility

Telework Before the COVID-19 Pandemic. (2021). *OECD productivity working papers*. https://doi.org/10.1787/d5e42dd1-en

Telework. (2002). *Teleworking*, pp. 115–137. https://doi.org/10.4324/9780203053089-13

Teleworking in the COVID-19 Pandemic: Trends and Prospects. (2016). *OECD*. https://www.oecd.org/coronavirus/policy-responses/teleworking-in-the-covid-19-pandemic-trends-and-prospects-72a416b6

The Evolution of Corporate Social Responsibility. (2022). *The evolution of Corporate Social Responsibility*. Center for Strategic and International Studies. https://www.csis.org/analysis/evolution-corporate-social-responsibility

The National Code of Corporate Governance for Mauritius—NCCG. (2003). https://www.nccg.mu/sites/default/files/files/the-national-code-of-corporate-governance-for-mauritius_2016.pdf

The New Corporate Social Responsibility (CSR) Framework ... —IONNEWS. (2016). https://ionnews.mu/wp-content/uploads/2016/08/New-CSR-Framework.pdf

The Practice of Corporate Social Responsibility (CSR) Around the World. (2015). *The practice of CSR around the world*. https://www.managementstudyguide.com/csr-practice-around-the-world.htm

The State of Video Conferencing in 2022. (2022). *Best VoIP providers: User reviews, expert guides*. https://getvoip.com/blog/2020/07/07/video-conferencing-stats/

Timmins, B. (2021). *Working from home: 'We get more done in the office', BBC News*. BBC. https://www.bbc.com/news/business-59634245

Trust and the Virtual Organization. (2014). *Harvard Business Review*. https://hbr.org/1995/05/trust-and-the-virtual-organization

Türkeş, M. C., & Vuţă, D. R. (2022). Telework: Before and after COVID-19. *Encyclopedia, 2*(3), 1370–1383. https://doi.org/10.3390/encyclopedia2030092

Unitrends. (2021). *BCDR: How business continuity and disaster recovery can improve business resilience*. Unitrends. https://www.unitrends.com/blog/bcdr-business-continuity-disaster-recovery

Work-at-Home After Covid-19—Our Forecast. (2022). *Global workplace analytics*. https://globalworkplaceanalytics.com/work-at-home-after-covid-19-our-forecast

Zimmermann@stlouisfed.org, Etheridge, B., Wang, Y., & Tang, L. (2020). *Worker productivity during lockdown and working from home: Evidence from self-reports* (ISER Working Paper Series). Institute for Social and Economic Research. https://ideas.repec.org/p/ese/iserwp/2020-12.html

Part III
Corporate Approaches

Chapter 8
Are Companies in Madagascar Sensitive to CSR?

Hajaina Ravoaja, Justin Nathanaël Andrianaivoarimanga, and Lantoniaina Béatrice Ralijerson

Abstract This study aims to identify the levels of commitment of companies in Madagascar to Corporate Social Responsibility (CSR) through their practices and to propose a typology of these practices. A categorisation of the CSR practices of thirteen companies in Madagascar was carried out through a theory check. Scales from 0 to 6 were determined for each of the ten dimensions of CSR to find the CSR institutionalisation and the profile of each company. A combination of the latter two elements forms the CSR model of each company. Four categories of CSR models were found: institutional inconsistency, lack of policy-performance coherence, strategic inconsistency and policy-performance coherence. All these practices can be improved. However, companies that are involved in CSR have to optimise their performance in this sense by making more efforts to sustain the results while integrating human resources (HR). Companies that do not assume their social responsibility, in order to face the recessionary situation, will find a way to strengthen their resilience by initiating and committing to a CSR approach that is calibrated to their capacities and resources. And the ideal would be to ensure at the same time sociological and psychological CSR. This has contributed to and expanded the literature on CSR. This paper advances the research in CSR throughout a modelisation of CSR practices and strengthens the resilience of companies through the CSR approach. It shows the way on the actions to be taken in this direction. Nonetheless, there may be other models of CSR practices in Madagascar.

Keywords CSR · Sustainable development · Madagascar · Sustainability · Dimensions · Models · Resilience

---

H. Ravoaja (✉) · J. N. Andrianaivoarimanga · L. B. Ralijerson
ISCAM Research Centre, Antananarivo, Madagascar

D. Crowther and S. Seifi (eds.), *Corporate Social Responsibility in Difficult Times*, Approaches to Global Sustainability, Markets, and Governance,
https://doi.org/10.1007/978-981-99-2591-9_8

8.1 Introduction

In Madagascar, in 2021, a study sponsored by the Ministry of the Environment and Sustainable Development (MESD), the Economic Development Board of Madagascar (EDBM) and the United States Agency for International Development (USAID) Madagascar found that the term CSR is known by the majority of companies. But it is sometimes associated with sponsorship, patronage, philanthropy or legal obligation (UNICEF, 2011). In fact, 80% of large international companies operating in Madagascar have endorsed their CSR. These are companies that employ between 250 and 500 people and operate in Madagascar. Companies that are weakly active towards CSR employ less than 50 people. With the exception of the agro-industrial, extractive and textile sectors, which are export-oriented, the level of commitment of companies to CSR remains low (Ur-CSR, 2021). CSR is thus perceived as an activity reserved for large companies and a reputational investment not accessible to small and medium-sized enterprises (SMEs). In Madagascar, the economic fabric is based on small and medium-sized industries/enterprises. Hence the interest of this study, as this category also benefits from maintaining its CSR in order to be able to continue its activities in the long term.

The world is halfway to the 2030 Agenda of the SDGs where companies have a role to play in achieving these goals (Schönherr et al., 2017). In Madagascar, the private sector has always been called upon to contribute to the government's objectives, which are notably aligned with the SDGs (Madagascar, 2022). The intensification of climate, health, social and environmental disruptions not only generates a need to strengthen the resilience of enterprises, especially SMEs, but also a need to optimise the impacts of CSR activities in terms of sustainability and efficiency (MIDSP, 2013).

These multiple challenges lead to the need to advance participants and improve CSR contributions to the pursuit of the SDGs. From this, two main questions emerge: how can companies that are doing CSR contribute more to sustainable development (SD) with resilience? And how should small and medium-sized industries (SMIs)/SMEs approach their CSR in the framework of SD and the post-COVID-19 economic crisis?

The main objective of this study is to identify ways to strengthen the resilience of companies in the CSR approach. Companies that are active in terms of CSR constitute models. Two specific objectives are thus pursued by this study: modelling the CSR profiles of companies active in this field and developing a CSR concept calibrated to the context of SMIs/SMEs in Madagascar.

Thus, in the first instance, this study will lead to recommendations for the sustainability of CSR-related activities and their impacts in terms of SD. Then, a proposal for an alternative and resilient CSR model for SMIs and SMEs will be made.

8.2 The Importance of CSR for Domestic Companies in the Context of SD

Recession and hardship are often cited as excuses for not practising CSR when the focus is on cost reduction and improving results. In recent decades, articles and opinion pieces on sustainability have increased dramatically. The word «sustainable» has been increasingly used as time goes by (Aslaksen et al., 2021).

In 1990, SD was often mentioned, compounding economic and environmental concerns. The broad discussion surrounded development issues, primarily in developing countries, combined with environmental problems, such as pollution, destruction of the ozone layer, the loss of biodiversity, the non-renewal of energy and climate change. The tone was distant and impersonal, relying on experts and collective units. But CSR or individual responsibility was not yet discussed at that time, as the duty towards sustainability was left to governments, business sectors and international organisations (Aslaksen et al., 2021). The ecological crisis and the organisation of society remained topical. It was generally accepted that companies and society should be transformed, but the form of this transformation was not specified. There was a tendency to put the responsibility for this transformation on the companies and to evaluate it from this angle (Aslaksen et al., 2021). CSR as a business imperative should not be accepted reluctantly or without conviction. On the contrary, it should be practised with all the vigour and passion of the heart, which will certainly help companies in the long run. After all, business is not just about the next quarter. Even so, domestic companies still lack knowledge and acquaintance with the instruments that facilitate the effective enforcement of responsible business criteria and concepts (Koladkiewicz, 2009). Leaders' understanding of the term CSR, as well as their stance and motivation, have an impact on the outcome of introducing CSR. Their position and motivation influence the outcome of the introduction of CSR in the company. Furthermore, the results reveal that the introduction of the term CSR in the vocabulary of companies does not necessarily reflect changes in the company's activities (Ditlev-Simonsen, 2010).

In general, CSR performance shapes a company's image. It is a means to generate a good image. From this perspective, CSR not only promotes a positive corporate image, but also helps to counteract negative influences. Corporate investment in CSR can improve the company's reputation and brand image. CSR positively affects the citizenship behaviour of customers. CSR affects directly the satisfaction of customers. CSR contributes positively to customer satisfaction. This is primarily due to the fact that a good reputation for CSR enhances the evaluation of the company by its customers. In fact, products sold by a responsible company are known to be more satisfying (Zhang, 2022). There is thus a need to research how to apply the concept of responsible business within SMEs sector (Koladkiewicz, 2009). In everyday language, sustainability has often been associated with the link between business and society. The scope of the term CSR has been extended. It has moved from internal affairs to a societal focus on sustainability. From 2008 onwards, and with force in 2018, sustainability was analysed with reference to social issues. Sustainable well-being has become the predominant element of the centre-right government's political programme. Economic growth, inclusive workplace, poverty alleviation, welfare provision, minorities integration and the climate disaster are the main issues, showing a mix of themes that form the foundations of a sustainable welfare state. References to social sustainability are recurrent (Aslaksen et al., 2021).

In practice, superficial attempts such as "green washing" were noted. They provide an example of how CSR objectives are subverted. Green washing refers to the branding practice used by a company that claims to promote environmentally friendly policies when in reality the company does not live up to its rhetoric. Criticism of unsustainable behaviour has been increasingly frequent and intense since 2008. Accusations of greenwashing have grown. It was claimed that the companies' statements about their environmental and social concerns were bogus. The discourses on CSR, society and sustainability were intertwined. Over time, the meaning of the term CSR has become more and more comprehensive in level, breadth and depth for the past three decades. Companies have committed themselves to consider more social and political aspects. The growing interest in sustainability has challenged their behaviour. Thanks to changing views on sustainability, business is increasingly seen as the driver of the green transformation. Businesses are key players in environmental sustainability. Indeed, they are at the heart of the problem and also part of the solution. Unsustainable behaviour is one of the barriers to sustainability, which has become broader and more complex. The responsibilities of economic actors have been made more explicit in sustainability than in CSR discourses. In this way, thoughts on sustainability have transformed and sometimes even replaced CSR discourses (Aslaksen et al., 2021). This increased emphasis on sustainability leads to the logic of resilience in the implementation of CSR in small and medium-sized enterprises.

CSR has four phases of evolution: conceptualisation, introduction, growth and consolidation. Its implementation requires internal practice and the commitment of managers and employees. It is crucial to put words into action and to impact the local community in the same way as purchasing and hiring at the local and community level. CSR in its development phase should lead the company to build a cordial relationship with key stakeholders such as suppliers, government agencies, employees, consumers and society at large as well as government agencies to promote sustainable practices and mitigate serious environmental and social problems. Companies should actually look beyond their bottom line and have a social component in their accounting statements as a way to measure the environmental and social impacts of their activities on the future. Businesses, through their CSR, have a duty to contribute fully to the promotion of a world fit for future generations (Mishra, 2020).

8.3 Triple Bottom Line

In the late 1990s, thanks to a survey on CSR and SD used internationally, the term "triple bottom line" or TBL emerged (Henriques & Richardson, 2004). This is the formulation of CSR as "people, planet and profit". The performance of US companies was assessed by John Elkington through their sustainability. This framework, called the "triple bottom line", went beyond measures of revenue, environmental returns and shareholder value. It considered social and environmental dimensions. It was an awareness of the overall outcomes of investments, including performance from the interrelated dimensions of profits, people and planet. It was a broader view that enabled sustainability objectives to be achieved. For-profit, not-for-profit and public organisations have increasingly embraced TBL accounting. Many companies and non-profit organisations have adopted the TBL sustainability framework to assess their performance. This trend has spread to governments at the local and state level.

Long before the TBL, environmentalists debated sustainability measures and the related framework. Academic fields have turned to sustainability. The term has attracted increasing attention over the last thirty years. A sustainable business generates profit for its shareholders while protecting the environment and improving the lives that interact with it. It works for its own interests, for those of the environment and of society. Such a company succeeds across decades and generations. It is part of the solution to environmental and social problems and turns responsibility into opportunity. The TBL captures the substance of sustainability by measuring the impacts of the activities of the organisation under review on the world. This includes profitability, shareholder values and social, economic and environmental impacts.

To this end, variables related to the social, economic and environmental dimensions have been identified to assess CSR performance. The economic variables are outcomes and cash flow. They may relate to income or expenditure, taxes, business climate drivers, employment and business diversity determinants. Similarly, personal income, underemployment's cost, turnover, size of the organisation, employment growth, employment's distribution by sector, firms distribution by sector and revenues by sector that contribute to gross state product are relevant to the economic dimension of CSR (Slaper & Hall, 2011).

Environmental variables measure the natural resources used that affect the sustainability of organisations. These may include water and air quality, energy and natural resources use, solid and toxic waste, land use and occupation. Long-term trends in each of these environmental variables allow organisations to recognise the environmental impacts of their projects and policies at a regional level. Sulphur dioxide concentration, nitrous oxide accumulation, selected stormwater priority pollutants, surplus nutrients, electricity use, fossil fuel consumption, solid waste handling, dangerous and toxic waste management, land use and land occupation are all environmental indicators. Social variables relate to the social facets of a community or region and concern education, equity, access to social resources, health, well-being, quality of life and social capital. Indicative social indicators include unemployment rate, female labour force participation rate, median household income, relative poverty, absolute poverty, rate of holders of tertiary degrees or certificates, average commuting time, violent crime per capita and health-adjusted life expectancy.

Economic performance issues encompass corporate governance, political domination, notoriety, risk handling, intellectual capital, supply chain, market share and eco-efficiency. Social performance issues contain economic expansion, responsible marketing, labour conditions, human rights and diversity. Environmental issues are composed of product stewardship, climate change and biodiversity. And for a company, the TBL mobilises stakeholders. This include government, investors, suppliers, customers, employees, future generations, the communities connected with it and the environment (Slaper & Hall, 2011).

8.4 Theoretical Framework

Between 1950 and 2000, numerous literatures attempted to specify the concept of CSR and to flesh out its components (Ansklok, 2016). These concepts cover several dimensions and the studies did not stop there. They are mainly oriented towards CSR policy (Gond & Moser, 2021), the orientations of CSR activities (Awan, 2015; Gond & Moser, 2021), the integration of CSR into the business (Roszkowska-Menkes, 2018; Singh et al., 2018), the commitment of management and HR (Athanasiadou & Theriou, 2021), human capital (Awan, 2015), preservation of the environment (Schönherr et al., 2017), positive impacts (Gond & Moser, 2021), the sustainability of outcomes (Gond & Moser, 2021), the holistic nature of activities in the framework of CSR (Schönherr et al., 2017) and the capitalisation of CSR achievements (Schönherr et al., 2017; Singh et al., 2018). In addition, two types of CSR have been identified: sociological CSR and psychological CSR, which need to be reconciled in practice to embrace a broad spectrum footprint (Gond & Moser, 2021). According to these authors, psychological CSR is more focused on mechanism and organisational pride, while sociological CSR is more oriented towards practices for building a socially, environmentally and ethically responsible image. Consequently, this study is based on these theoretical foundations.

Ten dimensions were identified:

- The choice of a policy and the adoption of a CSR approach for the sustainability of the business, the integration of the development needs of the organisation's territory in its CSR policy, the reason for adopting this policy, the purpose of the policy, the related areas of intervention and the consideration of all these elements in its vision, mission and values (Gond & Moser, 2021);
- The strategic dimensions of CSR orientations or the areas in which the organisation aspires to be integrated: market, environment, society or HR (Awan, 2015; Gond & Moser, 2021);
- The integration of ethical, social and environmental concerns into the core strategy and business operations (Roszkowska-Menkes, 2018; Singh et al., 2018);

- Employee and management commitment to CSR (Athanasiadou & Theriou, 2021);
- Human capital development focusing on well-being, gender, dialogue, security and health (Awan, 2015);
- Environmental preservation: the management of resources, the environment and pollution, as well as the reduction of greenhouse gas emissions (Schönherr et al., 2017);
- The positive impact on the ecosystem and the territory through the involvement of stakeholders in the consideration of the community and its expectations (Gond & Moser, 2021);
- Sustainability of impacts through a mechanism for the perpetuation of activities (Gond & Moser, 2021);
- The holistic nature of the activities and impacts, which represents the orientation towards several Sustainable Development Goals (SDGs) (Schönherr et al., 2017);
- CSR monitoring and evaluation practice: measurement of CSR performance, social, environmental, financial, reputational and relational impacts; reporting, communication and planning in this respect (Schönherr et al., 2017; Singh et al., 2018).

This theoretical framework constitutes a reference for this case study of CSR of companies operating in Madagascar.

8.5 Methodology

The purpose of this work is to conduct case studies based on data from the Research Centre of the ISCAM Business School (IBS), Antananarivo, Madagascar. It focuses on thirteen formal companies operating in Madagascar in the telecommunication, digital, textile, agri-food, mining, handicraft, hotel and export sectors. The methodological approach of the study includes the elaboration of the theoretical framework comprising the ten dimensions mentioned previously, the composition of measurement scales for these dimensions, the identification of the companies that constitute the cases, the processing of data on CSR of these companies and the analysis of the results. Table 8.1 shows the scores obtained by the thirteen companies on the ten dimensions mentioned above, the companies are named C1 to C13.

In doing so, scales from 0 to 6 were determined for each of these dimensions to find the CSR profile of each company. A value was then assigned to each dimension for each of these thirteen companies. This made it possible to identify categories according to the points awarded to them. As the CSR policy is the basis, the score on this policy determines the level of institutionalisation of CSR within each company. The total of the scores for the remaining nine dimensions that can be traced through the activity of the companies gives their CSR profiles. The combination of the level of institutionalisation of CSR and this profile for each case leads to a matrix representation where this profile is subdivided into psychological CSR and sociological

Table 8.1 Rating of the CSR activities of the thirteen companies

Rubrics\Companies	C1	C2	C3	C4	C5	C6	C7	C8	C9	C10	C11	C12	C13
CSR policy	6	6	6	4	4	4	2	2	2	2	2	0	0
Directions of activities	1,5	4,5	3	4,5	6	6	4,5	1,5	4,5	6	4,5	3	4,5
CSR & Business integration	4	2	4	2	2	6	4	2	2	6	6	2	4
HR Engagement	0	6	6	0	0	6	0	0	0	0	6	0	0
HR Well-being	0	0	6	0	0	6	0	0	0	6	6	0	0
Preservation of the environment	0	6	6	6	6	6	6	0	0	6	6	0	6
Positive impact	6	6	4	4	4	6	6	4	4	6	2	2	2
Sustainability of outcomes	4,5	4,5	4,5	4,5	3	3	4,5	4,5	4,5	4,5	3	3	3
Holistic approach to CSR	6	6	5	1	1	6	6	3	2	5	3	3	3
Capitalisation on achievements	4	6	2	4	2	2	2	2	1	2	2	2	2

CSR (Gond & Moser, 2021). Each resulting CSR model was analysed and discussed for improvement.

8.6 Results

The results presented as follows concern the level of institutionalisation of the cases studied and their respective profiles.

Table 8.2 shows the values given to the thirteen companies in terms of CSR policy adoption.

With regard to the institutionalisation of CSR, three distinct groups were identified, namely (i) companies with no CSR policy or with a CSR policy bud (score = 0), (ii) companies with a CSR policy and/or a CSR strategy (score = 2) and (iii) companies with a dedicated CSR structure with a formal budget allocation (score = 4 to 6). The total of the scores corresponding to the nine dimensions representing the CSR profiles of the companies gives Table 8.3.

In this second table, companies were ranked according to their scores in descending order. As a result, three CSR profiles were identified: low involvement in CSR where the scores are less than or equal to 24, medium involvement in CSR where the scores are between 24 and 26 and higher involvement in CSR where the scores are strictly above 26. Table 8.4 summarises the typology of CSR models of the cases studied according to their levels of institutionalisation of CSR policy and their

Table 8.2 Level of institutionalisation of the CSR policy in the cases studied

Companies	Institutionalisation of CSR
C1	6
C2	6
C3	6
C4	4
C5	4
C6	4
C7	2
C8	2
C9	2
C10	2
C11	2
C12	0
C13	0

Table 8.3 CSR profiles of the cases studied

Companies	CSR profiles
C6	47
C10	41.5
C2	41
C3	40.5
C11	38.5
C7	33
C1	26
C4	26
C13	24.5
C5	24
C9	18
C8	17
C12	15

CSR profiles. The combination of the two criteria, namely the institutionalisation of the CSR policy and the CSR profile, resulted in Table 8.4 of CSR models.

The four models resulting from these combinations are:

- LC: lack of coherence between policy and performance,
- CP: coherence between policy and performance,
- II: institutional incoherence,
- SI: strategic incoherence.

II and LC models have the lowest level of institutionalisation of CSR with an average of 2 for II and 1 for LC. The general average CSR policy is 3.08. Then the average of the SI model is 4.7, that of CP is 5.3. For CP, SI, LC and II respectively, the average

Table 8.4 Classification of CSR models of the cases

Companies	Institutionalisation	CSR profiles	CSR models
C13	0	24.5	LC
C8	2	17	LC
C12	0	15	LC
C9	2	18	LC
C2	6	41	CP
C3	6	40.5	CP
C6	4	47	CP
C11	2	38.5	II
C7	2	33	II
C10	2	41.5	II
C1	6	26	SI
C5	4	24	SI
C4	4	26	SI

CSR profiles are 29.33, 25.33, 12.50 and 11. For the LC model, environmental preservation is not carried out by companies C8, C9 and C12. HR engagement and HR well-being have the lowest average for all companies or for all CSR models: it is 1.85 for both criteria. Next comes the capitalisation of realisations with an overall average of 2.55. Then CSR and business integration for 3.54, CSR holisticity for 3.85, sustainability of outcomes for 3.92, business orientation and environmental preservation for 4.15 each and finally positive impact for 4.31. There is a difference between the CSR profile and the CSR model: the profile is about the nine dimensions of CSR apart from the related policy, whereas the model is the combination of the policy and the profile.

The matrix configuration of these profiles results in the typology shown in Fig. 8.1.

8.7 Discussions

For companies that have honoured their CSR, optimising their CSR performance is essential. For SMI/SMEs that have not yet taken on CSR, their initiation in this direction is necessary. As the economic fabric of Madagascar is based on SMI/SMEs, they should fully assume their CSR.

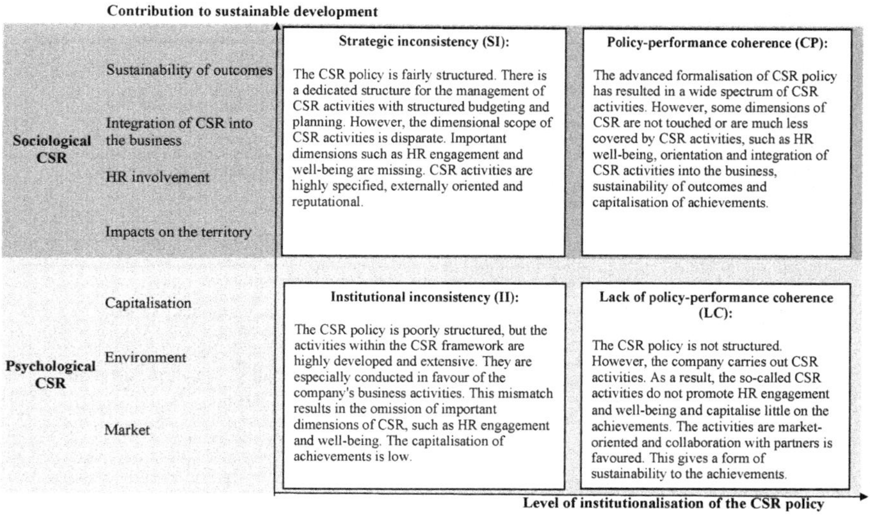

Fig. 8.1 CSR models of the companies

8.7.1 *Optimising the CSR Performance of Companies that Are Already Involved*

While the majority of companies in Madagascar have some knowledge of CSR (Ur-CSR, 2021), what differentiates all companies is the degree of institutionalisation of the CSR policy. Some companies have adopted a structured CSR policy, while others do not have a CSR policy. What is similar to the implementation or non-implementation of a CSR management system (Ur-CSR, 2021). Between these two profiles are the companies that have a budding CSR policy. What these three types of companies have in common is the practice of visible CSR activities. The level of institutionalisation of the CSR policy is already a differentiating criterion. It is clear that some companies that do not have a CSR policy are nevertheless engaged in a broad spectrum of CSR in terms of SD. On the other hand, others have implemented their CSR policies, but their impacts on SD are not commensurate with their scope. In other words, the institutionalisation of policy does not guarantee the sustainability performance of companies' CSR activities. Figure 8.2 proposes improvements for a better coherence between the policy and the performance of companies with regard to their CSR.

For companies that are involved in their CSR, adjustments and improvements need to be made in terms of basic CSR frameworks. These are the fundamentals of CSR, the management of a CSR approach, the commitment of stakeholders, CSR-oriented governance, responsible marketing, consumers and customers, waste management, labour relations and conditions, eco-design and life cycle analysis (Ur-CSR, 2021). These improvements need to be undertaken in a spirit of shared responsibility where

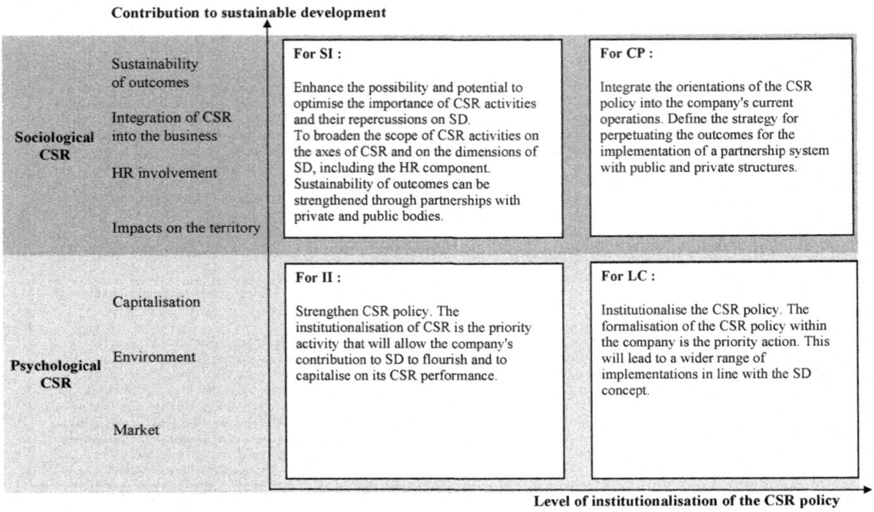

Fig. 8.2 Areas for improvement in corporate CSR models

CSR is an entry point for civil society and the public sector to support companies in the pursuit of their objectives and to secure their partnerships, which could influence their positioning on areas of general interest (MIDSP, 2013). The need to support the structuring of CSR within advanced companies in terms of CSR and to encourage them to publish their activities is necessary in this sense (UNICEF, 2011), all the more so as companies will have to look for all the means to be more resilient to face the context of economic recession post-COVID-19 (World Bank Group, 2020).

8.7.2 Need to Engage in a Resilient CSR Approach for SMIs/SMEs

The business world is increasingly influenced by standardisation (Koladkiewicz, 2009), by certifications and by the constraints linked to the pursuit of the SDGs. In addition to this, the economic crisis caused by COVD-19, where a first recession in the region in 25 years is highly likely, is a factor (World Bank Group, 2020). Companies will have to face this to survive, especially those companies that have declined their CSR: SMI/SMEs. It is in their interest to find ways and means to become more resilient to economic and health shocks (MIDSP, 2013). CSR is part of the solution for building competitive advantages, managing risks, reducing costs and maintaining corporate image and reputation. SMIs/SMEs can use CSR as a tool for competitiveness and for promoting sustainable and responsible investments (Ur-CSR, 2021). In this sense, it is in the interest of SMI/SMEs to initiate a CSR approach that is calibrated to their financial capacities and resources. It is recommended that SMI/SMEs set up CSR projects that do not necessarily require heavy financial investments (UNICEF, 2011). In return, they would have the additional motivation of employees (Athanasiadou & Theriou, 2021), improving the company's reputation (Gond & Moser, 2021), production economy, adherence to sectoral CSR objectives (Ur-CSR, 2021) and by far a financial return for the company (Awan, 2015).

The process of integrating CSR and SD into the company's strategy must be simplified with a long-term commitment and a desire for continuous improvement. The integration can be done in five classic steps. It involves committing to the CSR approach, planning objectives, moving to implementation, measuring achievements, reporting and communicating in a spirit of transparency and accountability in accordance with CSR/SD principles (MIDSP, 2013). Criteria on governance of the practice, societal impact, feasibility and adaptability will need to guide the approach and activities.

Due to COVID-19, companies and their customers are more interested in environmental protection, food safety and health. Corporate image reflects the public's overall assessment of the company. Contentment is the response of an individual to a feeling, especially the extent to which consumers perceive the forecasts of a product or a service. CSR has an impact on customer satisfaction (Zhang, 2022).

Four kinds of social responsibility are included in CSR from bottom to top of the pyramid: economic, legal, ethical and philanthropic. A company can achieve full CSR if it manages to fulfil these four responsibilities, starting with economic responsibility, then moving on to legal then ethical then philanthropic responsibilities. In the pyramidal hierarchy of CSR types, economic responsibility is the foundation. The company has only one option to survive and serve society: to make a profit. Without profit, there is no return on investment and no continuity in the production of quality products or services. This economic responsibility must have a vision of long-term progress while respecting not only the law and regulations, but also ethical and philanthropic standards. The economic component forms the basis. The other responsibilities are based on it. The legal responsibility of the company is related to the law, which provides the codification of good and bad by society. It is a matter of respecting the rules. Legal responsibility is the obligation of a company to comply with all relevant laws and regulations, along with those on employment, taxation, occupational health, safety and those fighting unfair competition. What goes with fair trade practices at local, regional and national levels. Ethical responsibility implies an obligation on the part of the company to take the right, fair and equitable action and, above all, to prevent harm. This level is more moral. Philanthropic responsibility leads the company to be a civic entity that contributes to the management and optimisation of the community's resources, and even the improvement of its quality of life (Carroll, 1991).

The economic and legal responsibilities correspond to the psychological CSR model by relying on the mechanism and focusing on, among other things, the market, the environment and the capitalisation of experience and knowledge to ensure the economic and legal survival of the company. Structural efficiency is essential to enable the company to meet legal and economic regulatory requirements and thus to have the necessary information and documents. Above all, it is the company's compliance with the various standards through the implementation of an adequate mechanism that is at the heart of these responsibilities.

Ethical responsibility is about respecting the environment, adopting an ethical code of conduct in dealing with stakeholders and carrying out activities and following standards that comply with the law. Ethical responsibility is about recognising and following moral standards and acting in accordance with society's expectations. Being ethically responsible means operating with integrity and in an ethical manner. Philanthropic responsibility supports the community and meets the needs of stakeholders. It leads to doing the most to improve lives. It is not only about doing the right thing, but also and above all about upholding the company's values and principles and bringing value to society. This leads to donations, volunteering and community development (Carroll, 1991).

Ethical and philanthropic responsibilities are more than regulatory responsibilities. They are more voluntary and more oriented towards the community, territory and sustainability that are among the main components of the sociological CSR model. These responsibilities optimise the company's level of contribution to SD. In order to ensure the sustainability of its CSR practice, the company needs to address the institutionalisation of its CSR in a more formal way. The relevance of CSR activities to the needs of stakeholders is of paramount importance and protects the company from CSR deviations such as green and social washing. The ultimate goal for companies in CSR is to achieve all four responsibilities: economic, legal, ethical and philanthropic, in other words, a company that combines both psychological and sociological models. Total CSR implies that companies optimise their contribution to SD through CSR activities integrated into their own activities and institutionalise them within their structure.

This study identified four types of CSR for the companies studied. Progressively, these are institutional incoherence, strategic incoherence, lack of policy-performance coherence and policy-performance coherence. The recommendation is that companies, in a continuous improvement process, can gradually achieve institutional coherence, then strategic coherence through policy-performance coherence and finally optimal policy-performance coherence in SD.

As institutional coherence consists of strengthening the CSR policy, the institutionalisation of CSR is the priority activity that will subsequently allow the company's contribution to SD to flourish and to capitalise on its CSR performance. Strategic coherence is reflected in the recognition of the possibility and potential to optimise the importance of CSR activities and social and sustainability footprints. At this stage, the company should try to broaden the scope of activities on CSR and SD dimensions, such as HR engagement, HR well-being and the sustainability of outcomes through partnerships with private and public organisations. The aim of policy-performance coherence is to institutionalise the CSR policy. The formalisation of the CSR policy within the company is the priority action. This will lead to broader implementation and will respond to the concept of SD. The final stage is the optimum policy-performance coherence in SD where the company tries to integrate the orientations of the CSR policy into the company's current activities and to define the strategy for the perpetuation of the outcomes for the implementation of a partnership mechanism with public and private structures. The combination of this typology with the concept of the TBL line leads to a progressive CSR approach model that includes twelve CSR levels:

In order to engage in CSR, SMEs should first try to find out where their CSR stands. This will allow them to identify and define the steps to be taken in order to scale up their own CSR and achieve a total CSR that is calibrated to their situation and context. It is important to progress without missing a step in order to be at the same level as other companies. In other words, to ensure the effectiveness of CSR regardless of the company's CSR profile. This progressive CSR approach is an approach that starts from within the company and allows it to avoid the trap of mimicking the CSR actions of other companies. The progressive approach favours innovation and sustainability of the structure. Sustainability can be seen from two perspectives: the "top-down" approach and the "inside-out" approach. Top-down approach focuses on management, quantification and control. Measuring the degree of sustainability of an organisation is difficult. Pursuing sustainable growth can be challenging. In doing so, there may not be enough action within structures and systems. Environmental management systems are sometimes ineffective and non-performing. Inside-out approach relies on change and innovation. To innovate and achieve a higher level of sustainability, new systems and methods are needed. It requires thinking outside the box and the structures of the traditional paradigm while paying attention to and building relationships with other actors (Henriques & Richardson, 2004).

While CSR, in the true sense of the word, concerns the responsibility of companies towards society, this notion has been broadened. The literature on CSR has evolved. Economic, legal, ethical and philanthropic responsibilities, and then the TBL and sustainability have been discussed. Stakeholder needs must be taken into account. At the corporate level, responsibility was associated with sustainability. Theories on CSR have diversified and complemented each other. In practice, professionals characterise CSR through corporate philanthropy, corporate contributions to the SDGs and the impacts of such activities on the environment while considering the local and national contexts. In addition, some companies focus on certain aspects of CSR, while others focus on other facets. Each company has chosen a number of dimensions and has committed to them at the level they consider necessary. Some have prioritised certain SDGs and some have turned to other SDGs. And this may be due to mimetic isomorphisms motivated by the desire to be part of the companies with enhanced images because they are doing CSR. In these cases, CSR has become a fad. However, companies should focus on their missions and include their CSR activities. Thus, this article offers a breadth of this concept to inform their choice of activities. Indeed, this inductive article proposes a model based on actual facts observed which in turn have been identified in the CSR literature. This term is subject to several interpretations. Everyone attributes their own meaning to it. In doing so, this work helps to better define and formalise it.

8.8 Conclusion

The study of the CSR cases of the thirteen companies operating in Madagascar highlights the existence of three types of companies: those that have institutionalised their CSR, those that do not have a CSR policy and those that have a budding CSR approach. But the performance of companies' CSR activities in relation to the SDGs is not a logical consequence of their level of participation in CSR. Following the ranking of companies according to their CSR momentum, four characteristics distinguish their CSR-related models: lack of coherence between policy and performance, coherence between policy and performance, institutional incoherence and strategic incoherence. Strategic incoherence and coherence between policy and performance are geared towards sociological CSR, whereas institutional incoherence and coherence between policy and performance are oriented towards psychological CSR. This dichotomous classification into psychological CSR and sociological CSR encompasses the elements classified in the TBL and the pyramid. The present study suggests ways to improve and strengthen each of these models to take them to the next level and to achieve optimal performance in terms of CSR and SD. The axis of HR engagement and well-being, sustainability of the outcomes of CSR activities, the integration of management and human resources in the approach and the capitalisation on achievements are among the tracks that are put forward. In addition, measures at the inter-organisational level should be put in place to encourage and support companies in achieving CSR.

SMI/SMEs can less and less escape the reality of the internationalisation of standards and the post-COVID-19 economic recession. Further, the ISO 26000 is an international standard dedicated to the social responsibility of organisations. It provides guidelines for socially responsible and environmentally friendly behaviour. Engaging in CSR that is calibrated to their potential and circumstances could enable them to be as resilient and sustainable as possible. The criteria of governance, societal impact and adaptability are to be considered for this category of companies in their commitment to follow the CSR approach. This commitment of companies to adopt CSR puts in perspective a further study to find out if the march towards CSR is natural and automatic with contextual influence or if a support structure or even a platform is needed to initiate and sustain the promotion of CSR in the private sector. To answer the question "Are companies in Madagascar sensitive to CSR?", this study shows that among the selected cases and in a decreasing order, some are listed under the strategic incoherence model, as well as others that are listed under the models of coherence between CSR policy and performance, institutional incoherence and lack of coherence between CSR policy and performance. But intermediate values could be found in other cases, which would increase the variety of categories. There could be models in between these four and even below and above them, as the policy-performance coherence is still improvable. Indeed, the notion of CSR is widespread, but the sensitivity of the thirteen companies in Madagascar with regard to CSR is diverse in these four models. And the ideal would be to ensure at the same time sociological and psychological CSR. Moreover, business leaders have a role to play in this implementation. Indeed, the CSR policy they choose has implications for the other nine dimensions of CSR which are: directions of activities, CSR and business integration, HR engagement, HR well-being, preservation of the environment, positive impact, sustainability of outcomes, holistic approach to CSR and capitalisation on achievements. This article offers a clarification of the scope of the term CSR to companies so that they can more conscientiously pursue their CSR. It proves that the theory can be practised and that companies should refer to it. It contributes to a review and advancement of knowledge and practice on CSR. Thus, a statistical study on these models and on all companies in Madagascar or even in the world would provide more information on the CSR situation.

References

Ansklok, K. (2016). The social responsability of international business: From ethics and the environnement to CSR and sustainable development. *Journal of World Business, 51*(1), 23–34.

Aslaksen, H. M., Hildebrandt, C., & Johnsen, G. (2021). The long-term transformation of the concept of CSR: Towards a more comprehensive emphasis on sustainability. *International Journal of Corporate Social Responsibility, 6*(1).

Athanasiadou, C., & Theriou, G. (2021, June). Corporate Social Responsibility (CSR) employee outcomes in the aviation industry during the COVID-19 pandemic era. A conceptual framework. *Management and Business Research Quarterly, 18.*

Awan, A. G. (2015). Impact of CSR on firms' financial performance: A case study of Ghee and Fertilizer industry in Southern Punjab-Pakistan. *European Journal of Business and Management, 7*(7), 375–384.

Carroll, A. B. (1991). The pyramid of corporate socal responsability: Toward the moral management of organisational stakeholders. *Business Horizons, 34*(4), 39–48.

Ditlev-Simonsen, C. D. (2010). From Corporate Social Responsibility awareness to action. *Social Responsability Journal, 6*(3), 452–468.

Gond, J.-P., & Moser, C. (2021). Critical Essay: The reconciliation of fraternal twins: Integrating the psychological and sociological approaches to 'micro' corporate social responsibility (T. T. Institute, Ed.). *Human Relations, 74(1)*, 5–40.

Henriques, A., & Richardson, J. (2004). *The tripple bottom line: Does it all add up?* Routledge.

Koladkiewicz, I. (2009). Corporate social responsibility in Poland: The Responsible Business Forum 2002–2007 report perspective 2009. *Social Responsibiity Journal, 5*(1), 48–61.

Madagascar. (2022, June 8). *Politique Générale de l'Etat.* https://www.presidence.gov.mg/: https://www.presidence.gov.mg/19-a-la-une/66-la-ligne-directrice-de-la-pge.html

MIDSP. (2013). *De l'entreprise responsable à l'entreprise durable.*

Mishra, S. (2020). Evolution of corporate social responsibility: Two sets of explanation.

Roszkowska-Menkes, M. T. (2018). Integrating strategic CSR and open innovation. Towards a conceptual framework. *Social Responsibility Journal, 14*(1), 950–966. https://doi.org/10.1108/SRJ-07-2017-0127

Schönherr, N., Findler, F., & Martinuzzi, A. (2017, December). Exploring the interface of CSR and the sustainable development goals. *Transnational Corporations, 24*(3), 33–47.

Singh, S., Holvoet, N., & Pandey, V. (2018). Bridging sustainability and corporate social responsibility: Culture of monitoring and evaluation of CSR initiatives in India. *Sustainability, 10*(7), 2353 (The Special Issue *Corporate Social Responsibility (CSR) in Developing Countries: Current Trends and Development*).

Slaper, T. F., & Hall, T. J. (2011). *The triple bottom line: What is it and how does it work?* I. U. Indiana Business Research Center.

UNICEF. (2011). *Corporate social responsibility in Madagascar.*
Ur-CSR. (2021). *Etat des lieux et identification des bonnes pratiques RSE.*
World Bank Group. (2020). *Evaluation de l'impact économique du covid-19 et des réponses politiques en Afrique subsaharienne.* Retrieved June 9, 2022, from https://www.food-security.net/wp-content/uploads/2020/04/Banque-Mondiale-Evaluation-Impact-Economique-COVID-19-Afrique_FRX.pdf
Zhang, N. (2022). How does CSR of food company affect customer loyalty in the context of COVID-19: A moderated mediation model. *International Journal of Corporate Social Responsibility, 7* (1).

Chapter 9
Determinants of Integrated Reporting Assurance: Evidence from Australia

Girish Napaul and Dineshwar Ramdhony

Abstract Traditional reporting has failed to meet evolving needs of stakeholders in the aftermath of the global financial crisis. A combination of financial and non-financial data reporting using the organisation's holistic approach was required. The integrated reporting (IR) concept emerged with a global coalition, the IIRC (International Integrated Reporting Council), coming up with its framework. This paper investigates the determinants of IR in the Australian context. Data were collected for the top 100 companies listed on the ASX for 2018–2019. The source includes annual reports from companies' websites and the Thomson Reuters Refinitiv Eikon database. Logistic regression was used to test hypotheses. Consistent with pre-defined hypotheses, firm size, growth opportunities and board activity positively influenced companies to have their integrated reports assured. The other exogenous variables used in the study, such as profitability, industry category, board size and board independence, were statistically not proven to bear any significant effect on the assurance of IR. This study contributes to the existing literature by investigating the idiosyncratic factors contributing to external assurance of integrated reports in a developed economy context.

Keywords Integrated reporting · Assurance · Boards · Logistic regression · ASX · Stakeholder theory

Abbreviations

AIR	Assurance of Integrated Reports
ASX	Australian Securities Exchange
CR	Corporate reporting
IASB	International Accounting Standards Board
IIRC	International Integrated Reporting Council

G. Napaul · D. Ramdhony (✉)
University of Mauritius, Reduit, Mauritius

D. Crowther and S. Seifi (eds.), *Corporate Social Responsibility in Difficult Times*, Approaches to Global Sustainability, Markets, and Governance,
https://doi.org/10.1007/978-981-99-2591-9_9

IoDSA Institute of Directors South Africa
IR Integrated reporting

9.1 Introduction

Traditionally, Financial Reporting uniquely rested on financial statements, which essentially offer a historical version of companies' financial position and performance. These financial statements have been used to make deductions about the amount, timing and uncertainty of a firm's future cash flows and other budgetary instruments (IASB, 2010). The contemporary shift towards environmental cognisance and social and ethical responsibility has imposed an additional burden on companies to disclose non-financial matters (Mock et al., 2007). Thus, to overcome the drawbacks and ineffectiveness of conventional corporate reporting, an integrated reporting framework was conceived with value creation as its gist (IIRC, 2013). Eccles and Krzus (2010) described this single report bearing the incidence of higher integrated reporting capability when encompassed with sustainability as their principal strategy.

Compared to its precursors, IR is undoubtedly dominating the headlines of the corporate world. IR differentiates itself through its "integrated thinking" approach, which blends concepts such as ESG and sustainability reporting. IR has emerged as the turning point of corporate reporting (CR) by including non-financial information. According to Maroun (2017), IR is "interpretively constructed" and comprises a mixture of qualitative and quantitative information. IR depicts a more objective and forward-looking description of firms based on several capital transformations.

Nevertheless, integrated reports are internally generated documents which could contain misleading and inaccurate information. Therefore, to add credibility and to enable stakeholders to place reliance on integrated reports, assurance should be carried out over the sustainability reporting in disclosures contained in the IR (IoDSA, 2009). Several researchers echo this view, who believe that without third-party assurance or other credibility-enhancing mechanisms, the integrated report may become a public relations/marketing tool (Simnett & Huggins, 2015).

Against this backdrop, this paper sets out to analyse the company-level factors which lead businesses to conduct assurance of their integrated reports. For this purpose, we sample the top 100 quoted companies in Australia. Our paper contributes to the scarce empirical evidence on the subject matter. Given the novelty of IR, our contribution to existing scholarly work requires significant elaboration at the legal and accounting framework level. Consequently, the results will direct regulators and standard setters towards the specific aspects that need to be targeted in the regularisation of IR.

Many studies have analysed the extent of application and assurance to integrated reporting. Alfiero et al. (2018) used gender diversity within the board and deduced a positive and significant relationship with IR. Other studies remain focused on disclosure characteristics or even ESG disclosures (Lai et al., 2016) and the implementation of IR. Frías-Aceituno et al. (2013), at their end, employed an external determinant and concluded that companies present in countries with strong legal enforcement are more inclined to implement IR. However, an excruciatingly slim research segment explored the factors which contribute to conducting the assurance of IR.

The main exogenous variables used in previous studies include board composition, board activity and board independence (Frías-Aceituno et al., 2013), board size (Alfiero et al., 2018), profitability (Vitolla et al., 2019), firm size (Ghani et al., 2018) and growth opportunities (Frías-Aceituno et al., 2014). The industry variable is challenging to capture and standardise due to sectoral differences. Companies in different industries disclose their performance to varying extents per pre-defined regulations or public pressure. This study is expected to fill the void in constructing a viable set of determinants of IR.

Australia has been selected amidst the pool of industrialised countries as it remains a politically and legally stable high-income economy with a sound investment climate. Among the Organisation for Economic Co-operation and Development (OECD) countries, Australia is the only country that withstood the financial crisis by not being driven into recession, explaining its resilient economy. Additionally, Australia has been at the forefront of upgrading to the latest international accounting and financial norms, thus an ideal choice for data collection. The firms under study must produce comprehensive annual reports in line with Australian legislation and accounting standards. Larger organisations, most of which are listed, are subject to greater accounting requirements than smaller firms. For instance, listed companies on the ASX are obliged to provide continuous and periodic disclosures, and their annual reports have to meet the technicalities of the ASX Listing Rules.

9.2 Background of the Australian Economic and Financial Landscape

Australia is a high-income economy which yields a good investment climate. Therefore, firms must produce comprehensive annual reports in line with Australian legislation. A federal system of government was established in Australia by its constitution in 1901. According to Nordea (no date), Australia has witnessed 26 years of continuous economic growth. The strong free-market financial system has enjoyed effective governance mechanisms that induce entrepreneurial development.

Among the Organisation for Economic Co-operation and Development (OECD) countries, Australia was the only country that withstood the financial crisis by not being driven into recession, explaining its resilient economy. This is supported by Australia's ranking 5th on the Index of Economic Freedom. According to Davies et al. (2018), Australia stands out globally with the highest median wealth per adult at USD 191,450 per capita. It is worth noting that Australia is rich in natural resources and is reputed for its massive coal and natural gas exports. On the other hand, the resources have attracted a high influx of foreign investment.

The Australian Securities and Investments Commission (ASIC) and the Reserve Bank of Australia (RBA) are the two independent authorities empowered to regulate financial markets in Australia. Companies in Australia may report to the Australian Taxation Office (ATO), the Australian Securities and Investments Commission (ASIC) and listed companies to the ASX.

The legal framework and the accounting framework provide the basis for the preparation of financial reports in Australia. The legal framework comprises the ASX listing rules and the Corporations Act. The Australian Accounting Standards consist of reporting entities' requirements and are aligned with the International Financial Reporting Standards (IFRS).

According to the JCPAA (2010), the Australian Accounting Standards Board (AASB) is responsible for the technical development work related to accounting standards. The framework regarding this is found in the Australian Securities and Investments Commission Act 2001. It is worth noting that since 1996, Australia has trod on a harmonisation policy with international accounting standards. In 2005, it was announced that the AASB started implementing international accounting standards fully.

Larger organisations, most of which will be listed, are subject to greater accounting requirements than smaller firms. Listed companies on the ASX are obliged to provide continuous and periodic disclosures, and their annual reports have to meet the technicalities of the ASX Listing Rules.

Following the IIRC guidance and IR evolutions in the global business environment, companies in Australia have also adopted the principles of IR. IR is not yet mandatory there. Australian companies are familiar with IR basics. For instance, corporate governance is one key element of IR. Since the ASX Corporate Governance Council was set up in 2002, companies have followed its rules. According to research by the Net Balance Foundation and ACCA Australia and New Zealand in 2011, 70% of surveyed companies implemented policies for maintaining good governance. After seven years, much improvement has taken place. This study will investigate assurance of IR among the selected listed companies in Australia.

9.3 Literature Review

9.3.1 Assurance of Integrated Reporting

The IIRC (2013) states that several mechanisms, including independent external assurance, influence the reliability of information furnished to stakeholders. Assurance of IR enhances credibility as the market requires a "stamp of approval" for the integrated reports (Maroun & Atkins, 2015). Without a credibility-enhancing mechanism, reporters may not attain the goal of giving users relevance and reliability of information (Simnett & Huggins, 2015). Therefore, assurance adds value by enhancing external transparency (Rossi & Tarquinio, 2017) and improving internal management systems, which can generate greater investment willingness (Reimsbach et al., 2018).

Given the lack of studies on the assurance of IR, we also rely on strands of the literature focusing on the assurance of sustainability/CSR reporting. Sam and Tiong (2015) and Gürtürk and Hahn (2016) examined the extent of assurance statements for sustainability reports. Moreover, Rossi and Tarquinio (2017), with a sample of Italian-listed companies, evaluated the factors affecting the quality of assurance statements in sustainability reporting. However, very few studies focused on the assurance of integrated reports. Reimsbach et al. (2018) examined the perception of professional investors on the assurance of reporting through an online questionnaire.

A recent study by Briem and Wald (2018) examined the reasons that motivate companies to obtain independent assurance for integrated reports through interviews with representatives of auditors and companies. Their results claim that both accounting firms and regulators in Germany are still far from applying a standardised IR assurance process.

Maroun (2019) also concluded that external assurance could be used to enhance the credibility and reliability of integrated and sustainability reports with the need for more detailed guidance on exactly how an integrated or sustainability report could be the subject matter of an assurance engagement.

Some studies have highlighted the challenges in the assurance process. Simnett and Huggins (2015) probed into the practical and technical challenges in applying conventional standards for assurance of IR and future-oriented information. Likewise, Eccles et al. (2012) studied the issues of accounting firms on the liability of assurance. Stubbs and Higgins (2014) have doubted the IIRC framework and whether its principles are appropriate for assurance. Moreover, Simnett and Huggins (2015) focus on the issues of assurance in terms of the need for updated assurance skills and a rethinking of auditors' mindsets. This researcher has also established a public consultation process and published a discussion paper on IR assurance considering external assurance to ensure the reliability and credibility of the reports.

9.3.1.1 Types of Assurance

Three of the proposed models for the assurance of IR are restricted assurance, integrated assurance and interpretive assurance. Under restricted assurance, auditors read the integrated report to ensure that information inconsistent with the financial statements is not included (Atkins & Maroun, 2015). The objective of the integrated assurance model is to depict how various sources of assurance are combined to ensure integrated reports contain reliable information (Maroun, 2017). Maroun (2018) proposed the interpretive assurance model based on existing risk-based and strategic systems audits. The interpretive assurance model evaluates the completeness of a firm's value creation process. In addition, it involves investigating the system implemented by the governance structure to review management discussion and analysis.

9.3.1.2 Value Creation

In IR, value creation is the main principle that has been mentioned more than 50 times within the IIRF (Flower, 2015), and it is defined as the process which leads to the rise, decline or alterations of the capital by the organisation's business activities and outcomes (IIRC, 2013). The prime objective of an integrated report is to make it clear to the supplier of financial capital in what way an organisation creates value after some time (IIRC, 2013, p. 7). Then we may go more deeply into the IIRF and realise that the value concept has two elements, "value built for organisation" and "value set up for others", a concept that is firmly linked together. The primary element could be equivalent to Shareholder Value as it "allows financial returns to the suppliers of financial capital", and the second point would be referred to Stakeholder or Public Value as the examples given for "others" are "stakeholders and society as a whole" (IIRC, 2013, p. 10).

9.3.2 Theoretical Framework

Stakeholder, legitimacy, agency and signalling theories are the guiding theories to understand the reasons behind information disclosures relating to economic, social and environmental issues.

9.3.2.1 Stakeholder Theory

The stakeholder theory recognises the existence of a fiduciary obligation between the company and society (Mathews, 1993). The company has the autonomy to employ human and natural resources for production. In this process, the organisation should generate capital and external stakeholder benefits. Companies should attempt to produce value for each stakeholder rather than focusing on only the shareholder under traditional reporting. From the organisation's perspective, the stakeholder theory is built on a model of accountability for all players (Gray et al., 1996). At any point, individuals or groups are having or claiming rights related to an organisation or its operations. These rights arise from a legal or moral nature (Clarkson, 1995). Given the importance of stakeholders, they should be imparted ESG information through additional company reports (Hess, 2008). KPMG (2013) purports that assurance reduces firms' pressure and provides stakeholders confidence in sustainability reporting.

9.3.2.2 Legitimacy Theory

According to this theory, legitimacy is paramount for a firm's continued operations. The theory asserts that firms will always aim to operate according to the norms of the "social contract" (Deegan, 2009). Based on Mathews (1995) study, a business may be moved to provide further disclosures in its annual report to create or step up the organisation's legitimacy towards a target group or the general public. Deegan and Unerman (2011) insisted that if there is no adherence to legitimacy by organisations, there could be the annulment of the social contract with penalties. The content of a company's report is of critical importance. It will assure society of the legitimacy of the business and ensure that the relations between investors and society are safeguarded. Casey and Grenier (2015) concurred that firms obtained assurance of their reports to control the pressures on maintaining the contract. According to Dumay et al. (2018), legitimacy theory is used to explain social and environmental accounting practices. Legitimacy theory helps to understand how organisations adopt, and justify SR practices like assurance as it helps to develop trust between stakeholders and managers through its confirmation of the reliability of information (Dumay et al. 2016). Studies on the legitimacy theory show how external pressures influence management decisions in adopting assurance practices in SR (Perego & Kolk, 2012) and aim to improve reputation and legitimacy (Gürtürk & Hahn, 2016; Michelon et al., 2015). A recent study by Corrado et al. (2019) uses the legitimacy theory to show how assurers tend to provide their services to improve the image of organisations rather than to make organisations more accountable. It also raises questions on whether the framework meets investors' needs as the latter tend to rely more on financial reports, representing a high level of assurance since it is a more mature and standardised practice.

9.3.2.3 Agency Theory

The agency theory advocates that the more information disclosures occur, the better stakeholders can make decisions. Agency problems crop up when collaborating parties have diverging objectives (Eisenhardt, 1989). From the point of view of this theory, assurance engagements are suited for mitigating agency costs (Ruhnke & Gabriel, 2013). Jensen and Meckling (1976) contented that these costs represent welfare losses arising from conflicts of interest and information asymmetry cropping up due to the principal-agent relationship. According to Zhou et al. (2017), enhancing the information disclosed through IR can mitigate uncertainty and estimations risks in a firm's performance valuation. They also explore IR's benefits from an investors' point of view and find that analysts' forecast error reduces if the report follows the IIRC framework. Moreover, this alignment also lowers the cost of capital. Hence, IR helps to communicate a company's overall performance and strategy by not neglecting relevant non-financial information (Sierra-García et al., 2015). A recent study by Briem and Wald (2018) highlights the importance of the IR assurance process to gain more transparency in corporate reporting and decrease information asymmetry between investors and company representatives.

9.3.2.4 Signalling Theory

According to Connelly et al. (2011), it isn't very easy for external stakeholders to evaluate the company's sustainability performance. By signalling distinct characteristics unrevealed to stakeholders, management will be able to differentiate the firm from other market players. Therefore, the latter must decide which information to provide and the medium to use. While the public must decide on the interpretation of the signal, it can be induced that firms provide positive information rather than negative information, as these will affect individuals' decision-making. Therefore, assurance adds credibility to positive information; otherwise, it could be seen as a medium to misinform the public. The transparency and connectivity of financial and non-financial information by IR exert a signalling effect on capital providers, which encourages managers to adopt a long-term value-creation strategy beneficial to investors (Lys et al., 2015). Recently Maulidya et al., (2019) concluded that companies disclose only positive information, mainly about their financial capital. It also claimed that when companies refer to the value they have created, they signal stakeholders to maintain their legitimacy to operate as a company serving society's interests. Thus, information about value creation can be considered as need signals.

9.3.3 Hypothesis Development

9.3.3.1 Profitability

Profitability can be a significant determinant of integrated reporting, since companies engaged in lucrative businesses tend to disclose sustainability information to win over the public (Alsaeed, 2006; Legendre & Coderre, 2013). Profitable firms are, by nature of their scale, exposed to closer public scrutiny than their competitors and are thus more likely to be scapegoated for any negative externalities on society, requiring conscious, sustainable advances incorporated in their business model (Artiach et al., 2010; Haniffa & Cooke, 2005). A recent study by (Wong et al. 2016) noted a positive relationship between profitability and sustainability reports' assurance implying that corporate profits are not yielded at the expense of social welfare. Ruhnke and Gabriel (2013) and Branco et al. (2014) even substantiate that a company earning high profits carry a higher propensity of assuring their sustainability reports.

From the signalling theory perspective, profit is a clear signal of investment value. Successful businesses are inclined to publish supplementary information to deliver positive signals in the financial market (Dienes et al., 2016). Advocates of political cost theory suggest that a company will be enthusiastic about providing more information in its reporting. This information polarises successful companies from less successful ones and helps to reduce their capital costs (Frías-Aceituno et al., 2014) and reporting costs (Jennifer Ho & Taylor, 2007). Signalling mechanisms such as sustainability reporting assurance further reduce agency costs, especially experienced by firms with strict compliance to corporate governance norms (Ruhnke & Gabriel, 2013).

Conversely, Zorio et al. (2013) analysed all listed companies on the Spanish Stock Exchange. They found that while size and industry are significant in explaining sustainable reporting assurance, leverage and profitability are not. Sierra et al. (2013) focused on the IBEX 35 companies and propounded that while assurance of sustainability reports depends on the company's size, leverage and profitability, it has no significant relationship with the industry or audit firm. We, therefore, hypothesise that:

H1: A relationship exists between a firm's profitability and the assurance of IR.

9.3.3.2 Firm Size and Assurance

Large companies are subject to greater pressure from major stakeholders to disclose their social activities due to their reputational risk in the face of elevated high public exposure (Veronica Siregar & Bachtiar, 2010). Reference is increasingly made to the legitimacy theory whereby public approval of business set-up and objectives is crucial to developing an ownership advantage (Kolk & Perego, 2010). Moreover, larger firms have readier access to capital markets and thus borrow more extensively than smaller ones. This aspect of internal economies of scale increases the importance of integrating partly confidential information for increased transparency and improved stakeholder-firm relationships from a stewardship theory perspective (Frías-Aceituno et al., 2013). Simnett et al. (2009) propounds that larger-sized companies are more inclined to voluntarily assure their integrated or sustainability reports as their production processes bear a considerable impact on the environment, an omission of consideration which might result in unwanted backlash. In this view, Sierra et al. (2013), with a sample of IBEX 35 companies, found that assurance of sustainability reports largely depends on the company's size, leverage and profitability.

H2: A relationship exists between the size of a business and the assurance of integrated reporting.

9.3.3.3 Growth Opportunities

Growth opportunities are arguably another relevant contributor to sustainability reporting (Ameer & Othman, 2012; Artiach et al., 2010; Lourenço & Branco, 2013). Artiach et al. (2010) posit that more growth opportunities will seduce management into sustainable business practices in their strategic future expansionary projects.

Economic sustainability should thus be backed by environmental and social sustainability as a pre-requisite of going concern (Ameer & Othman, 2012; Artiach et al., 2010). In line with this, firms with an ambitious future are inclined to publish their sustainability or consider the same in view of their integrated reports and having the same externally assured to win the people's trust.

Based on the agency theory, in a situation of potential expansion, a company may adopt an extensive disclosure policy to overcome information asymmetry, which may increase investor optimism in the company's future prospects. This is true as information asymmetry deters investors from entering a potentially valuable investment. According to Myers and Majluf (1984), these external factors contribute to companies securing external corporate debts at a concessional rate of interest. Considering the above, firms anticipating growth opportunities will find the assurance of their incumbent integrated reports bringing in numerous advantages from a financial and business expansion point of view. Bushman and Smith (2001) suggested that this will reduce the cost of debt, accompanied by an enhancement of investment efficiency. Standard setters and regulators should thus pay particular attention to parts of the IR that relate to strategic focus and future orientation. We, therefore, hypothesise that:

H3: A relationship exists between a company's growth opportunities and assurance of IR.

9.3.3.4 Activity of the Board

One of the activities boards can carry out to manage and indulge in firm value enhancive sustainability actions is establishing a sustainability committee (Michelon & Parbonetti, 2012). With experience, skill and knowledge, this committee addresses stakeholders' demands geared towards modernised concepts of stakeholder capitalism (Amran et al., 2014). These responsibilities and duties include assisting the management in strategy formulation and growth, integrating the sustainable aspect and reviewing its reporting strategy (Post et al., 2002), including the assurance process. Hence, this committee deals with legitimacy issues regarding company decisions and can thus be seen as an appropriate mechanism to improve the credibility of non-financial and sustainability reporting by disseminating an external assurance statement (Martínez-Ferrero, J., & García-Sánchez, I. M. (2017b)). The agency cost theory argues that board activity positively impacts strategic disclosure. According to Lipton and Lorsch (1992), directors are inclined to be more active in proving their efforts to stakeholders, resulting in higher information provision. This leads to the preparation and assurance of integrated reports. Xie et al. (2003) contended that companies with frequent board meetings are less likely to manipulate their accounts. It can be inferred that they would report on the capitals of IR.

H4: There exists a relationship between the level of activity on the board and the assurance of IR.

9.3.3.5 Size of the Board

The key role of a board is to engage in the overall supervision of the management of the business. Due to the complexity of the management function, it proves to be more problematic to make reliable data available in all instances. Hence, the need arises for highly competent and seasoned directors to carry out the supervision function, thereby increasing information credibility. According to Sanchez et al. (2011), a large board size will result in greater strategic information disclosure to indicate their performance. Dalton et al. (1999) and Coles et al. (2008) are major proponents of large boards, claiming the added skillset and experience baggage (Markarian & Parbonetti, 2007). Numerous studies (Jackling & Johl, 2009; Kiel & Nicholson, 2003; Yammeesri & Herath, 2010) provide empirical evidence that a larger board of directors offering more expertise and experience strengthen the business pillar of corporate governance.

Nonetheless, another school of thought militates vehemently against having large boards in favour of company progress. Smaller boards are expected to bring efficiency in decision-making through minimising conflict of opinions and lethargic decision-making (Jensen, 1993; O'Reilly et al., 1989). Liao et al. (2017), in their study of Chinese listed companies engaging in the assurance of CSR reporting, found that large board size and gender diversity are the main determinants of assurance. We put forward the following hypothesis.

H5: There is a relationship between the size of the board and the assurance of IR.

9.3.3.6 Independence of the Board

An independent board is viewed as the key element for supervising managers' actions and ensuring the attainment of stakeholders' objectives (Agrawal & Knoeber, 1996; Fama & Jensen, 1983). Boards with more independent directors are more likely to monitor and control management. They are more efficient in directing management towards long-term value, given that they remain well-versed in the internal affairs of the business (Jizi et al., 2014). Board composition with more independent directors is highly sensitive and attentive to stakeholders' demands, thereby increasing the credibility and reliance on CSR reporting. External assurance thus emerges as an integral mechanism for reducing opportunistic behaviours by management (Liao et al. 2018) and is a feature of accountable governance (de Villiers et al., 2014; Tweedie and Martinov-Bennie, 2015). On the empirics side, a recent study by Martínez-Ferrero and García-Sánchez (2017a) illustrates that board independence is positively associated with the probability of assuring sustainability information. We, therefore, propose the following hypothesis.

H6: There is a relationship between the level of independence on the board of directors and the assurance of IR.

9.3.3.7 Industry

According to Gao et al. (2005), different industries will exhibit diverse characteristics arising from competition, growth potential, government intervention and job availability. Alsaeed (2006) held that manufacturing companies provide more information than non-manufacturing companies. Non-financial companies often generate negative externalities such as pollution and depletion of natural resources. However, Elzahar and Hussainey (2012) report that industrial companies report more risk disclosure than service companies. Their results also revealed that the entities in the service and finance industries disclose more forward-looking information compared to manufacturing companies. Thus, they will try to minimise these impacts and convey such information to stakeholders via annual reports. Therefore, assurance of integrated reports helps to confirm that the company's data are not misleading. Watts and Zimmerman (1986, p. 239) claimed that failure by companies to implement similar disclosure strategies as other firms in the same industry, the market could capture this as disturbing signals. Thus, non-financial firms seem prone to publishing and assuring their integrated reports.

H7: There is a relationship between the industry category and the assurance of IR.

9.4 Methodology

9.4.1 Sample Size

For this study, ASX100 companies have been targeted. Australia has been chosen due to the emergence of IR in its economy. The time frame under consideration is the period 2018 and 2019. Therefore, the number of observations amounts to 200.

9.4.2 Regression Model

A binary logistic regression was used to investigate the association between the dependent and independent variables. Logistic regression enables the testing of models to forecast categorical outcomes with two or more categories. Since the dependent variable is binary, i.e. 0 or 1, logistic regression is suitable as an alternative to linear regression analysis (Bircan, 2004: Özdamar, 2002). This type of regression aids in the classification and appointment process. It necessitates no pre-requisite, such as a normal distribution variance or continuous variance (Korkmaz et al., 2012).

Other studies, such as Aranda-Ordaz (1981) and Johnson (1985), advocate using logistic regression.

The formulation of the equation is as follows:

$$\begin{aligned} AIR = {} & b + b_1 ROC + b_2 LNSALES + b_3 PRICETOBOOK \\ & + b_4 BMEET + b_5 BSIZE + b_6 BNONEXE \\ & + b_7 INDUSTRY + e \end{aligned}$$

9.4.2.1 Dependent Variable

AIR (Assurance) takes value 1 if a company's integrated report is assured and 0 otherwise.

9.4.2.2 Independent Variables

ROC is the return on capital employed of the firm used as a proxy for profitability.

LNSALES represents firm size measured by the firm's natural logarithm of sales.

PRICETOBOOK represents growth opportunity measured by the ratio of price to book of the company's share.

BMEET represents board activity determined by the number of board meetings the company holds.

BSIZE is the company's board size, determined by the number of directors on the firm's board.

BNONEXE represents board independence, determined by the percentage of non-executive directors on the company's board.

Industry represents the industry category of the firm; it takes a value of 1 for non-financial companies and 0 otherwise.

9.5 Results and Discussion

9.5.1 Descriptive Statistics

We provide an overview of the statistical characteristics of the data in Table 9.1.

The mean of non-executive directors is 84.1740%, while the minimum percentage stands at 44.4400%. The highest standard deviation is at 12.0561, represented by the return on capital employed, while the lowest standard deviation is 1.8413, standing for board size.

Table 9.1 Descriptive statistics

	Minimum	Maximum	Mean	Std. Deviation
LNSALES	13.3047	24.9493	21.6070	1.6456
ROC	−31.6600	71.3500	12.1372	12.0561
PRICE-TO-BOOK	−35.5500	24.7600	2.9163	5.2408
BMEET	4.0000	31.0000	11.2800	3.7606
BSIZE	4.0000	15.0000	8.0800	1.8413
BNONEXE (%)	44.4400	100.0000	84.1740	8.2142

Table 9.2 Correlation matrix

	BMEET	BSIZE	BNONEXE	INDUSTRY NON FINANCIAL	LNSALES	PRICE TO BOOK	ROC
BMEET	1.000						
BSIZE	−0.263	1.000					
BNONEXE	−0.022	0.024	1.000				
INDUSTRY NON FINANCIAL	0.060	−0.280	0.021	1.000			
LNSALES	0.000	0.421	0.179	−0.044	1.000		
PRICE TO BOOK	0.082	−0.104	−0.165	0.131	−0.081	1.000	
ROC	0.062	−0.242	−0.268	0.026	−0.123	0.189	1.000

9.5.2 Correlation

Correlation analysis is utilised to depict the strength and direction of the linear relationship between two variables. Correlation coefficient values can range from −1 to +1 (Pallant, 2011). According to Tabachnick and Fidell (2001), a worrying level of multicollinearity does not prevail until the correlation coefficient attains close to 0.80 or 0.90. Based on the results, it can be seen that most independent variables are not strongly correlated. The highest correlation value was 0.421. Thus, there is no indication of multicollinearity among independent variables (Table 9.2).

9.5.3 Regression Results

Binary logistic regression was used to determine the factors which lead a company to assure its integrated report. The model comprised seven independent variables (size, profitability, industry category, growth opportunities, board activity, board size and

Table 9.3 Logistic regression results

Variable	Coefficient	Probability	Odds ratio
ROC	0.063	0.070	1.065
LNSALES	0.345	0.033	1.412
PRICE TO BOOK	0.135	0.028	1.145
BMEET	0.343	0.031	1.409
BSIZE	−0.026	0.901	0.975
BNONEXE	0.053	0.150	1.054
INDUSTRY	0.105	0.905	1.111
Hosmer and Lemeshow Test:			
Chi-square	14.132		
Significance	0.78		
Cox & Snell R Square	0.11		
Nagelkerke R Square	0.318		
Correctly classified	95.50%		

independence). The Hosmer and Lemeshow Test is reliable for evaluating the model fit (Pallant, 2011). For this test, a poor fit is represented by a significance value lower than 0.5, requiring a value greater than 0.5 in favour of the model. In this case, the chi-square value is 14.132 with a significance level of 0.078. It is larger than 0.5, thereby representing support for the model (Table 9.3).

From the values of the Cox & Snell R Square and Nagelkerke R Square, it can be observed that the amount of variation in the dependent variable represented by the model ranges between 11.0% and 31.8%. The two values from these tests give an overview of the variation of the dependent variable explained by the model. The model's sensitivity was 95.5%, representing the percentage that the model has accurately identified, having assured their integrated report.

9.5.3.1 Profitability and AIR

It can be observed that profitability has no relationship with assurance of integrated reports. At 5% significance level, the probability is insignificant at 7%, depicting no link between profitability and assurance of IR. Thus, the return on capital employed cannot influence companies to have their reports assured. However, according to Tagesson et al. (2009), profitability leads to better firm performance, extending to sustainability activities and making management less hesitant to provide more sustainability information (Haniffa & Cooke, 2005). This is not consistent with the studies like Ruhnke and Gabriel (2013) and Legendre & Coderre, (2013), which report that companies with higher profit margins are likely to have reports being assured. The reason for this result could be stakeholders in Australia consider business size more important rather than profitability. Therefore, we reject H1.

9.5.3.2 Firm Size and AIR

The natural log of sales is positively and significantly associated assurance of IR. Thus, H2 is accepted ($p = 0.33$), suggesting that the probability of assuring an integrated report is positively related to firm size. As a firm's size grows, available resources increase. Large firms will want to distinguish themselves in the market and uphold their reputation and prestige. The findings on size correlate with previous studies (García-Benau et al., 2013; Sierra et al., 2013; Simnett et al., 2009; Zorio et al., 2013). Therefore, when setting up a legal framework for assurance of IR, regulators can use companies' sales revenue for mandatory benchmark assurance. There are approximately 2000 listed companies in Australia, and it has the market index ASX300 for the largest 300 listed companies in market capitalisation. The regulators can use the companies with the lowest sales revenue among ASX300 to set the minimum benchmark for mandatory assurance. The investigation procedures of the value creation process should also be incorporated in the legal framework to check the objectivity in the determination of the capitals' values of IR.

9.5.3.3 Growth Opportunities and AIR

Further, it can be seen that the price-to-book ratio is significantly associated ($p = 0.28$) with assurance of IR. Therefore, we accept H3 and confirm a positive association between potential business growth and assurance of integrated reports. Growth opportunities indicate prosperous avenues. This reflects the mindset of companies to mitigate information asymmetry and agency costs. By overcoming information asymmetry, a business retains investors' confidence, attracts significant investment and increases a firm's market capitalisation. In addition, they can differentiate themselves. The findings corroborate previous research by Bushman and Smith (2001).

9.5.3.4 Board Activity and AIR

Moreover, board activity seems to have a positive and significant relationship with the assurance of integrated reports. The number of board meetings has been utilised as a proxy for board activity, and it is significant at 5% significance level. H4 is accepted. This is in line with the findings of Martínez-Ferrero and García-Sánchez (2017a), who illustrate that board activity is positively associated with the probability of assuring sustainability information. Hence, it can be said that establishing a sustainability committee can enhance the assurance process by mitigating the agency issue and also handling the legitimacy theory, which is clearly stated by (Amran et al., 2014; Michelon & Parbonetti, 2012; Post et al., 2002). The positive association demonstrates the board's efficiency, implying higher frequency of meetings enables the monitoring of AIR by the board. In addition, the positive association implies that the more meetings that occur, the more likely they will assure their report. A proactive board can produce better decisions and discussions. It is consistent with the study by Lipton and Lorsh (1992). The standard setters for assurance should incorporate in their procedures to inspect the board minutes related to the preparation of IR.

9.5.3.5 Board Size and AIR

Regarding board size, the latter has no significant relationship ($p = 0.901$) with the assurance of integrated reports. Hypothesis H5 is therefore rejected. The result does not corroborate with research by Frias-Aceituno et al. (2013). Moreover, it contradicts Mintzberg (1993) who claimed that an increase in board size would link firms to their external environment and secure critical resources, including prestige and legitimacy, which is in line with the legitimacy theory. Moreover, the findings of Castelo Branco et al. (2014) illustrate that board size is positively associated with the probability of assuring sustainability information. He also stated that larger boards are expected to show a greater assurance demand with the legitimacy goal and the findings regarding sustainability disclosure. It can be argued that since there are only 200 observations, the results may differ if a larger sample of companies are considered.

9.5.3.6 Board Independence and AIR

Furthermore, it can be noticed that board independence and assurance of integrated report are not significantly associated ($p = 0.150$). H6 is rejected as the link between the percentages of non-executive directors, and AIR has not been established. This finding is not in accordance with the study of Martínez-Ferrero and García-Sánchez (2017a), as independent directors encourage companies to disclose higher levels of voluntary information (Michelon & Parbonetti, 2012). A study by Qu et al. (2015) also found that companies with many independent directors disclosed precise sales forecasts. Thus, it can be inferred that in Australia, non-executive directors do not vouch for having reports assured externally to ensure information credibility.

9.5.3.7 Industry and AIR

In addition, it can be observed that industry category has no significant relationship ($p = 0.905$) with AIR. As a result, we have to reject H7 and accept that there is no link between non-financial companies and AIR. These findings are not consistent with the results of the majority of previous studies Zorio et al. (2013) and Gomes et al. (2015), which found that industry and assurance of sustainability reports have a significant link. However, this result is coherent with a previous study by Sierra et al. (2013), which found that assurance of sustainability reports has no significant relationship with industry.

9.6 Conclusions

The flaws of traditional reporting have led to the emergence of IR. As integrated reporting is gradually becoming the norm of financial reporting worldwide, it will soon receive much attention from legislators and regulators. This research was conducted to determine the company-level variables that induce companies to have their integrated reports assured.

We found no association between assurance of integrated reports and board size, board independence and industry category. However, company profitability is found to contribute towards AIR. The link is not direct, as it is not the availability of funds that essentially incentivises companies to assure their annual reports. It is instead because of the call for higher accountability and better transparency from various stakeholder classes, which yields to having IR assured by external auditors. The company's size has been positively and significantly linked to assurance of integrated reports. This demonstrated that large companies would be willing to assure their reports maintaining credibility over their reporting and avoid any financial contingencies arising from the reputational loss.

In Australia, there are approximately 2000 listed companies, with a market index ASX300 for the largest 300 listed companies in terms of market capitalisation. Therefore, when setting up a legal framework for assurance of IR, regulators can use companies' sales revenue to benchmark the mandatory threshold for assurance. The regulators can thus earmark companies with the lowest sales revenue among ASX300 to set the minimum benchmark for mandatory assurance. The investigation procedures of the value creation process should be incorporated in the legal framework to check the objectivity in determining the capital's values of IR.

Moreover, growth opportunities prove to impact companies to have their reports assured. They want to exploit the full opportunities IR provides them to mitigate information asymmetry and agency costs. Previous studies have shown that information asymmetry may dissuade potential investors, harming a company's stock of capital. Thus, through assurance of integrated reports, firms can ooze their reports' credibility and reliability. Key stakeholders such as shareholders and investors will feel more confident when increasing their stake in the business in situations where companies forecast good prospects and proposed strategic plans in their assured integrated reports.

Furthermore, the research shows that board activity has a significant positive relationship with assurance. It can be inferred that more meeting enables time to track the preparation and assurance of reports. A better planning and discussion strategy for the report can thus be developed. Through assured integrated reports, investors are provided credible information on the firm's operation. A concept such as the value creation process can signal important information on the ability and potential of the organisation. All these can only be possible if an active board can direct and monitor overall operations. In addition, assurance can mitigate the risk of subjectivity and over-optimism of contents in an integrated report.

Our findings for the relationship between board size and AIR remain consistent with the propositions of O'Neil et al. (1989) and Jensen (1993). They contest the blind belief in the positive correlation between board size and AIR. Board size should ideally not be a determining factor of AIR as its quantitative nature prohibits a well-covered analysis of its effects on AIR. In other words, board size does not reflect the directors' skillset, experience or business judgement capability. Instead, a large board might be construed as comprising less seasoned directors to fill the void of adequate mastery and experience.

As for industry affiliation, the rationale is to encourage more moral judgement by the board and management in constructing or re-designing business models to "greenwash" their operations (Lyon & Montgomery, 2015). Thus, regularising the assurance of IR to make it mandatory for non-financial firms would be a milestone for restoring deteriorating climatic conditions and supporting ethical investors' growing momentum as they remain major surplus units of funds. The rationale behind this occurrence is that both ESG or Integrated Reporting disclosures and their assurance bear anticipative results only when they promote a positive image of the company in question, irrespective of sectoral affiliation. Ethical investors are more concerned with steps taken to mitigate and reduce the negative externalities that businesses are causing rather than them coming clean to them at the expense of brand image. The industry affiliation becomes important when dissected between major polluting companies and environmentally sound operative companies.

While IR gathers momentum, we should not lose sight of the issues faced to maintain the credibility of audit reports and auditors in the post-Enron era. From the standpoint of a consulting firm, integrated reporting assurance is a competitive market for several assurance providers, all of whom have significant economic interests at stake (Cohen & Simnett, 2015; O'Dwyer et al., 2011) and it is feared that assurance providers may tend to support those who appointed them (boards). Notwithstanding the previous argument, the assurance of integrated reports is fraught with challenges. As compared to financial reports, the assurance of integrated reports suffers from a lack of globally accepted standards implying that assurance providers are unable to apply reliable methodologies and procedures to forward-looking information. Consequently, comparability of information is compromised (Adams, 2015). A recent research found that investors rely more on financial reports, which already provide a high level of assurance due to their maturity and standardisation. Furthermore, stakeholders perceive assurance to be a managerial tool for enhancing their self-confidence in narrative reporting rather than a credibility boosting tool (Corrado et al., 2019). Nonetheless, the assurance of integrated reports is still at an early stage and there is plenty room for improvement to meet user needs.

9.6.1 Limitations

The study's main shortcomings comprise sample size and time under consideration. Only a hundred companies have been included over two years. Due to time constraint, a restricted sample has been considered. The sample comprised only Australian-listed companies. This study has only been carried out at the firm level, thereby missing out on some factors. Secondly, given that the field of assurance of Integrated Reporting is entirely groundbreaking, as Integrated Reports are, per se, mandatory in the present context, our review of previous literature is relatively narrow. References were mainly taken from scholars' points of view for the assurance of sustainability reports.

9.6.2 Future Research

There exist several avenues which can be the subject of future research. Very few studies have been carried out in the area of assurance. A larger sample of companies from different countries or a mix of listed and unlisted companies can be considered. The variables that influence the assurance of integrated reports, could be further examined for their extent and quality in assurance of IR. In addition, the application of different models of assurance by firms can be investigated. The factors influencing the assurance providers can also be determined. Moreover, the determinants impacting the assurance of IR at the country level could be examined. These could be legal or political issues. Furthermore, the effect of COVID-19 on the assurance of IR could be investigated.

References

Adams, C. A. (2015). The international integrated reporting council: A call to action. *Critical Perspectives on Accounting, 28*, 23–28.

Agrawal, A., & Knoeber, C. R. (1996). Firm performance and mechanisms to control agency problems between managers and shareholders. *Journal of Financial and Quantitative Analysis, 31*(3), 377–397.

Alfiero, S., Esposito, A., Doronzo, R., & Cane, M., 2018. Determining characteristics of boards adopting Integrated Reporting. *Financial Reporting, 2*, 37–71.

Alsaeed, K. (2006). The association between firm-specific characteristics and disclosure: The case of Saudi Arabia. *Managerial Auditing Journal*.

Ameer, R., & Othman, R. (2012). Sustainability practices and corporate financial performance: A study based on the top global corporations. *Journal of Business Ethics, 108*, 61–79.

Amran, A., Lee, S. P., & Devi, S. S. (2014). The influence of governance structure and strategic corporate social responsibility toward sustainability reporting quality. *Business Strategy and the Environment, 23*(4), 217–235.

Aranda-Ordaz, F. J. (1981). On two families of transformations to additivity for binary response data. *Biometrika, 68*(2), 357–363.

Artiach, T., Lee, D., Nelson, D., & Walker, J. (2010). The determinants of corporate sustainability performance. *Accounting & Finance, 50*(1), 31–51.

Atkins, J., & Maroun, W. (2015). Integrated reporting in South Africa in 2012: Perspectives from South African institutional investors. *Meditari Accountancy Research, 23*(2), 197–221.

Bircan, H. (2004). Lojistik regresyon analizi: Tıp verileri üzerine bir uygulama. *Kocaeli Üniversitesi Sosyal Bilimler Dergisi, 8*, 185–208.

Branco, M. C., Delgado, C., Gomes, S. F., & Eugénio, T. C. P. (2014). Factors influencing the assurance of sustainability reports in the context of the economic crisis in Portugal. *Managerial Auditing Journal, 29*(3), 237–252.

Briem, C. R., & Wald, A. (2018). Implementing third-party assurance in integrated reporting: Companies' motivation and auditors' role. *Accounting, Auditing & Accountability Journal, 31*(5), 1461–1485.

Bushman, R. M., & Smith, A. J. (2001). Financial accounting information and corporate governance. *Journal of Accounting and Economics, 32*(1–3), 237–333.

Casey, R. J., & Grenier, J. H. (2015). Understanding and contributing to the enigma of Corporate Social Responsibility (CSR) assurance in the United States. *Auditing: A Journal of Practice and Theory, 34*(1), 97–130.

Castelo Branco, M., Delgado, C., Ferreira Gomes, S., & Eugénio, C.P.T. (2014). Factors influencing the assurance of sustainability reports in the context of the economic crisis in Portugal. *Managerial Auditing Journal, 29*(3), 237–252.

Clarkson, M. E. (1995). A stakeholder framework for analyzing and evaluating corporate social performance. *Academy of Management Review, 20*(1), 92–117.

Cohen, J. R., & Simnett, R. (2015). CSR and assurance services: A research agenda. *Auditing: A Journal of Practice & Theory, 34*(1), 59–74.

Coles, J. L., Daniel, N. D., & Naveen, L. (2008). Boards: Does one size fit all? *Journal of Financial Economics, 87*(2), 329–356.

Connelly, B. L., Certo, S. T., Ireland, R. D., & Reutzel, C. R. (2011). Signaling theory: A review and assessment. *Journal of Management, 37*(1), 39–67.

Corrado, M., Demartini, P., & Dumay, J. (2019). Assurance on integrated reporting: A critical perspective. In *Integrated reporting: Antecedents and perspectives for organizations and stakeholders* (pp. 199–217). Springer.

Dalton, D. R., Daily, C. M., Johnson, J. L., & Ellstrand, A. E. (1999). Number of directors and financial performance: A meta-analysis. *Academy of Management Journal, 42*(6), 674–686.

Davies, J., Shorrocks, A., & Lluberas, R. (2018). *Global Wealth Report 2018* [online]. https://www.credit-suisse.com/media/assets/private-banking/docs/uk/global-wealth-report-2018.pdf

de Villiers, C., Rinaldi, L., & Unerman, J. (2014). Integrated reporting: Insights, gaps and an agenda for future research. *Accounting, Auditing & Accountability Journal.*

Deegan, C. (2009). *Financial accounting theory* (3rd ed.). McGraw Hill.

Deegan, C., & Unerman, J. (2011). *Financial accounting theory* (2nd European ed.). McGraw-Hill Higher Education.

Dienes, D., Sassen, R., & Fischer, J. (2016). What are the drivers of sustainability reporting? A systematic review. *Sustainability Accounting, Management and Policy Journal, 7*(2), 154–189.

Dumay, J., Bernardi, C., Guthrie, J., & Demartini, P. (2016, September). Integrated reporting: A structured literature review. In *Accounting forum* (Vol. 40, No. 3, pp. 166–185). No longer published by Elsevier.

Dumay, J., de Villiers, C., Guthrie, J., & Hsiao, P. C. (2018). Thirty years of Accounting, Auditing and Accountability Journal: A critical study of the journal's most cited articles. *Accounting, Auditing & Accountability Journal.*

Eccles, R. G., & Krzus, M. P. (2010). *One report: Integrated reporting for a sustainable strategy.* Wiley.

Eccles, R. G., Ioannou, I., & Serafeim, G. (2012). *The impact of a corporate culture of sustainability on corporate behavior and performance* (Vol. 17950, No. 1). National Bureau of Economic Research.

Eisenhardt, K. M. (1989). Agency theory: An assessment and review. *Academy of Management Review, 14*(1), 57–74.

Elzahar, H., & Hussainey, K. (2012). Determinants of narrative risk disclosures in UK interim reports. *The Journal of Risk Finance, 13*(2), 133–147.

Fama, E. F., & Jensen, M. C. (1983). Separation of ownership and control. *The Journal of Law and Economics, 26*(2), 301–325.

Flower, J. (2015). The international integrated reporting council: A story of failure. *Critical Perspectives on Accounting, 27*, 1–17.
Frías-Aceituno, J. V., Rodríguez-Ariza, L., & García-Sánchez, I. M. (2013). The role of the board in the dissemination of integrated corporate social reporting. *Corporate social responsibility and environmental management, 20*(4), 219–233.
Frías-Aceituno, J. V., Rodríguez-Ariza, L., & Garcia-Sánchez, I. M. (2014). Explanatory factors of integrated sustainability and financial reporting. *Business Strategy and the Environment, 23*(1), 56–72.
Gao, S. S., Heravi, S., & Xiao, J. Z. (2005, June). Determinants of corporate social and environmental reporting in Hong Kong: A research note. In *Accounting Forum, 29*(2), 233–242. Taylor & Francis.
García-Benau, M. A., Sierra-Garcia, L., & Zorio, A. (2013). Financial crisis impact on sustainability reporting. *Management Decision, 51*(7), 1528–1542.
Ghani, E. K., Jamal, J., Puspitasari, E., & Gunardi, A. (2018). Factors influencing integrated reporting practices among Malaysian public listed real property companies: A sustainable development effort. *International Journal of Managerial and Financial Accounting, 10*(2), 144–162.
Gomes, S. F., Eugénio, T. C. P., & Branco, M. C. (2015). Sustainability reporting and assurance in Portugal. *Corporate Governance, 15*(3), 281–292.
Gray, R., Owen, D., & Adams, C. (1996). *Accounting & accountability: Changes and challenges in corporate social and environmental reporting*. Prentice hall.
Gürtürk, A., & Hahn, R. (2016). An empirical assessment of assurance statements in sustainability reports: Smoke screens or enlightening information? *Journal of Cleaner Production, 136*, 30–41.
Haniffa, R. M., & Cooke, T. E. (2005). The impact of culture and governance on corporate social reporting. *Journal of Accounting and Public Policy, 24*(5), 391–430.
Hess, D. (2008). The three pillars of corporate social reporting as new governance regulation: Disclosure, dialogue, and development. *Business Ethics Quarterly, 18*(4), 447–482.
IASB. (2010). *The conceptual framework for financial reporting* [online]. http://eifrs.ifrs.org/eifrs/files/238/bv2012_conceptual_framework_part%20a_161.pdf
IIRC (International Integrated Reporting Council). (2013). *The International Framework* [online]. http://integratedreporting.org/wp-content/uploads/2015/03/13-12-08-THE-INTERNATIONAL-IR-FRAMEWORK-2-1.pdf
Institute of Directors in Southern Africa (IoDSA). (2009). *King Report on Governance for South Africa (King III)* [online]. https://cdn.ymaws.com/www.iodsa.co.za/resource/resmgr/king_iii/King_Report_on_Governance_fo.pdf
Jackling, B., & Johl, S. (2009). Board structure and firm performance: Evidence from India's top companies. *Corporate Governance: An International Review, 17*(4), 492–509.
Jensen, M. C. (1993). The modern industrial revolution, exit, and the failure of internal control systems. *The Journal of Finance, 48*(3), 831–880.
Jensen, M. C., & Meckling, W. H. (1976). Theory of the firm: Managerial behavior, agency costs and ownership structure. *Journal of Financial Economics, 3*(4), 305–360.
Jennifer Ho, L. C., & Taylor, M. E. (2007). An empirical analysis of triple bottom-line reporting and its determinants: Evidence from the United States and Japan. *Journal of International Financial Management & Accounting, 18*(2), 123–150.
JCPAA. (2010). *Review of Independent Auditing by Registered Company Auditors: Financial reporting* [online]. https://www.aph.gov.au/parliamentary_business/committees/House_of_Representatives_Committees?url=jcpaa/indepaudit/chapter3.pdf
Jizi, M. I., Salama, A., Dixon, R., & Stratling, R. (2014). Corporate governance and corporate social responsibility disclosure: Evidence from the US banking sector. *Journal of Business Ethics, 125*, 601–615.
Johnson, W. (1985). Influence measures for logistic regression: Another point of view. *Biometrika, 72*(1), 59–65.

Kiel, G. C., & Nicholson, G. J. (2003). Board composition and corporate performance: How the Australian experience informs contrasting theories of corporate governance. *Corporate Governance: An International Review, 11*(3), 189–205.

Kolk, A., & Perego, P. (2010). Determinants of the adoption of sustainability assurance statements: An international investigation. *Business Strategy and the Environment, 19*(3), 182–198.

Korkmaz, M., Güney, S., & Yiğiter, Ş. (2012). The importance of logistic regression implementations in the Turkish livestock sector and logistic regression implementations/fields. *Harran Tarım Ve Gıda Bilimleri Dergisi, 16*(2), 25–36.

KPMG. (2013). *The KPMG Survey of Corporate Responsibility Reporting 2013* [online]. https://assets.kpmg/content/dam/kpmg/pdf/2015/08/kpmg-survey-of-corporate-responsibility-reporting-2013.pdf

Lai, A., Melloni, G., & Stacchezzini, R. (2016). Corporate sustainable development: Is 'integrated reporting' a legitimation strategy? *Business Strategy and the Environment, 25*(3), 165–177.

Legendre, S., & Coderre, F. (2013). Determinants of GRI G3 application levels: The case of the Fortune Global 500. *Corporate Social Responsibility and Environmental Management, 20*(3), 182–192.

Liao, L., Lin, T., & Zhang, Y. (2018). Corporate board and corporate social responsibility assurance: Evidence from China. *Journal of Business Ethics, 150*, 211–225.

Liao, P. C., Xia, N. N., Wu, C. L., Zhang, X. L., & Yeh, J. L. (2017). Communicating the corporate social responsibility (CSR) of international contractors: Content analysis of CSR reporting. *Journal of Cleaner Production, 156*, 327–336.

Lipton, M., & Lorsch, J. W. (1992). A modest proposal for improved corporate governance. *The Business Lawyer*, 59–77.

Lyon, T. P., & Montgomery, A. W. (2015). The means and end of greenwash. *Organization & Environment, 28*(2), 223–249.

Lys, T., Naughton, J., & Wang, C. (2015). Signaling through corporate accountability reporting. *Journal of Accounting and Economics, [e-journal], 60*(1), 56–72. https://doi.org/10.1016/j.jacceco.2015.03.001

Markarian, G., & Parbonetti, A. (2007). Firm complexity and board of director composition. *Corporate Governance: An International Review, 15*(6), 1224–1243.

Maroun, W. (2017). Assuring the integrated report: Insights and recommendations from auditors and preparers. *The British Accounting Review, 49*(3), 329–346.

Maroun, W. (2018). Modifying assurance practices to meet the needs of integrated reporting: The case for "interpretive assurance". *Accounting, Auditing & Accountability Journal.*

Maroun, W. (2019). Does external assurance contribute to higher quality integrated reports? *Journal of Accounting and Public Policy, 38*(4), 106670.

Maroun, W., & Atkins, J. (2015). *The challenges of assuring integrated reports: Views from the South African auditing community.* The Association of Chartered Certified Accountants.

Martínez-Ferrero, J., & García-Sánchez, I. M. (2017a). Coercive, normative and mimetic isomorphism as determinants of the voluntary assurance of sustainability reports. *International Business Review, 26*(1), 102–118.

Martínez-Ferrero, J., & García-Sánchez, I. M. (2017b). Sustainability assurance and assurance providers: Corporate governance determinants in stakeholder-oriented countries. *Journal of Management & Organization, 23*(5), 647–670.

Mathews, M. R. (1993). *Socially responsible accounting.* Chapman & Hall.

Mathews, M. R. (1995). Social and environmental accounting: A practical demonstration of ethical concern. *Journal of Business Ethics, 14*, 663–671.

Maulidya, E. W. S., Sukoco, A., Suyono, J., & Elisabeth, D. R. (2019). Analysis of financial performance based on financial ratio and economic value added. *IJIEEB International Journal of Integrated Education, Engineering and Business*, 2(2), 115–122. eISSN 2615–1596; pISSN 2615–2312.

Michelon, G., & Parbonetti, A. (2012). The effect of corporate governance on sustainability disclosure. *Journal of Management & Governance, 16*(3), 477–509.

Michelon, G., Pilonato, S., & Ricceri, F. (2015). CSR reporting practices and the quality of disclosure: An empirical analysis. *Critical Perspectives on Accounting, 33*, 59–78.
Mintzberg, H. (1993). *Structure in fives: Designing effective organizations*. Prentice-Hall, Inc.
Mock, T. J., Strohm, C., & Swartz, K. M. (2007). An examination of worldwide assured sustainability reporting. *Australian Accounting Review, 17*(41), 67–77.
Myers, S. C., & Majluf, N. S. (1984). Corporate financing and investment decisions when firms have information that investors do not have. *Journal of Financial Economics, 13*(2), 187–221.
O'Dwyer, B., Owen, D., & Unerman, J. (2011). Seeking legitimacy for new assurance forms: The case of assurance on sustainability reporting. *Accounting, Organizations and Society, 36*, 31–52.
O'Neill, H. M., Saunders, C., & McCarthy, A. (1989, August). Board members background characteristics and their level of corporate social responsiveness orientation: A multivariate investigation. In *Academy of Management Proceedings* (Vol. 1989, No. 1, pp. 32–36). Academy of Management.
O'Reilly III, C. A., Caldwell, D. F., & Barnett, W. P. (1989). Work group demography, social integration, and turnover. *Administrative Science Quarterly*, 21–37.
Özdamar, K. (2002). *Paket Programlar Ýle Ýstatistiksel Veri Analizi*. Eskiþehir: Kaan Kitabevi.
Pallant, J. (2011). Survival manual. *A Step by Step Guide to Data Analysis Using SPSS, 4*, 4.
Perego, P., & Kolk, A. (2012). Multinationals' accountability on sustainability: The evolution of third-party assurance of sustainability reports. *Journal of Business Ethics, 110*(2), 173–190.
Post, J. E., Preston, L. E., & Sachs, S. (2002). Managing the extended enterprise: The new stakeholder view. *California Management Review, 45*(1), 6–28.
Reimsbach, D., Hahn, R., & Gürtürk, A. (2018). Integrated reporting and assurance of sustainability information: An experimental study on professional investors' information processing. *European Accounting Review, 27*(3), 559–581.
Rossi, A., & Tarquinio, L. (2017). An analysis of sustainability report assurance statements: Evidence from Italian listed companies. *Managerial Auditing Journal, 32*(6), 578–602.
Ruhnke, K., & Gabriel, A. (2013). Determinants of voluntary assurance on sustainability reports: An empirical analysis. *Journal of Business Economics, 83*(9), 1063–1091.
Sam, C. Y., & Tiong, P. N. (2015). An investigation of the corporate responsibility report assurance statements of the Big Four banks in Australia. *Journal of Economics Library, 2*(1), 3–14.
Sierra, L., Zorio, A., & García-Benau, M. A. (2013). Sustainable development and assurance of corporate social responsibility reports published by Ibex-35 companies. *Corporate Social Responsibility and Environmental Management, 20*(6), 359–370.
Simnett, R., & Huggins, A. L. (2015). Integrated reporting and assurance: Where can research add value? *Sustainability Accounting, Management and Policy Journal*.
Sierra-García, L., Zorio-Grima, A., & García-Benau, M. A. (2015). Stakeholder engagement, corporate social responsibility and integrated reporting: An exploratory study. *Corporate Social Responsibility and Environmental Management, 22*(5), 286–304.
Simnett, R., Vanstraelen, A., & Chua, W. F. (2009). Assurance on sustainability reports: An international comparison. *The Accounting Review, 84*(3), 937–967.
Stubbs, W., & Higgins, C. (2014). Integrated reporting and internal mechanisms of change. *Accounting, Auditing & Accountability Journal*.
Tabachnick, B. G., & Fidell, L. S. (2001). *Using multivariate statistics* (4th ed.). Allyn and Bacon.
Tagesson, T., Blank, V., Broberg, P., & Collin, S. O. (2009). What explains the extent and content of social and environmental disclosures on corporate websites: A study of social and environmental reporting in Swedish listed corporations. *Corporate Social Responsibility and Environmental Management, 16*(6), 352–364.
Tweedie, D., & Martinov-Bennie, N. (2015). Entitlements and time: Integrated reporting's double-edged agenda. *Social and Environmental Accountability Journal, 35*(1), 49–61.
Veronica Siregar, S., & Bachtiar, Y. (2010). Corporate social reporting: Empirical evidence from Indonesia Stock Exchange. *International Journal of Islamic and Middle Eastern Finance and Management, 3*(3), 241–252.

Vitolla, F., Raimo, N., & Rubino, M. (2019). Appreciations, criticisms, determinants, and effects of integrated reporting: A systematic literature review. *Corporate Social Responsibility and Environmental Management, 26*(2), 518–528.

Watts, R. L., & Zimmerman, J. L. (1986). Positive accounting theory.

Wong, J., Wong, N., Li, W. Y., & Chen, L. (2016). Sustainability assurance: An emerging market for the accounting profession. *Pacific Accounting Review, 28*(3), 238–259.

Xie, B., Davidson, W. N., III., & DaDalt, P. J. (2003). Earnings management and corporate governance: The role of the board and the audit committee. *Journal of Corporate Finance, 9*(3), 295–316.

Yammeesri, J., & Kanthi Herath, S. (2010). Board characteristics and corporate value: Evidence from Thailand. *Corporate Governance: The International Journal of Business in Society, 10*(3), 279–292.

Zhou, S., Simnett, R., & Green, W. (2017). Does integrated reporting matter to the capital market? *Abacus, 53*(1), 94–132.

Zorio, A., García-Benau, M. A., & Sierra, L. (2013). Sustainability development and the quality of assurance reports: Empirical evidence. *Business Strategy and the Environment, 22*(7), 484–500.

Chapter 10
Environmental Strategy & Management and Accounting Information System's Relationship: A Portuguese Case Study

Sónia Monteiro and Verónica Ribeiro

Abstract Literature review suggests that environmental strategic alignment and the environmental management accounting practices' adoption are influenced not only by institutional pressure (coercive, mimetic and normative), but also by the organization's characteristics. The aim of this paper is twofold: (a) to analyse, from a theoretical point of view, the implications of considering the environmental variables into the companies' strategy, management and accounting information systems; (b) to develop a case study in order to understand the strategies, practices, management tools and environmental/sustainability disclosure adopted by a large Portuguese group, operating in an environmental sensitive industry, and the role performed by its accounting information system. Environmental issues have been incorporated into the group's strategy and management practices as result of external pressures, from legislative and stakeholders demands. This proactive strategy was materialized by (a) an organizational restructuring, including an environmental/sustainability; (b) the changes in the production process, introducing clean technologies and a circular economy approach; and (c) the environmental management systems' implementation and certification in all industrial centres. The information generated by the accounting information system reflects the relevance of environmental variables for the group, as for the cost accounting and in the financial accounting. However, the status quo of environmental management accounting (EMA) development is unsatisfactory, perhaps as result of the lack of common guidelines to implement EMA in a business context.

Keywords Environmental strategy · Environmental management accounting (EMA) · accounting Information system · Case study · Environmental management practices · Institutional pressures

---

S. Monteiro (✉) · V. Ribeiro
Research Centre on Accounting and Taxation (CICF), Polytechnic Institute of Cavado and Ave, Barcelos, Portugal

D. Crowther and S. Seifi (eds.), *Corporate Social Responsibility in Difficult Times*, Approaches to Global Sustainability, Markets, and Governance,
https://doi.org/10.1007/978-981-99-2591-9_10

10.1 Introduction

The growing and general awareness on sustainable development matters has manifested itself in a greater social and institutional concern about the environmental protection and preservation. As a result, companies, like one of the major polluters, are motivated to consider their responsibilities and to act in reducing their negative impacts. The environmental responsibility's assumption by companies is shown by the integration of environment variables into their strategy and management practices. Some companies take on a sustainable proactive attitude, by developing environmental strategies towards the sustainable development. This proactivity is shown not only on the industrial implementation of clean, environment friendly production systems, but also considering ecologic issues on the company management and its implementation on the accounting information system. It allows to obtain environmental management support, but also to an external demonstration that the company has successfully evolved, in a sustainable manner.

In this matter, the corporate environmental management has developed and experienced changes in its organizational structure over the last few decades. The companies' culture, procedures and products have changed, as well as the adoption of new tools and strategies regarding the environmental issues, specifically, concerning the adoption and certification of Environmental Management Systems (EMS).

On the other hand, the integration of environmental issues in the strategy and management of companies, as well as the interest to make visible their environmental commitment, has motivated new information needs by the several stakeholders. Therefore, it is required the change of the corporate information systems, including the accounting system, to generate environmental information that is suitable and convenient for the decision-making process. In this regard, the contents and configuration of the information produced must also adapt, either by integrating non-financial information in the annual financial reports or through ad hoc reports, such as environmental reports and/or sustainability reports.

In this context, there are two main purposes for this research. On the one hand to analyse, on a theoretical viewpoint, the implications include environmental variables into the companies' strategy, management and accounting information systems. Another goal is to carry out a case study, to understand the strategies, practices, management tools and environmental/sustainability disclosure adopted by a large Portuguese group, operating in an environmental sensitive industry, and the role performed by its accounting information system.

The paper is structured as follows: after the introduction, the first section presents a literature review on the relationship between environmental strategy, management and accounting information system. The remaining of the paper is dedicated to the case study, explaining the research design, namely the methodology and the selection and characterization of the case. Afterwards, we present and discuss the results. The last section summarizes the main conclusions and limitations of the study, and some suggestions for future research.

10.2 Literature Review

10.2.1 Environmental Strategies and Management

Companies have grown conscious about the benefits of formulating environmentally friendly strategies, to generate competitive advantage, at a cost level, as well as by differentiation (Porter & Van der Linde, 1995; Westley & Vrendenburg, 1991). In this line, Azzone and Manzini (1994) consider the obtained advantages can be of external origins (by cleaning the company's public image and by showing social concern), as well as internal (consequence of cost saving due to a more efficient natural resources usage and the reduction of penalties regarding environmental laws incompliance).

The environmental strategic positioning of a company may be influenced by internal (e.g. organizational culture) and external factors (legislative pressures and/or stakeholders, trends, country's cultural trades, etc.) (James et al., 1999). According to Azzone et al. (1997), the combination of these factors will determine that an environmental strategy taken by a certain company is or is not sustainable. Bennett and James (1998) present three categories of environmental strategic positioning:

- Passive strategy: When the managers and the main stakeholders are not aware of the importance of the environmental impacts caused by their activities, companies tend to adopt a passive or inactive behaviour regarding environmental matters. Sometimes, companies adopt this strategic positioning because they lack financial, technical and human capabilities to deal with their environmental issues and, consequently, they choose to ignore them.
- Reactive strategy: Companies only seek to answer to external pressures (from stakeholders or legislation) to take actions in order to reduce their negative impacts on the environment. Thus, they address environmental concerns in reaction to increased public exposure. They actually seek to project an image of themselves as companies engaged in environmental protection, but do not effectively integrate environmental issues into their management models or decision-making processes. Therefore, companies adopt an approach focused on compliance with environmental legislation and external pressures, but there is no real environmental commitment.
- Proactive strategy: Companies fully integrate environmental issues into their decision-making and management processes by making a genuine commitment to environmental protection. A proactive environmental behaviour supposes being ahead of changes in the environment and establishing an agenda of environmental actions (such as recycling, waste reduction). The objective is not only to solve problems or reduce environmental impacts, but also to prevent them and provide additional value to the company. Thus, these companies seek to obtain competitive advantages anticipating the evolution of competitors' actions, legislation and customers' needs. These companies go beyond the environmental legislation compliance, by implementing environmental management practices (e.g. environmental auditing, product-life-cycle analysis, etc.) to improve their environmental

performance. Their organizational structure usually has an environmental department and they have implemented an Environmental Management System (EMS) (Déniz Mayor & Pérez Alemán, 2003).

EMS is considered a systematic and global mechanism to improve company's environmental performance (Florida & Davison, 2001). The main motivations and related benefits of the implementation and certification/registration of EMS are: the improvement of the company public image, its relationship with the stakeholders, the improvement of legal commitment (fulfilment of legislation) and the obtention of competitive advantage and environmental improvement (Bansal & Bogner, 2002; Darnall et al., 2000; Pan, 2003).

The ISO 14001 enables organizations to manage and improve their environmental aspects related to their activity, as to fulfil compliance obligations and achieve environmental objectives. The systematic management of the environmental aspects imposed by ISO 14001 contributes to sustainability, by improving environmental performance and complying with laws, but it can also improve organizational, operational, people and customer results (Fonseca, 2015). Besides, one reason that leads a company to develop and/or certificate its EMS according to ISO 14001 standard is the external recognition, as a way of claiming their environmental responsibility before society.

10.2.2 Environmental Accounting Information System

The inclusion of environmental variables in the companies' management brings up new needs and information demands, to which the traditional accounting system cannot attend. For this reason, the change or redefinition of some of the postulates of traditional accounting to embrace the environmental issues is crucial.

Environmental accounting can be divided into environmental financial accounting (EFA) and environmental management accounting (EMA) (Jalaludin et al., 2011). Regarding EFA, the focus is on environmental reporting. To disclose environmental information two alternatives are possible: (a) information disclosed in the traditional financial statements (e.g. within the management report) and (b) environmental information disclosed in a specific separate report (such as environmental report, CSR report, sustainability report).

The first option has been the solution for many European companies in the in the early 2000s, due to the recommendation of the Commission of European Communities (2001) on the recognition, measurement and disclosure of environmental information in the annual accounts of EU companies.[1] In Europe, several

[1] Following the European Recommendation, Portugal approved the Accounting Standard 29: Environmental Matters (2002) which makes compulsory for Portuguese companies to disclose environmental information in their annual reports. Later, the Accounting Standardization System was approved by DL no. 158/2009, of July 13th, repealing this guideline. The Portuguese Accounting Standardization System is composed of 28 accounting and financial reporting standards, adapted

studies have analysed environmental disclosure practices (Barros & Monteiro, 2012; Costa & Agostini, 2016; Monteiro & Guzmán, 2010). Like Portugal, many other countries (e.g. USA, Canada, Norway, Spain, Belgium, France, the UK, Sweden, Denmark, etc.) have accounting standards that require the recognition of social and environmental matters in financial reporting (Ribeiro & Monteiro, 2015).

Findings corroborate the accounting standards' influence on the increase and improvement of the environmental information disclosed. Most of the studies provide empirical evidence that company size and/or environmentally sensitive industry are determinants factors of mandatory environmental disclosure in annual reports (Barros & Monteiro, 2012). Environmental or social reporting was primarily a matter of companies strongly committed to the idea of sustainability because of operating in a sustainability-related sector. Current sustainability reporting has become common practice for many more firms because their competitors issue such reports as well or society expects firms to report on sustainability performance regardless of their sector affiliation KPMG (2020).

However, we have witnessed a gradual increase of the number of organizations that disclosure environmental information through a stand-alone environmental report (Costa & Agostini, 2016; Fortes, 2002) and, in the last years, more and more through sustainability reports (KPMG, 2020). In the sustainability reporting field, the Global Reporting Initiative (GRI) intends to empower organizations' transparency worldwide and encourage them to take responsibility for their impacts through their sustainability reports. GRI guidelines/standards are highlighted as the world's most recognized and globally accepted sustainability reporting framework (KPMG, 2020).

Environmental or social reporting was primarily a matter of companies strongly committed to the idea of sustainability because of operating in a sustainability-related sector. Currently, sustainability reporting has become common practice for many more companies because their competitors publish sustainability reports as well or society expects companies to report on sustainability performance regardless of their sector activity (Dienes et al., 2016).

Nowadays, the 2030 Agenda approval and the definition of 17 Sustainable Development Goals (SDGs) provide an opportunity to link organizational strategies and global priorities and, therefore, to articulate the organizations' strategy and reporting with the goals (Monteiro et al., 2020). Target 12.6 encourages organizations to adopt sustainable practices and to integrate sustainability information into their reporting cycle. However, there is a lack of a common framework for measuring and reporting companies' contribution to the SDGs. To this end, the GRI published a linkage document that shows the disclosures within the GRI Standards that can be used to report on specific SDGs and their targets. In the report state of progress: business contributions to the SDGs, GRI (2022), using a sample of GRI reporters, presents an analysis and evaluation of how they are acting in relation to the SDGs and disclosing information on the SDGs, in a pandemic period (2020–2021). Most of the companies surveyed seem to have a good understanding of the goals, including they are able to identify

---

from IAS/IFRS and accepted in the EU. It includes the standard 26—*Environmental Matters*, which is a full transcription of the previous Accounting Standard 29.

those that are most relevant to their business. However, most companies have not yet set targets explicitly aligned with the SDGs.

Research on the linkage of the SDGs to corporate reporting is still in its infancy. Most studies consider listed companies and/or from different industries, and also certified companies (Fonseca & Carvalho, 2019; Monteiro et al., 2022; Tsalis et al., 2020). The studies agree that the number of companies mentioning the SDGs in their corporate reporting is increasing, but still bellow from desirable. Under the non-financial reporting European regulation (Directive 2014/95/EU, which requires certain large companies to report on non-financial information), companies are increasingly reporting on the SDGs (Gazzola et al., 2020; Hummel & Szekely, 2022).

Several studies in the field of environmental accounting have focused on the issues of corporate reporting, but little attention has been given to explore on how environmental issues are managed internally. Abdalla's et al. (2014)'s study emphasize the importance of engage in environmental accounting research.

Although many companies give priority to externally meant models of environmental/sustainability/SDGs reporting, the development of guidelines such as the ISO 14001 or EMAS has highlighted that accounting management can play in environmental management support. Management accounting practices operate as an enabler mechanism for the environmental management by reinforcing the ISO 14001/EMAS elements: environmental legislation compliance, commitment to the continual improvement of the environmental performance and communication with stakeholders (Albelda, 2011).

Again, it is required that the adaptation of the accounting information system follows a new philosophy of environmental management and strategic environmental definition, so that information is presented clearly and allows the managers to take on certain decisions, that are suitable and also convenient for the environmental performance evaluation (FMAC, 1998).

Environmental management accounting (EMA) deals with the management of environmental costs that directly impact corporate performance (also called internal costs). EMA can help companies to apply cleaner and more productive procedures such as carbon emissions reduction and the efficient usage of physical resources (e.g. water, material, energy, emissions and waste). Furthermore, an accounting system can recognize, estimate and classify environmental-related costs and liabilities. It can also help with product prices decisions and costs calculation related to environmental projects, among others (Bresciani et al., 2022; Olalekan & Jumoke, 2017).

In this sense, management accounting could play an important role in environmental management support (Albelda, 2011), for example, through the definition of indicators that collect important information on the different environmental performance aspects that allow the analysis of companies' performance improvement (or worsening) over time, between distinct organizational units, or companies within the same industry or sector (Blanco Dopico et al., 2000; Young, 1996).

However, the management accounting role as a system in charge of submitting information for the decision-making process and control over the environmental performance of the organizations sometimes has been reduced, pointing for a weak connection (sometimes not at all) between accounting and environmental management (Bouma & Wolters, 1999; Martín et al., 2002). This lack of connection gives place to a variety of problems, which solutions require a strict cooperation between accounting professionals and managers. On the other hand, this gap may also be reduced through the adaptation of traditional costs procedures to the environmental management's real needs and, at an opportune time, with the introduction of more updated systems, based on the activities (ABC/ABM) or in the calculation and analysis of costs of a product life cycle (Life Cycle Costing).

Thus, environmental management accounting practices (EMAPs) have been developed as alternatives to conventional practices. These practices can bring transparency to the environmental costs and improve environmental performance and decision-making process leading to sustainable development (Bresciani et al., 2022; van der Poll, 2022).

There are several contributions from the literature focused on EMAPs in the business context (Bartolomeo et al., 2000; Baumann et al., 2015; Chathurangani and Madhusanka, 2019; Crespo Soler, 2002; Ferreira and Moulang, 2010; Fuadah et al., 2021; Jalaludin et al., 2011; Latif et al., 2020; Phan et al., 2017; Olalekan & Jumoke, 2017; Setthasakko, 2010; Wachira & Wangombe, 2019; Wang et al., 2019), investigating the drivers and/or the barriers of EMA adoption. These studies have used as research methodologies questionnaires and case studies, focusing on companies from environmentally sensitive industries, such as manufacturing.

10.3 Research Design

10.4 Methodology and Prepositions

Research on Environmental Management Accounting has been carried out using many different methods, both qualitative and quantitative. Qualitative methods emphasize case study-based research (Fuadah et al., 2021). We have selected as our research methodology, the case study. This method allows deepening on the appearance, functioning and real impact of environmental management in the companies, its prior and consequences, its attitude towards the development and release of environmental information, and the role, on this subject, that the accounting information system takes on. These are known ledges that can only be obtained by developing an intensive and continued study of the objective unit to analyse, which has limited us in the number of companies to study.

Sharma and Vredenburg (1998) consider that the case study is a proper method when the phenomena at hands (in our case, the environmental management and its connection to the accounting information system) cannot be easily separated from the organizational context in which it develops its activity. On the contrary, the organization must be viewed as a whole, since only the analysis of the phenomena at hands in its own context will allow comprehending the existing interrelation between the company and the mean that circumscribes it.

Since one of the advantages of case studies is to allow the use of multiple techniques and sources to obtain information, to conduct our study we have used the triangulation as research method. In qualitative research, triangulation adds depth to the data that are collected. It consists of a mix of qualitative and quantitative methods, such as interviews, detailed observations and fieldwork, documentary evidence (Ormin, 2020). Thus, we use document analysis (reports, website, media, etc.), direct and participative observation, personal interviews to responsible directors in the environmental/sustainability and accounting fields. The interviews were held between June and September of 2019.

The obtained data was organized according to a coherent logic, considering the study's purpose, questions and propositions formulated. To do so, we have taken on a coding procedure, with the main goal of manipulating the information obtained through interviews and documental analysis, to convert the "raw data" in a more reduced number of variables, in the sense of facilitating its analysis, interpretation and confrontation with the propositions in study, specifically:

- P1: Some internal variables and/or external contextual factors influence the environmental management.
- P2: The environmental management leads to changes in the organizational structure and in the management and information accounting systems.
- P3: The environmental management is positively correlated with the quantity and type of environmental information, used internally and externally disclosed to stakeholders.

10.4.1 Selection and Characterization of the Case

The election of the unit for which we would analyse and conduct this case study was not random, since we chose company that, in our opinion, could be considered what Yin (1994) defines as "critical case". In the sense, its suitability to the goals of our study will allow us to verify the formulated propositions, from the conducted theoretical analysis. To elect the unity to analyse in this case study, we have considered the following criteria:

- To be a large group (the variable size is broadly considered in the literature). In this sense, Azzone et al. (1997) have demonstrated that the company's size affects the process of developing an environmental strategy, in a way that small-sized companies tent to adopt passive or inertia behaviours towards environmental issues. On the other hand, larger companies have more resources (financial, technical and human) to address the environmental issue through the implementation or adoption of systems and tools to manage the environmental impacts of their activities. Therefore, it is expected that the group's size influences the relationship between accounting and environmental management (Bouma & Wolters, 1999;

Wachira & Wangombe, 2019). Large companies are more exposed to external stakeholders and pressures from regulatory bodies, environmental groups and the society, which may lead to increased involvement with EMA activities (Baumann et al., 2015; Christ & Burrit, 2013).
- To operate in a more environmentally sensitive sector. In environmental accounting studies, industry is often measured with regard to how environmentally sensitive different sectors are considered to be (Christ & Burrit, 2013). Sensitive industries, such as forest, paper and pulp, must be more regulated and, therefore, are more likely to use environmental management tools (Blanco Dopico et al., 2000). It has also been suggested that environmental accounting practices, including EMA, are more common in companies operating in environmentally sensitive industries (Wilmshurst & Frost, 2000).
- To have, at least, an Environmental Management System (EMS) certified, which demonstrates the industry's concern over environmental issues. Some literature notes that the ISO 14001 or EMAS certifications have a positive and significant impact on environmental performance (Erauskin-Tolosa et al., 2019) and on environmental information disclosure (Barros & Monteiro, 2012; Costa & Jesus, 2019).
- To be listed in the stock market, because quotation in a stock market is a determinant factor of environmental information disclosure (Monteiro & Guzmán, 2010).
- To apply the Portuguese Accounting Standard on Environmental matters (NCRF 26), based on the proposition that mandatory environmental accounting standards influence reporting practices, improving the disclosures quality (Barros & Monteiro, 2012).

After analysing the fulfilment of those requirements, we have selected to our study, a company group with strongest presence in the world, playing a structuring role for the Portuguese national economy by vertically integrating its business model: applied research, cellulose pulp, forestry, renewable energy, paper and tissue. The group's productive structure relies in 4 industrial centres, which are a reference in Europe, both in size and at the technology level. The sector that this group belongs to generates a high impact over nature, but at the same time, presents a high environmental awareness, with a considerable experience as far as developing environmental actuations.

According to Yin (1994), our company's selection can be defined as a "critical case", in the sense that its suitability to the objectives pursued in our study, and it will allow us to verify the propositions formulated above.

10.5 Case Description

10.6 Environmental Strategy and Management

The group has as mission "To be a global company, admired for the innovative and sustainable way it transforms the forest into products and services that contribute to people's well-being". Thus, their business model includes industrial, social and environmental sustainability.

Environmental protection is essential for the group to assert itself in demanding international markets. Thus, since the end of the 80s, the group has a responsible over the environmental issues, at each industry centre, and at the year 2005, it was created, at the organization chart level, a specific area for the environment. Later, in 2015, a sustainability department replaces the environmental department. This is an autonomous area that reports directly to the board, in a transversal manner to the companies that integrate the group. This allows an integrated and coordinated performance, as far environmental, social, quality and safety. As part of the board structure, there is also: (a) an environmental consultant organ, which assists the board on the environmental aspects related to the group's activity and formulates recommendations on the environmental impacts, keeping a close eye on the legislation on this matter; (b) a Sustainability Forum, an initiative that aims to strengthen collaboration and dialogue between the group and its main stakeholders, from civil society organizations, universities, to customers and suppliers, as well as associations and forestry producers.

The group's commitment to environmental responsibility means they have improved the eco-efficiency of their production processes, to minimize their environmental impacts, leading to remarkable results, such as the natural resources use reduction, as well as emissions levels, water consumption reduction, increased use of renewable energy, improved waste management, etc. The group's environmental actuation reveals a proactive attitude towards the environment protection.

The group has placed a strong investment in technological development, to modernize equipment and to prevent and reduce contamination, recurring in some cases to cutting-edge technology. Whenever possible, the group uses integrated or preventive purposes technology, even though in some situations, the usage of "end of cycle" equipments is justified. Regarding energy, we highlight the investments in photovoltaic solar energy as well as the energy generated from a local renewable source, which allows for costs reduction in energy.

Even though the economic reliability is a key element in their general strategy, the group considers that the economic prosperity and environmental responsibility balance, respecting the principles of the sustainable development are fundamental pieces for success. In this way, its strategic positioning concerning the environment is characterized over time by the adoption of a proactive attitude, which tries to go beyond the simple environmental legislation compliance and anticipate itself to external pressure, both legislative and by the different stakeholders, carrying out measures that lead to the continuous improvement of their environmental performance. Therefore, the group considers the environmental issue to be an opportunity, since over the years it has shown evidence of a proactive strategic positioning, concerning the environment. As an example, we highlight that the studied group:

- Has been pioneer in the usage of certified raw materials and employment of alternative materials, that generate a smaller environmental impact.
- Has voluntarily implemented an EMS in the several industry centres according to ISO 14000, being pioneer in its sector in the obtaining of an environmental certificate.
- Has received the Environmental licence two years and half before the deadline set by the applicable European directive.
- Has anticipated the Portuguese environmental accounting standard adoption before it became mandatory.
- Became the first Portuguese group and one of the first worldwide, to set the ambitious goal of achieving carbon neutrality at its industrial complexes by 2035.
- The group is among the world's best sustainable companies, according to the ESG Risk Rating produced by Sustainalytics.
- It was one of the first groups to join the Circular Bioeconomy Alliance in 2021. As part of Prince of Wales' Sustainable Markets Initiative, it is a platform to accelerate the transition to a circular, climate-neutral bioeconomy that is inclusive and in harmony with nature.

The main guidance lines of the group's environmental strategy are based in three axes: (a) the strict following of legislative demands for the environment; (b) the adoption of a policy of transparency and complete open-mindedness to the surrounding community; and (c) the appliance of techniques and tools that allow to pursue and improve the environmental performance.

In the environmental strategy's definition, there are several influences, namely the sector that the group operates on (since the environmental issues cannot be ignored and the group must respond to environmental legislative demands) but also the pressures of the several stakeholders (particularly, the customers, the environmental activists and the community), to which interests and demands, the group tries to respond in the better manner. In an internal level, the organizational culture of the group withholds values of environmental protection and a high awareness for the use of new opportunities to improve their environmental performance and to anticipate solutions for the problems that might come ahead.

As far as management, the environmental proactive strategic positioning of the group has led to the implementation of an EMS in all industrial centres. The group started the process of implementation of management systems at the end of the 80s, with the Quality Management Systems (QMS) implementation in the industrial centres. Concerning the environment, the implementation of EMS in the group was gradual, from the late 90s on. Has a result of this process, environmental measures were taken to minimize the environmental risks and, in this way, to prevent any law breaking. This implied several significant changes in solid waste management, atmospheric emissions and industrial effluents. In this sense, among the benefits of implementing EMS, we can refer: the improvement of environmental performance (through a better energetic, hydro and solid waste management); the cost reduction associated to smaller consumptions and emissions; better organizational control of the environmental issues and the assurance that the obtained data are reliable and disclosure throughout the organization.

Once concluded the implementation process of EMS in each industrial centre, the group has searched for an environmental certificate, to improve its image and to respond to the growing pressures and demands of the customers, on environmental issues. In this regard, the group has taken a leadership role in the movement for environmental certification based on the ISO 14001 standard, within their respective sector of activity.

Group's policies are embodied in certified management systems, accredited by external bodies on the basis of annual audits, in line with internationally recognized ISO standards. Besides ISO 14001 certification, the group has also certifications on: Quality Management System (under ISO 9001), Health and Safety at Work Management System (under OSHAS 18,001) and Multisite Chain of Custody certification schemes (under the Forest Stewardship Council and Programme for the Endorsement of Forest Certification schemes).

The group approach to sustainability management is based on its sustainability policy and on other policies which address its main environmental, social and economic risks and opportunities. The group collects a large amount of data related to its sustainability performance, which is the base for the elaboration of internal documents, supporting the management process. Generally, there are technical data (and therefore expressed in physics units), which elaboration is the responsibility of the sustainability department.

The environmental performance evaluation is conducted through the elaboration of technical indicators, whose goal is to evaluate the fulfilment of internal goals, as well as the legal requirements fulfilment. Although concerning the group's solid waste, the group also keeps financial information (associating the costs of the solid waste treatment), for the remaining aspects, it is considered difficult to keep monetary indicators, and therefore, no such data is kept. The follow-up and review of the environmental indicators are conducted monthly by the environmental area and management systems, being also reviewed yearly by the administration. It is also a competence of the area of environment and management systems to elaborate documents and internal reports to collect these indicators.

On the other hand, with the purpose of helping the environmental management, the group recurs from time to time to a set of techniques and management tools. Therefore, aiming the quality improvement of the different areas of the group, it developed a project of Total Quality Management (TQM) in all its industrial centres, based upon the EFQM model, which embraced several programmes. The implementation of such practice has produced significant improvements in the productivity index, the reduction of production costs and the improvement of the product quality. This tool has helped to develop the integrated quality and environment systems, at the industrial centres.

In the context of its policy of research and development (R&D), the group developed an analysis model of Life Cycle Assessment, to identify and analyse the environmental impact of the changes of production that integrate the life cycle of copy paper. As far as benchmarking, this group casually uses this technique to analyse the environmental practices taken on by other companies of the sector (both national and international), to evaluate its ranking on this subject.

10.6.1 Environmental Management and Accounting Information System's Relationship

In the context of a technological modernization policy, the group has developed from the late 90s, a programme of inversion related to the modernization of the information systems, with the goal of profiting from the general integration of these systems. Concerning the accounting information system, the relationship between financial accounting and cost accounting is ensured by the computer system, facilitating the information flow between both areas (including the environmental data). The group has a cost accounting system based on cost centres, using the complete costs system. The implementation of EMS has not changed in a significant manner the cost accounting system, since the group has restricted itself to add eventual environmental data to the already existing data. The operational costs concerning protection/conservation of the environment are collected in the costs centre where these activities take place. The group does not include in the product cost, the environmental-related costs, since in their opinion that this information is not of interest. Therefore, the environmental costs information is considered globally. The costs related to the environmental management are usually classified as "environmental costs" by the group's accounting system usually classify as environmental, while there were many hidden environmental costs included in other accounts.

Concerning the financial accounting, the group's accounting plan reflects the environmental issues separately, having been created sub-accounts that allow the identification and recognition of the environmental expenditures. The environmental expenditures identified and recognized by the group are several: materials, personnel costs related with the environmental area and the handling of equipments designed for the prevention or reduction of environmental damage, subcontracts and external services (including among others: energy consumption, solid waste management, cleaning, maintenance, etc.). The costs of the equipment's depreciation related to prevent/reduce environmental damage take on a significant role. For this reason, special care is taken in identifying these equipments, to facilitate the calculation of the annual depreciation and their posterior assignment to the respective cost centre. On the other hand, the group performs the capitalization of environmental expenditures whenever their meant to preserve resources or prevent/reduce environmental damage and whenever it is considered that they extend the asset life, increase ability or improve the safety/efficiency of other assets.

Although the group has an insurance of civil responsibility for environmental damages, which purpose is to cover the risks of environmental damage connected to its activity, within each semester, the costs associated with responsibilities and environmental risks are calculated and, whenever needed, the allocation of environmental provisions is made. Therefore, the evaluation of environmental contingencies is made.

Finally, concerning the disclosure of environmental information, even before the existence of accounting standard on environmental matters, it was group's policy to recognize the contingent liabilities and environmental expenditures. Most of the environmental-related information is disclosed in the management report, in a specific section for environmental issues, even though there are some environmental references in other sections of that document. The environmental information on the management report is mainly of narrative nature and positive, referring to: the strategy/policy and environmental programmes defined by the group; the process of implementation of EMS in each industrial centre and the corresponding auditing for the obtention/maintenance of the ISO 14001 certificate; the environmental investments; the environmental protection and corrective/preventive measures (implemented or in progress); environmental performance information, etc.

Additionally, the group discloses environmental information through their webpage. Thus, not only does it make public its policies of management systems, sustainability and forest management, but also provides information on the obtained certificates by each centre, the forest activity of the group, the R&D on environmental matter and the group actuation towards the environment protection. The first sustainability reports, according to the GRI guidelines, have been published in 2005. The reports are divided into three main areas: Forest and Industry (covering sustainable forest management, energy and climate, and industrial environmental management), People (emphasizing occupational health and safety as well as talent management) and Partnerships (encompassing sustainable management of suppliers, client satisfaction and community involvement). The theme of "innovation" is covered throughout the reports, due to its relevance to all areas. In 2017, the first Sustainability Roadmap was published, setting out commitments, targets and the group's response to the SDGs. The sustainability reports also address the impact of the group on the SDGs, aligning the group's commitments with the 2030 Agenda. The group has established commitments and goals for 2030 in the three strategic action areas defined in its Agenda: Nature, Climate and Society.

Concerning the main reasons to motivate the disclosure of environmental and sustainability information, the group highlights the stakeholders' right to information and the fact that it is the group policy to rigorously fulfil the existing legislation, the transparency of the group in general and in the environmental/sustainability issues, particularly. The use of the standards on environmental/sustainability matters and the promotion of a better image are also reasons considered to justify the increased improvement of the corporate reporting, since the group wishes to show its actions to the community and the effort being made to improve their environmental/sustainability performance.

As explained, the group's accounting area has a certain role in the treatment (preparation and disclosure) of environmental-related information. However, the degree of interaction between the accounting department and the environmental area is not high, even though both parts share information, in the future it is expected that their cooperation will increase. Therefore, from time to time, they establish contact and the environmental/sustainability and systems of information areas provide data to the accounting/financial department, so that it can confront the treatment expenditure and solid waste management (since these are areas with a high incident in the terms of total expenditures on the environmental questions) with other information; apply the accounting legislation in terms of the environment; clear up the purpose of certain equipments or spending with the environment, so that the accounting team can distinguish the environmental expenditures or inversions. They also submit information on judicial processes in progress that may originate future expenditures, reflecting in the annual accounts the environmental responsibilities of the group, either by provisions or by contingencies.

On their part, the accounting area reflects, in the most accurate way possible, the environmental questions by means of a suitable recognition and disclosure of relevant environmental information. Occasionally, the environmental area asks the accounting department information on the environmental inversions and expenditures, not only to elaborate reports and questionnaires, but also to support the decision-making process.

10.7 Analysis and Results Discussion

In this section, we take on the analysis and confrontation of the obtained information with the theoretical propositions elaborated.

- *P1: Some internal variables and/or external contextual factors influence the environmental management*

From the interviews, we identified the main external and internal determinant factors that explain the attitude of the group towards the environment, and therefore, the strategy and type of environmental management developed. Among the external factors, we stand out the industry to which the group belongs to. Pulp and cellulose industry is characterized by a high impact on the environment and a great awareness of the importance and need to operate in an ecological and responsible manner, adopting new strategies and technologies to protect the environment. Therefore, in a certain way, the group's environmental commitment may be seen as a reflection of the general situation that characterizes the sector in which it operates. The environmental concern of the group dates to its own beginning, taking on a growing importance over the time and assuming greater visibility from the 80 s, with important changes in Technologies and Information systems, to improve its environmental performance.

On the other hand, this industry also had influence in the quantity and demand legislative requirements to which the companies must attend to, and which fulfilment is an important factor of the kind of environmental management developed. Effectively, following the worldwide trend, the group began to react against the contamination of the seventies, by selecting production gear that had lower contamination and searching for (and implementing) procedures that would lead to the reduction of contaminating emissions.

In third place, the pressure of the several stakeholders (in this case, the customers, the ecological groups and the community), whose interests and demands of the group try to fulfil, is another determinative factor in the environmental management, since we may consider that the conduction of environmental actions by the group meets the purpose of improving the group's public image and the relationship to the community. These findings are in accordance with Delmas and Toffel (2014) which found that environmental strategies and environmental management practices' adoption are influenced by several stakeholders (such as governments, regulators, customers, competitors, community and environmental groups, and industry associations).

Based on the foregoing, we consider that the external motivations that have led the group to adopt environmental practices are included in one of the categories set by Bansal and Roth (2000), relational motivations, according to which, the group adjusts its actions to the legislation and values that regulate the society. Therefore, in meeting the legal demands and in trying to establish friendly relationships with the main stakeholders, the group reveals a desire to be legitimated. These factors are like those observed by Dias-Sardinha and Reijnders (2005).

Concerning the internal factors that influence of environmental management developed by this group, we particularly stand out the presence and overall weight of the values of continuous improvement of the environmental performance, as well as protection/preservation values in the organizational culture. It is also important to stand out the strong commitment of the top administration that holds the environment in their main concerns and interests. In this sense, the administration is aware that a proper environmental performance is an opportunity to obtain and keep competitive advantage, as well to get a series of important benefits (such as tax incentives, public funding for technological investments). In the line of thought of Bansal and Roth (2000), these initiatives of environmental protection reveal a true ecological awareness by the group and the desire to improve its environmental performance.

Finally, the financial resources availability and the existence of environmental abilities (technological and know-how) are also considered determinant factors on the environmental management developed by this group.

Based on the foregoing, the obtained empirical evidence allows us, in a certain measure, to confirm the thesis of Delmas and Toffel (2004) that suggest that environmental management practices' adoption, not only is influenced by institutional pressure (coercive, mimetic and normative),[2] but also by the organizational characteristics of the company itself.

---

[2] Coercive pressure refers to both formal and informal pressures originating from laws and influential stakeholders,such as governments, suppliers, and customers; normative pressure stems from collective expectations, norms and standards within a particular organizational context; mimetic pressure involves voluntary imitation from leaders companies (DiMaggio & Powell, 1983).

All these factors, internal and external, have motivated this group to adopt over time a proactive attitude towards the environment, taking on actions and adopting measurements to improve its environmental performance, and at the same time, obtain better financial results and productivity improvement. In our opinion, this attitude is evident, among other aspects, in: the importance given to R&D and the innovation in products and procedures, with the goal of keeping within the best available techniques in the sector; their focus more on the prevention of contamination than on the repair of environmental damages; and the promotion of the participation and implication of the staff in the environmental goals, through intensive training and raising of awareness in environmental issues.

In this sense, we consider that the group acts as a leader in its sector, as far as the environmental protection and preservation. This group has been pioneering in the usage of materials that generate a smaller environmental impact, as well as in incorporating "clean" technologies and production processes, such as the adoption and certification of their EMS, and also the adoption of a circular economy approach in their production cycles.

- *P2: The environmental management leads to changes in the organizational structure and in the management and information accounting systems.*

The group's positioning towards the environment has had a clear and evident reflection in its organizational structure, particularly since the year 2005, when an autonomous environmental department was introduced in the organization chart. The main reasons that motivated its creation are linked to the growing attention that the environmental issues had within the group and to the need to ensure a better coordination of the developed action, which would allow a better control and optimization of resources. The change of the organization chart wasn't, therefore, motivated by an interest of showing to the outsider a group that is socially and environmentally responsible, nor did it had the intention to copy other organizations. The creation of this department had the purpose of meeting the group's real needs. Later, in 2015, the environmental department has been replaced by the sustainability department, which include the environmental issues.

Institutional and legislative pressures are the main drivers for the adoption of environmental/sustainability management practices, which include the adoption and certification their management systems (Jennings & Zanbergen, 1995). Thus, the inclusion of environmental variables in the group's decision-making process originated that the ISO 14001 standard was considered by the board as an opportunity to carry on the reorganization and systematization of the several environmental procedures, and to implement a fully structured and formal EMS. In this sense, the process began at the late 90s with the purpose of not only to ensure the standard's commitment, but also to advance in the continuous improvement of the environmental performance. These motivations are in the line of those found in the literature and in the empirical studies on the matter (Bansal & Bogner, 2002; Darnall et al., 2000; Florida & Davison, 2001; Morrow & Rondinelli, 2002) and allow to corroborate the highlighted theory by Bansal and Bogner (2002), namely that the implementation of a EMS sets base for a company to develop in a coordinated and controlled manner, several environmental initiatives. Moreover, in line with González-Benito et al. (2011), the EMS appears to provide useful tools for group that want to satisfy the environmental demands of their stakeholders.

Nevertheless, the adoption and certification of the EMS were a long process that imposed considerable changes and required the cooperation of the group staff (multidisciplinary teams), as well as outside consultants. The obtained benefits (improvement of performance, cost reduction, better control and staff awareness on environmental protection…) are similar to those observed in other companies, as some studies on the subject have shown (Montabon et al., 2000; Poksinska et al., 2003; Ravikumar et al., 2002). Likewise, the reasons pointed by the group for the obtaining of an environmental certificate are aligned with those suggested in the literature and the results achieved in other previous studies (Pan, 2003; Poksinska et al., 2003).

The major obstacle associated to the implementation of the EMS was related to the bureaucratic weight of the ISO standard that demands the elaboration of a high number of technical documents. On this matter, the high bureaucracy associated to this system is one of the major critical points set by the literature (García Rodríguez & Pérez Chamorro, 1999).

It was also necessary to introduce changes in the group's information systems, as to provide them with the necessary conditions to answer to the new information requirements. In this matter, the group has elaborated several types of technical documents, from which they collect environmental information for internal usage (e.g. environmental performance indicators). Their elaboration is a competence of the environment/sustainability and management systems areas, and the accounting/financial department participates by submitting some information (mainly on the costs).

According to the literature (Jalaludin et al., 2011; Latif et al., 2020; van der Poll, 2022), coercive, mimetic and normative pressures and contingent factors played an important role in the adoption of environmental management accounting practices. Phan et al. (2017)'s study provides an insight into the contingent factors influencing the use of environmental management accounting (EMA). The authors found a positive influence of EMS on the use of EMA as well as positive impact of EMA use on environmental performance. Environmental strategy was also identified as one of the contingent factors that influence the adoption of EMA (Baumann et al., 2015; Christ & Burritt, 2013; Fuadah et al., 2021).

However, in our case study, an environmental proactive strategy and the EMS adoption did not produce many changes in the cost/management accounting system of the group. Nor it has established a specific cost centre for the environment, even though the cost centres that are more closely related to that area have been identified. In our opinion, the level of development of the EMS and the cost accounting system is not comparable. In the first case, the group has conducted an important effort to develop, implement and certificate its EMS, while in the case of the cost/management accounting system, we have witnessed a classical cost accounting system, which complexity is more motivated by the trades of the group itself (size and organizational structure) and with its production procedures, than the incorporation of techniques and sophisticated cost calculation and analysis tools, or the elaboration of reports

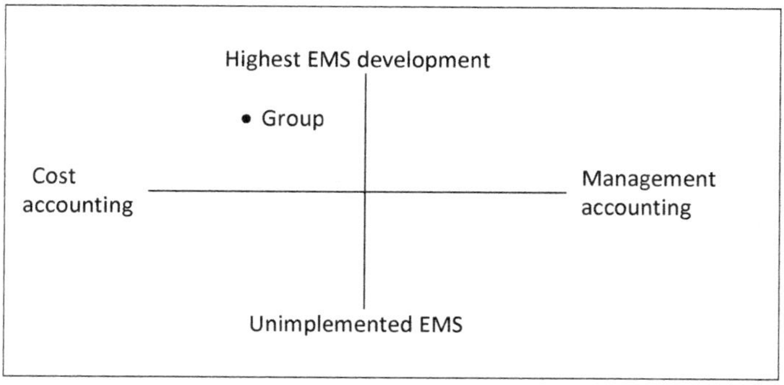

Fig. 10.1 Environmental management and accounting system's relationship: the group's placement. *Source* Own elaboration

with specific data, environmental indicators, etc. We agree with Wang et al. (2019) that due to the lack of consistent industry standards about EMA implementation, companies with high perceived benefit or top management support are less inclined to surrender to mimetic pressure and tend to implement EMA based on their own rules.

As a result, if both systems were to be presented in a coordinates axis, the group would be placed in the first quadrant, as reflected in Fig. 10.1, that corresponds to a highly developed EMS and a cost accounting system not much sophisticated.

From our point of view, this gap between the development of both systems may be justified, in a certain measure, by the low interaction between the group's environmental/sustainability department and the accounting/financial department, as occurred in the cases studied by other authors (Bouma & Wolters, 1999; Crespo Soler, 2002; Martín Samper & Vélez Elorza, 2002). Accountant involvement tends to be higher in areas that involve traditional accounting skills, such as financial reporting. Thus, environmental management accounting is not as advanced as other monitoring and measuring processes and practices of environmental management systems.

However, it is expected improvements in the future, to the point that cost accounting takes on new functions in the information supply for environmental management (e.g. through the elaboration of monetary indicators or of more specific and detailed information on the environmental costs) and incorporates techniques such as the ABC. According to Albelda (2011), an explicit identification of the environmental costs can make them more visible and comprehensible, therefore accounting information can be used not only to reduce environmental costs, but also to improve monitoring and reporting activities.

We agree with Setthasakko (2010) that the lack of guidance on environmental management accounting is one of the barriers to integrate the environmental issues into accounting systems. The IFAC (2005) guidance document on EMA suggests the most of early EMA experience has been in the manufacturing sector, and that sector-specific guidance may be required to assist professional accountants in adapting EMA practices to different industrial settings. According to Setthasakko (2010: 322) "to develop environmental management accounting, the pulp and paper companies need to provide accountants with organizational learning mechanisms, including environmental training and teamworking. The mechanisms would provide opportunities for significant interaction and intellectual exchange with other members of the organization and increase the understanding of the importance of environmental and social sustainability". These arguments are in line with the literature, which findings indicate that education or/and training play a vital role influencing accountants regarding to EMA adoption (Chathurangani & Madhusanka, 2019; Jalaludin et al., 2011).

- *P3:* The environmental management is positively correlated with the quantity and type of environmental information, used internally and externally disclosed to stakeholders.

The defined policies in the matter of protection and preservation of the environment, along with other environmental information, are collected in documents that are made public on the group's webpage. On the other hand, the Image and Communication area, together with the environment and management systems area, are in charge of disclosure to the outside the main environmental performance indicators, submitting to the information users that will not only allow the comparison of data between the centres, but also in relation with the values from the previous years. Concerning the external disclosure of information, the group has also taken on a proactive attitude, disclosing in their annual reports environmental even before the existence of a mandatory accounting standard on environmental matters. Also, since 2005 the group voluntary discloses environmental indicators through their sustainability reports, following GRI guidelines/standards, verified by an external entity. In 2017, the first Sustainability Roadmap was published, setting out commitments, targets and the group's response to the SDGs. Thus, the sustainability reports address the impact of group on the SDG, aligning the group's commitments with the Agenda 2030.

The highlighted reasons by the group to voluntarily disclosure environmental information in their financial reports (mainly the search for transparency and the satisfaction of the stakeholders demands) and also in their sustainability reports are in line with the literature and the findings obtained in some studies (Ahmad & Sulaiman, 2004; Wilmshurst & Frost, 2000). On the other hand, the concern of projecting an image of a company that is environmentally responsible through the disclosure of an increasingly larger amount of environmental information (mainly narrative and positive) is considered by some authors as an attempt to achieve social legitimacy (Ahmad & Sulaiman, 2004; Barros & Monteiro, 2012; Costa & Agostini, 2016; Patten, 1992).

Finally, with the aim of supporting the environmental management process, the group recurs to the employment of a set of techniques and management tools (Total Quality Management—TQM, Life Cycle Analysis—LCA, benchmarking,...) and elaborates a series of documents for internal usage, adapted to the specific needs of the internal users.

10.8 Conclusion

The increase of external pressures in favour of the company actuation being compatible with the sustainable development and the larger companies' environmental awareness has motivated the environmental issues integration into the companies' management and decision-making process, and therefore within the set of base factors to which the companies draw their strategies. In this sense, there is an increasing number of companies that consider that an environmental protection/preservation strategy may be a source of competitive, sustainable advantage. Nevertheless, not all companies present the same degree of integration of environmental values and, as a result, the type of environmental management process developed and the characteristics and functions of the instruments and tools adopted for such effect, are not homogeneous. Therefore, relying on the environmental situation diagnoses, and the type of strategic positioning taken towards the environment, each company must identify the instruments that would contribute for a better development of environmental management.

The general trend of the companies is to use tools and instruments as support to environmental management (such as the analysis of a product life cycle, the activity-based systems, benchmarking, TQM, ...). In this sense, in accordance with Bresciani et al. (2022)'s evidence, we consider that the knowledge of these tools and their adaptation to the specificities and own trades of the environmental management are a basic requirement to, effectively, constitute a support on accomplishing the goals for the sustainable development and environmental performance continuous improvement.

At the same time, the assumption of an environmental responsibility by some companies demands new informational needs, both internally and externally, to which the accounting information system should respond. Effectively, the low quality and credibility of environmental information submitted externally by some companies (that generally, doesn't represent the whole of the developed environmental performance) and the low rate of participation of accounting in the environmental management process has taken us to consider that the accounting information system response has been insufficient, as the interested stakeholders that wish to know the company's environmental performance must recur to other sources of information.

As a result, a review of the traditional accounting information system is needed, if it is to provide a more convenient and relevant information and at the same time, to provide the system with enough flexibility to adapt to the organizational and management changes, incorporating the environmental variables in the action and decision-making processes of an organization. In the case of the information for external stakeholders, it supposes the redefinition of some concepts, principles and hypotheses of the traditional financial accounting, as a starting point for the accounting processing of environmental issues. Concerning the cost/management accounting, it is required that they adapt to the new philosophy of environmental management and strategic design of the organization, so that they can present environmental information in a clear and systematic manner, allowing the managers to not only make the right decisions, but also to properly evaluate the environmental performance.

Regarding our case study, environmental issues have been incorporated into the group's strategy and some management practices, such as investment appraisals, performance measures, corporate reporting, but less in the internal costing systems. The external pressures (from legislation, clients, ecological groups and community in general) along with the importance given to the environmental values within the group have led to a high awareness in the high boards of administration, in matters related to the environmental protection, motivating an proactive attitude towards the environment, anticipating on many occasions the legislative and stakeholders demands, and actively participating in initiatives to improve its environmental performance, searching for a continuous prevention and reduction of the environmental impacts.

This proactive positioning towards the environment has taken to an increasingly bigger integration of the environmental issues in the management and decision-making processes, and therefore, the implementation of an EMS in all industrial centres and the obtaining of an environmental certificate, being a pioneer group in this aspect, for its sector.

Further, this proactive posture has had a clear and evident reflection in the organization's structure, with the creation of a department or environmental/sustainability area within the group's organization chart. There have also been produced changes in the production of paste and paper, specifically through the appliance of new technologies in preventing contamination and the usage of certified raw materials (or from controlled origins) and alternative materials (e.g. additives) to generate a smaller environmental impact, as well as the adoption of a circular economy approach into their production cycles. These findings are in line with Latif et al. (2020), which consider that in Europe, mimetic pressure is considered the best tool to ensure higher performance, since companies can respond to international demands by adopting or utilizing green technology or resources.

According to Wang et al. (2019), mimetic pressure plays an important role when the behavioural processes are highly complex and difficult to understand and adopt. Hence, the effect of mimetic pressure is reduced when the implementation of EMA is high (Latif et al., 2020). It was not the case of our group. Like Wang et al. (2019) results, the mimetic pressure has no significant effect on EMA adoption. In fact, the status quo of the environmental management accounting development is unsatisfactory, as similar to other studies (Chathurangani & Madhusanka, 2019). These results may be due to accountants' lack of environmental knowledge and experience. The lack of industrial guidelines to implement EMA may be a possible explanation for the insignificant effect of mimetic pressure (Wang et al., 2019).

Our study confirms the previous findings (Crespo Soler, 2002; Larrinaga-Gonzalez & Bebbington, 2001; Monteiro & Aibar-Guzmán, 2010), which found that accounting did not have significant impact on the process of organizational change within the context of the environmental agenda. However, the information generated by the accounting information system reflects the importance of environmental issues for the group, as for the cost accounting and in the financial accounting (through the environmental information disclosure in the annual report and the sustainability report). Even though there is no high interaction between the accounting/financial department and the environmental/sustainability area, both share some information, and it is expected that their cooperation will increase in the future. Professional accountants and environmental experts should share their skills to form a multifaceted team to address significant environmental issues to the group.

Our study presents as the main limitation, the fact that we have analysed only one group. Nevertheless, it is of our understanding that the degree of dept of our analysis allows, in a way, to compensate this limitation. With the present study, we do not expect to generalize any conclusions, but simply to study the reality of one group, considered to be a leader in Portugal, in the context of environmental management. In future research, it might be interesting to complement this study through the inclusion of multiple case studies (Bouma & Wolters, 1999; Crespo Soler, 2002). On the other hand, we propose to broaden this study to other companies from the paper paste sector since, according to Sharma and Vredenburg (1998), the study of organizations from the same industrial context makes it easier to compare them by the replication of results both literally (when similar responses occur) and theoretically (when different results occur, for predictable reasons).

Acknowledgements This study was conducted at the Research Center on Accounting and Taxation (CICF) and was funded by the Portuguese Foundation for Science and Technology (FCT) through national funds (UIDB/04043/2020 and UIDP/04043/2020).

References

Abdalla, Y., Siti-Nabiha, A., & Shahbudin, A. (2014). Social and environmental accounting research: The way forward. *International Journal of Economics and Management, 8*(2), 365–383.

Ahmad, N., & Sulaiman, M. (2004). Environmental disclosures in Malaysian annual reports: A legitimacy theory perspective. *International Journal of Commerce & Management, 14*(1), 44–57.

Albelda, E. (2011). The role of management accounting practices as facilitators of the environmental management: Evidence from EMAS organizations. *Sustainability Accounting, Management and Policy Journal, 2*(1), 76–100.

Azzone, G., & ManzinI, R. (1994). Measuring strategic environmental performance. *Business Strategy and the Environment, 3*, 1–14.

Azzone, G., Bianchi, R., Mauri, R., & Noci, G. (1997). Defining operating environmental strategies: Programmes and plans within Italian industries. *Environmental Management and Health, 8*(1), 4–19.

Bansal, P., & Bogner, W. (2002). Deciding on ISO 14001: Economics, institutions and context, *Long Rang. Planning, 35*(3), 269–290.

Bansal, P., & Roth, K. (2000). Why companies go green: A model of ecological responsiveness. *Academy of Management Journal, 43*(4), 717–736.

Barros, C., & Monteiro, S. (2012). Determinant factors of mandatory environmental reporting: The case of Portuguese primary metal and steel industry. *Studies in Fuzziness and Soft Computing, 286*, 123–147.

Bartolomeo, M., Bennet, M., Bouma, J., Heydkamp, P., James, P., Walle, F., & Wolters, T. (2000). Environmental management accounting in Europe: Current practice and future potential. *European Accounting Review, 9*(1), 31–52.

Baumann, S., Lehner, O., & Losbichler, H. (2015). A push-and-pull factor model for environmental management accounting: A contingency perspective. *Journal of Sustainable Finance and Investment, 5*(3), 155–177.
Bennett, M., & James, P. (1998). *Environment under the spotlight: Current practice and future trends in environment-related performance measurement for business*. The Association of Chartered Certified Accountants.
Blanco Dopico, M., & Maside sanfiz, J. & Aibar guzmán, B. (2000). *Hacia una perspectiva contingente del diseño del sistema de información de gestión medioambiental en base estratégica*. IX Encuentro de Profesores Universitarios de Contabilidad.
Bouma, J., & Wolters, T. (1999). Developments in eco-management accounting: an analysis of the case studies, in M. Bartolomeo, M. Bennet, J. Bouma, P. Heydkamp, P. James, F. Walle, & T. Wolters (Eds.),*Eco-management accounting*. Kluer Academic Publishers.
Bresciani, S., Rehman, S., Giovando, G., Alam, G. (2022). The role of environmental management accounting and environmental knowledge management practices influence on environmental performance: Mediated-moderated model. *Journal of Knowledge Management*. Vol. ahead-of-print No. ahead-of-print. https://doi.org/10.1108/JKM-12-2021-0953
Chathurangani, H., & Madhusanka, K. (2019). Environmental management accounting (EMA) adoption level among listed manufacturing companies in Sri Lanka: Institutional theory perspective. *Research in Social Sciences, 2*(1), 1–12.
Christ, K., & Burritt, R. (2013). Environmental management accounting: The significance of contingent variables for adoption. *Journal of Cleaner Production, 41*, 163–173.
Commission of European Communities. (2001). COM 2001/453/EC European Commission Recommendation on recognition, measurement and disclosure of environmental issues in the annual accounts and annual reports of EU companies. http://eur-lex.europa.eu/LexUriServ/LexUriServ.do?uri=OJ:L:2001:156:0033:0042:EN:PDF
Costa, C., & Jesus, T. (2019, novembro, 7–8). *A divulgação de informação financeira ambiental nas empresas*. Portuguesas entre 2010 e 2014. XVII Congresso de Contabilidade e Auditoria (CICA), Porto.
Costa, E., & Agostini, M. (2016). Mandatory disclosure about environmental and employee matters in the reports of Italian-listed corporate groups. *Social and Environmental Accountability Journal, 36*, 10–33.
Crespo Soler, C. (2002). *Internalización de la variable medioambiental en la gestión empresarialrespuesta estratégica, cambio organizativo e implicación en los sistemas de información contable para la gestión*. Universitat de València.
Darnall, N., Gallagher, D., Andrews, R., & Amaral, D. (2000). Environmental management systems: Opportunities for improved environmental and business strategy. *Environmental Quality Management, 9*(3), 1–9.
Delmas, M., & Toffel, M. (2004). Stakeholders and environmental management practices: An institutional framework. *Business Strategy and the Environment, 13*, 209–222.
Déniz Mayor, J., & Perez Alemán, J. (2003). Alternativas estratégicas frente al reto medioambiental *Jornal Do Técnico De Contas e Da Empresa, 449*, 90–94.
Dias-Sardinha, I., & Reijnders, L. (2005). Evaluating environmental and social performance of large Portuguese companies: A balanced scorecard approach. *Business Strategy and the Environment, 14*, 73–91.
Dienes, D., Sassen, R. J., & Fischer, J. (2016). What are the drivers of sustainability reporting? *A Systematic Review, Sustainability Accounting, Management and Policy Journal, 7*(2), 154–189.
DiMaggio, P., & Powell, W. W. (1983). The iron cage revisited: Collective ratio- nality and institutional isomorphism in organizational fields. *American Sociological Review, 48*, 147–160.
Erauskin-Tolosa, A., Zubeltzu-Jaka, E., Heras- Saizarbitoria, I., & Boiral, O. (2019). ISO 14001, EMAS and environmental performance: A meta-analysis. *Business Strategy and the Environment, 29*(3), 1145–1159.
Ferreira, A., & Moulang, C. (2010). Environmental management accounting and innovation: An exploratory analysis. *Accounting, Auditing & Accountability Journal, 23*(7), 920–948.

Financial Management Accounting Committee (FMAC). (1998). Environmental management in organizations the role of management accounting. *Study 6*

Florida, R., & Davison, D. (2001). Gaining from green: Environmental management systems inside and outside the factory. *California Management Review, 43*(3), 64–84.

Fonseca, L. (2015). ISO 14001:2015: An improved tool for sustainability. *Journal of Industrial Engineering and Management, 8*(1), 35–50.

Fonseca, L., & Carvalho, F. (2019). The reporting of SDGS by quality, environmental, and occupational health and the reporting of SDGS by quality, environmental, and occupational health and safety-certified organizations. *Sustainability, 11*(20), 5797

Fortes, H. (2002). The need for environmental reporting by companies. *An Examination of the Use of Environmental Reports by Swedish Public Companies, Green Management International, 40*, 77–92.

Fuadah, L., Kalsum, U., & Arisman, A. (2021). Determinants factor influence environmental management accounting and corporate environmental performance: Evidence in Indonesia. *Journal of Southwest Jiaotong University, 56*(3), 582–601.

García Rodriguez, A., & Pérez Chamorro, V. (1999). *Implicaciones de la gestión medioambiental en los sistemas contables de gestión* (VI Workshop 'Raymon Konopka' en Contabilidad de Gestión). Valencia, Enero.

Gazzola, P., Pezzetti, R., Amelio, S., & Grechi, D. (2020). Non-financial information disclosure in Italian public interest companies: A sustainability reporting perspective. *Sustainability, 12*(15), 1–16.

González-Benito, J., Lannelongue, G., & Dolores Queiruga, D. (2011). Stakeholders and environmental management systems: A synergistic influence on environmental imbalance. *Journal of Cleaner Production, 19*(14), 1622–1630.

GRI. (2022). *State of progress: Business contributions to the SDGs*. A 2020–2021 study in support of the Sustainable Development Goals. https://globescan.com/wp-content/uploads/2019/11/Driving_Corporate_Action_Towards_Accomplishing_the_SDGs_publication.pdf

Hummel, K., & Szekely, M. (2022). Disclosure on the sustainable development goals-evidence from Europe. *Accounting in Europe, 19*(1), 152–189.

Jalaludin, D., Sulaiman, M., & Ahmad, N. (2011). Understanding environmental management accounting adoption: A new institutional sociology perspective. *Social Responsibility Journal*, 7(4), 540–557.

James, P., Ghobadian, A., Viney, H., & Liu, J. (1999). Addressing the divergence between environmental strategy formulation and implementations. *Management Decision, 37*(4), 338–347.

Jennings, P. D., & Zanbergen, P. A. (1995). Ecologically sustainable organizations: an institutional approach. *The Academy of Management Review, 20*(4), 1015–1052.

KPMG. (2020). *The time has come: The KPMG survey of sustainability reporting 2020.*

Larrinaga-Gonzalez, C., & Bebbington, J. (2001). Accounting change or institutional appropriation—A case study of the implementation of environmental accounting. *Critical Perspectives on Accounting, 12*, 269–292.

Latif, B., Mahmood, Z., San, O. T., Said, R. M., & Bakhsh, A. (2020). Coercive, normative and mimetic pressures as drivers of environmental management accounting adoption. *Sustainability, 12*(11), 1–14.

Martín Samper, R., & Vélez Elorza, F. (2002). La gestión medioambiental en hoteles: el papel potencial de la Contabilidad de Gestión. *Un estudio de caso, XII Jornadas Luso-espanholas de gestão científica – Novos desafios na gestão: Inovação ou renovação.* Universidade da Beira Interior, Covilhã, 10–12 Abril.

Montabon, F., Melnyk, S., Sroufe, R., & Calantone, R. (2000). ISO 14000: Assessing its perceived impact on corporate performance. *Journal of Supply Chain Management, 36*(2), 4–16.

Monteiro, S., & Aibar-Guzmán, B. (2010). Organizational and accounting change within the context of the environmental agenda. *Journal of Accounting & Organizational Change, 6*(4), 404–435.

Monteiro, S., Ribeiro, V., & Lemos, K. (2020). Emerging trends on sustainability/integrated reporting: Public and private perspectives. In D. Crowther & S. Seifi (Eds.), *CSR and sustainability in the public sector. Approaches to global sustainability, markets, and governance* (pp. 137–149). Springer.

Monteiro, S., Ribeiro, V., & Lemos, K. (2022). Linking corporate social responsibility reporting with the UN sustainable development goals: Evidence from the Portuguese stock market. In Management Association (Ed.), *Research anthology on measuring and achieving sustainable development goals* (pp. 250–268). IGI Global.

Morrow, D., & Rondinelli, D. (2002). Adopting corporate environmental management systems: Motivations and results of ISO 14001 and EMAS certification. *European Management Journal, 20*(2), 159–171.

Olalekan, I. O., & Ogunleye, J. O. (2017). Identifying barriers to environmental management accounting practices: A comparative study of Nigeria and South Africa. *The Business Management Review, 9*(1), 168–179.

Ormin, K. (2020). Triangulation approaches in accounting research: Concerns, implications, and resolutions. *Applied social science approaches to mixed methods research* (pp. 186–200) IGI Global.

Pan, J. (2003). A comparative study on motivation for and experience with ISO 9000 and ISO 14000 certification among Far Easter countries. *Industrial Management & Data Systems, 103*(8), 564–578.

Patten, D. (1992). Intra-industry environmental disclosures in response to the Alaskan Oil Spill: A note on legitimacy theory. *Accounting, Organizations and Society, 17*(5), 471–475.

Phan, T. N., Baird, K., & Su, S. (2017). The use and effectiveness of environmental management accounting. *Australasian Journal of Environmental Management, 24*(4), 355–374.

Poksinska, B., Dahlgaard, J., & Eklund, J. (2003). Implementing ISO 14000 in Sweden: Motives, benefits and comparisons with ISO 9000. *The International Journal of Quality & Reliability Management, 20*(4/5), 585–606.

Porter, M., & Van der Linde, C. (1995). Green and competitive: Ending the stalemate. *Harvard Business Review, 73*(5), 120–134.

Ravikumar, S., Selukar, A., & Bansal, R. (2002, September–October). Indian Petrochemicals saves costs, gains competitiveness and employee commitment with ISO 14001-bases EMS. *Management Systems*, 43–48.

Ribeiro, V., & Monteiro, S. (2015). Public and private sector environmental reporting: Mandatory or voluntary regulation? *Revista De Ciências Empresariais e Jurídicas, 26*, 163–188.

Setthasakko, W. (2010). Barriers to the development of environmental management accounting: An exploratory study of pulp and paper companies in Thailand. *Environmental Management Accounting, 5*(3), 315–331.

Sharma, S. & Vredenburg, H. (1998). Proactive corporate environmental strategy and the development of competitively value of organizational capabilities, *Strategic Management Journal,* 19 (8), August, 729–753.

Tsalis, T., Malamateniou, K., Koulouriotis, D., & Nikolaou, I. (2020). New challenges for corporate sustainability reporting: United Nations' 2030 Agenda for sustainable development and the sustainable development goals. *Corporate Social Responsibility and Environmental Management, 27*(4), 1617–1629.

Van der Poll, H. (2022). The barriers and drivers of environmental management accounting practices' adoption in developed and developing countries for sustainable development. *Sustainable Development, 30*, 1222–1234.

Wachira, M., & Wangombe, D. (2019). The application of environmental management accounting techniques by manufacturing firms in Kenya. *Environmental Reporting and Management in Africa, 8*(1), 69–89.

Wang, S., Wang, H., & Wang, J. (2019). Exploring the effects of institutional pressures on the implementation of environmental management accounting: Do top management support and perceived benefit work? *Business Strategy & the Environment, 28*(1), 233–243.

Westley, F., & Vredenburg, H. (1991). Strategic bridging: The collaboration between environmentalists and business in the marketing of green products. *Journal of Applied Behavioral Science, 27*, 65–91.

Wilmshurst, T., & Frost, G. (2000). Corporate environmental reporting. *A Test of Legitimacy Theory, Accounting, Auditing & Accountability Journal, 13*(1), 10–26.

Yin, R. (1994). *Case study research.* Sage.

Young, C. (1996). Measuring environmental performance. In R. Welford (Eds.), *Corporate environmental management. Systems and strategies* (pp. 150–176). Earthscan.

Chapter 11
The Impact of COVID-19 on the Corporate Social Responsibility of Top 100 Companies in Mauritius

Sheistah Bundhoo-Deenoo

Abstract The purpose of this book chapter is to present the findings of a research aimed at analysing the strategies and Corporate Social Responsibility (CSR) activities of firms in Mauritius amidst the COVID-19 pandemic. 16 CSR Leads from "*Top 100 companies List*" in Mauritius have been interviewed with the aim of understanding the impact of the COVID-19 pandemic on the development and implementation of the companies' CSR actions. Various scholars have found gap in literature which demonstrates that social investment of companies through CSR and companies' contribution towards societal development have not been thoroughly researched and analysed. Therefore, this research adopts an ontological research philosophy with an interpretivism approach using a mono-qualitative research methodology. The findings show that companies have implemented new projects to combat the socio-economic impact of the COVID-19 pandemic through CSR thereby reinforcing their commitment towards the Sustainable Development Goals (SGDs). As a result, companies' contribution towards CSR actions during the pandemic have largely co-contributed towards the elimination of various social ills and upliftment of a harmonious society. Moreover, the CSR actions of companies also led to the enhancement of the brand's image. Lastly, it can also be analysed that companies have jointly worked with various stakeholders to combat the pandemic and avenues of collaboration between multiple stakeholders were noted.

Keywords COVID-19 preparedness · Social issues · Brand image · Corporate Social Responsibility Strategies · Marketing value · Stakeholders

S. Bundhoo-Deenoo (✉)
Charles Telfair Institute, Moka, Mauritius

D. Crowther and S. Seifi (eds.), *Corporate Social Responsibility in Difficult Times*, Approaches to Global Sustainability, Markets, and Governance,
https://doi.org/10.1007/978-981-99-2591-9_11

11.1 Introduction

11.1.1 CSR in Mauritius

Corporate Social Responsibility (CSR) has grown significantly on a global scale during the past two decades as a result of increased socio-political, environmental and stakeholders' pressure (Voegtlin et al., 2012). While there is no universally acknowledged definition of CSR, it remains a multi-dimensional concept grouping corporate and societal values (Navickas et al., 2021). Hence, despite the fact that CSR has been defined in various ways, a common global agreement is that firms and business managers need to participate in both economic and societal activities alongside showing commitment towards ethical behaviours, social justice and environmental sustainability (European Foundation for Management Development, 2005).

It has been recognized that during the last few years, several countries have altered from voluntary CSR to mandatory CSR (Ramdhony, 2018). Likewise, mandatory CSR was introduced in Mauritius in 2009 by the Minister of Finance (Ramdhony, 2018). Prior to 2009, a company operating in Mauritius had the right to spend its CSR funds in accordance with its own CSR strategies and then remit any unspent funds to the Mauritius Revenue Authority (MRA) (Mauritius Revenue Authority, 2021). With mandatory CSR, the Income Tax Act required companies to set up a CSR fund (Mauritius Revenue Authority, 2021). Companies now have to create and contribute to a CSR fund equal to 2% of their taxable income as per the 2016 Financial Law (Mauritius Revenue Authority, 2021). To ensure the management of the CSR funds, the National Social Inclusion Foundation (NSIF) was set up to receive, administer, and allocate CSR contributions collected by the MRA (National Social Inclusion Foundation, 2020).

11.1.2 CSR Expansion and Key General Concerns

Sklair and Miller (2010) believe that with the expansion of CSR, key questions and underlining issues have surfaced. Two such questions include—*Is CSR expansion an indicator of a growing humane capitalism? And is CSR a strategy for managers to sort out the capitalist paradox?* (Sklair & Miller, 2010). Consequently, it has been proved through various research that there is a growing managers' engagement in "doing good" and "avoiding harm" which are two different types of managerial behaviours towards CSR (Doh & Quigley, 2014; Stahl & Sully de Luque, 2014). Therefore, the debate about CSR, therefore, continues to amplify with new dimensions.

11.1.3 COVID-19 and CSR

The COVID-19 pandemic has left long-lasting impact on business operations (He & Harris, 2020) and which is still relevant and continues to expand today. As a result of the business challenges, it is undisputable that companies' social initiatives have either been reinforced (Raimo et al., 2021) or restricted due to financial constraints (Humphreys & Trotman, 2022). COVID-19 has exhibited who should be considered the most "critical" corporate stakeholders and this contributed to a new political economy for CSR managers (Crane & Matten, 2021). The differentiation between CSR theory and practice should, therefore, be investigated during the pandemic period to analyse the shift from an individualistic to a societal perspective (Crane & Matten, 2021). It has been predicted that with the financial impact of the pandemic, CSR initiatives of firms and their CSR reporting will largely determine ethical business behaviour (Albitar et al., 2021).

This research sheds light on the societal responsibilities and philanthropic actions (Ahmed et al., 2021) taken by companies to address social inequalities (Zhao, 2021). Thus, the research question has been formulated as followed: "*What is the impact of the COVID pandemic on the development and implementation of CSR strategies of firms from the Top 100 Companies list in Mauritius?*".

11.2 Literature Review

11.2.1 Background and Relevance of CSR

There are several assumptions about what CSR includes, which range from fundamental legal and economic commitments and accountability towards shareholders to broader obligations vis-a-vis larger social system in which a firm operates (Jamali, 2008). In fact, CSR complements the government's responsibility to uplift people's living standards and has a multiplier effect with the financial support of firms (Japhet et al., 2015). On the other hand, global capitalism theories position CSR as an approach which will allow companies to assume state-like functions, and CSR will eventually become Political CSR (PCSR) (Rhodes & Fleming, 2020). It is also debatable whether or not CSR is a self-interest approach of the firm (Crane & Matten, 2021).

Table 11.1 provides an overview of the different definitions of CSR proposed by various authors.

Table 11.1 CSR definitions

Definition of CSR	Author and year
CSR refers to the compulsory commitment that businessmen need to undertake to achieve desirable goals and values for society	Bowen (1953)
The only social responsibility of business is to maximize profits through resources usage within free competition	Friedman (1962)
CSR entails bringing business conduct along with prevalent societal norms and values	Sethi (1975)
CSR comprises society's economic, legal, ethical, and moral expectations on businesses at any point of time	Carroll (1979)
CSR is a concept whereby business and society are intertwined rather than separate entities	Wood (1991)
CSR is about the management practices of businesses to make a positive impact towards society	Baker (2003)
CSR includes an attitude towards society's economic and human resources, as well as a desire to ensure that those resources are being used for broader societal goals rather than narrowly defined individual interests	Frederick (1960)

Adapted from Mohammed (2020). Produced by Author

11.2.2 Theories

1. Corporate Social Performance

Corporate Social Performance (CSP) refers to changing business conduct to create fewer negative consequences and more positive outcomes for society and its people (Wood, 1991). This idea contends that in addition to economic growth, businesses bear the responsibility for societal issues caused by businesses themselves or by other factors in addition to its economic and legal obligations (Mohammed, 2020). This covers for ethical obligations as well as unilateral or charitable corporate activities which benefit society (Mohammed, 2020). Wood (1991) argues that the outcomes of businesses' corporate social performance can be measured through its policies, the CSR programmes and activities, and the CSR impact created by the company. It can, therefore, be said that CSP represents an indicator to measure the social impact of companies and can be used as a tool to analyse progress, address gaps and determine a comprehensive "*way-forward*" to combat social issues.

2. Shareholder Value Theory

Shareholder theory, also known as classical (Karake, 1998; Rugimbana et al., 2008) or fundamentalist theory, maintains that a company should be governed in the best interests of its shareholders (Clarkson, et al., 1994). On the other hand, the Shareholder Value Theory emphasizes that the sole aim of businesses is profit maximization in view of increasing the economic value for its shareholders (Crane, et al., 2008). According to this theory, companies may engage in CSR if they are mandated by applicable legal frameworks and regulations, or if the CSR activities would contribute towards the maximization of the shareholders' profit (Mohammed, 2020). According to this theory, the aim of a firm is to produce return on investment for its shareholders (Greenwood, 2001). This classical approach considers firm's CSR spending as a breach of management obligation towards increasing shareholder value and any social action leading towards non-value creation is not justified (Ruf et al., 2001).

3. Corporate Citizenship Theory

For decades, many business executives have been involved in charitable activities and/or actions towards the communities around which they operate and this has been acknowledged as good corporate citizenship (Mohammed, 2020). The Corporate Citizenship Theory links businesses as part of the societal structure (Crane, et al., 2008) and legitimizes active and participative engagement in welfare programmes (Mohammed, 2020) thereby qualifying for corporate citizenship within the managerial movement (Windsor, 2001).

11.2.3 COVID-19 Impact on CSR

The impact of the COVID-19 on businesses is multi-fold and inevitable. The engagement of a company's CSR activities varies because, at the core of it, some companies have been forced to close down due to the pandemic's financial implication (Navickas et al., 2021). Therefore, it has become essential to study socially responsible companies (Navickas et al., 2021) and evaluate the comparative effectiveness of its internal strategic planning (Zollo et al., 2009). Businesses have been pressured to '*do something*' about environmental issues and social inclusion (Frynas, 2005). This expectation became even more important and significant with the effects of the COVID-19 pandemic.

Table 11.2 provides an analysis of the recent literature on CSR during the COVID-19 pandemic and presents the views of several authors from selected articles published between 2020 and 2021.

11.2.4 CSR as a Social Investment

Corporate Social Investment (CSI) embodies the core shift away from corporate charity towards more deliberate and strategic social projects (Hinson & Tidings, 2011). An investment around the CSI concept indicates that an exchange is anticipated and this exchange can be in the form of a social uplift or a return on the business itself (Hinson & Tidings, 2011). In fact, the core pitch of a business case for CSR is that a company can perform better financially when contributing towards societal causes (Kurucz et al., 2008). CSI may help participating companies by

Table 11.2 COVID-19 and CSR implications

Authors	Analysis of current CSR situation during the pandemic	Recommendation to companies
He and Harris (2020)	The pandemic will leave long lasting socio-economic effects. With lack of resources, it is expected that firms will only implement short term CSR activities	Strong CSR strategies during the pandemic is forecasted to have a positive relationship on consumers and the brand image leading to creation of meaningful relationships
Panagiotopoulos (2021)	The two types of CSR implemented by companies include tactical and strategic CSR. Tactical CSR include short term engagement with limited resources while strategic CSR is an adoption of a holistic CSR perspective by the firms. The design of CSR strategies of firms during the pandemic will be either tactical or strategic depending on the firm's perception of the pandemic and availability of resources	To confront the pandemic, firms are forced to adopt a newly formed CSR concept which is the "critical CSR" which is a hybrid version of the tactical and strategic CSR
Mohammed (2020)	Employees working in firms which have shown commitment to CSR actions during the pandemic have higher job satisfaction. Globally, business and government have already come together to support vulnerable groups during the pandemic along with internal commitment for job security for their employees	Businesses should explore CSR and Human Resource Management during the pandemic given that it brings positive impact for the firm and its stakeholders
Humphreys and Trotman (2022)	With the financial implication on businesses related to the COVID pandemic and closure of some firms' significant challenges have been attributed towards attainment of strong CSR project outcomes	Companies should focus on demonstrating tangible outputs of sustainable and CSR actions as part of their performance measures to improve stakeholder's perception of the company
Raimo et al. (2021)	Companies' social initiatives during the pandemic has been about projects which are in line with the company's core business	Improved reputation and performance can be achieved through a win–win CSR strategy focused on subsidies and donations depending on the revenue level of the firm

(continued)

Table 11.2 (continued)

Authors	Analysis of current CSR situation during the pandemic	Recommendation to companies
Ahmed et al. (2021)	The pandemic created more scope for genuine philanthropic initiatives and socially commitment actions from firms	Positive brand associations can be linked with CSR activities of the firm aligned with sustainable practices. A positive relationship between Post CSR profitability and philanthropic action is forecasted

Produced by Author

strengthening their reputations, therefore preserving their integrity and legitimacy (Hinson & Tidings, 2011). Furthermore, with CSI, businesses establish a good working environment for their employees while also contributing to the government's social programmes (Hamann, 2009). Employees' evaluations of their firm's CSR participation are influenced by their liking of the company's CSR marketing strategies and clear vision embedded within the social identity theory (Schaefer et al., 2020). Therefore, employees' perception of their employer CSR action also has a great role to play in regard to their job satisfaction.

11.2.5 CSR within the Triple Bottom s (TBL)

Based on the Triple Bottom (TBL) theory, companies should look beyond its profit margin to ensure sustainability (Sustainability, 2021). The TBL theory focuses on three components which are essential to ensure corporate sustainability and they include—profit, people and planet (Księżak & Fischbach, 2017). Research shows that companies should upgrade their performance measuring system to include TBL and CSR because both frameworks represent an opportunity for companies to expand towards the global market and business ventures while at the same time benefit from improved brand image as well as consumers and employee satisfaction (Thakkar et al., n.d).

11.3 Research Objectives

Based on the research gap identified through literature, this research is framed to meet the following objectives:

1. To determine the link between the CSR strategies of firms in Mauritius and the socio-economic situation amidst the COVID-19 pandemic.
2. To highlight on the COVID-19-related CSR projects put in place by companies and
3. To assess the communication approach of CSR as a means to build the brand image.

11.4 Research Model

Based on the current literature on CSR and the COVID-19 pandemic along with the rising concerns and debate around the implication of COVID-19 on CSR strategies of firms, this research presents two propositions as detailed below (Fig. 11.1):

P1: *Firms are aligning their CSR strategies to provide relief and support to combat the diverse effects of COVID pandemic.*

Justification

The adverse impact of the pandemic on the economic and financial landscape cannot be disregarded (Srivastava et al., 2020). During the pandemic and the recovery period, collaboration on a cross-sectoral basis and diverse stakeholders joining hands to remedy disruptions (Lawton et al., 2020) have been noted. On the other hand, the workforce, products, services and costs were the most largely impacted in the business sector (Srivastava et al., 2020). The impact of the COVID-19 pandemic also

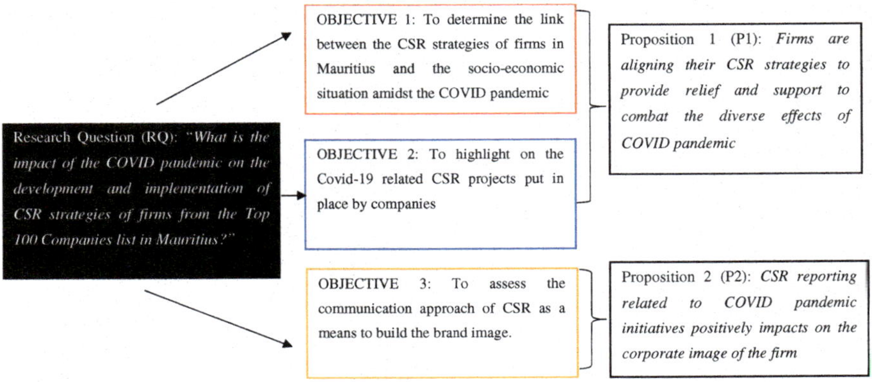

Fig. 11.1 Conceptual model. Produced by Author

resulted in a shift from traditional CSR to '*Strategic CSR*' (Lee, 2022) because companies were collectively participating with governments, civil society organizations and other non-profit institutions to provide support and relief (Lawton et al., 2020).

P2: *CSR reporting related to COVID pandemic initiatives positively impacts on the corporate image of the firm.*

Justification

CSR is now part of the core business strategies (Lee, 2022) because economic and societal factors emerging from the pandemic have changed interactions in the business world (Lawton et al., 2020). There is a need to explore the new dimension that CSR is taking to get a deeper insight on CSR actions being taken by firms (Lee, 2022), to understand the motivations and strategies of CSR managers in line with the corporate image of the company (Grewal & Serafeim, 2020), to create a differentiation strategy with the aim of increasing brand awareness (Maheshwari & Kumar, 2013) and to determine the pandemic impact on CSR strategies of firms (Bhattacharya et al., 2021).

Alongside, since CSR is now a core engagement of firms (Lee, 2022), it would add value to the literature of CSR by researching on the reporting of CSR during the pandemic as well as the control systems and disclosure of information regarding CSR (Grewal & Serafeim, 2020, Lawton et al., 2020).

11.5 Research Methodology

This research has adopted an inductive approach to answer the research question and meet the research objectives. An inductive approach allows the emergence of meanings through trends and relationships (Saunders et al., 2007).

11.5.1 Research Philosophies

An ontological research philosophy with an interpretivism approach has been used. Ontological philosophy allows for the study of reality (Slevitch, 2011) and describes the meaning of words and their connections (Muñoz-García et al., 2016). This philosophy matches with the research objectives since critical components such as organizational decision-making process and strategy implementation practices are being studied.

11.5.2 Research Design

The research is exploratory in nature and uses the case study strategy. The case study approach creates insights through intense and in-depth investigation out of the study of phenomena in its real-world setting, resulting in extensive, empirical descriptions and theory modelling (Saunders et al., 2007). Simultaneously, as part of the case study strategy, a mono-qualitative study approach has been used to gather data through semi-structured interviews with 16 firms from the Top 100 Companies list of Mauritius.

11.5.3 Sample

The sample population of this research are the CSR managers of firms in Mauritius, and the target population are CSR managers of firms from the Top 100 Companies list in Mauritius. Hence, a sample of 16 CSR managers of firms from Top 100 Companies in Mauritius has been selected, and the CSR managers have been interviewed individually through a semi-structured interview. Each interview lasted between 45 and 90 min. A non-probability sampling technique has been used to identify the 16 interviewees.

11.6 Findings

The findings of this research have been analysed through Nvivo and manually. As such four underlying themes related to the two propositions emerged from the findings.

On a general note, it has been analysed that most companies attribute their CSR in terms of donations to charitable organizations, Non-Governmental Organisations (NGOs) and 'force vives'. Some companies have their own "*CSR Foundation*" set up as part of representing the CSR pillar of the company whereby they have their own CSR projects run by employees that the company recruit and the projects are in line with specific areas of intervention and the strategic vision and mission of the company. Only one company out of the 16 interviewed highlighted that they have an internal CSR policy while the remaining companies' strategy is mostly axed on the Sustainable Development Goals (SDGs) set by the United Nations and which has been signed by the State of Mauritius.

Furthermore, it can be noted that companies doing CSR position their projects mainly on social interventions towards the external community through NGOs. There is a lack of focus and communication on projects for employees' well-being as part of CSR. As such, CSR is being mostly perceived as a concept of social investment in external context rather than an internal practice. The strategic plan mainly comes from the CSR committee set up by companies, with the financial and monitoring abilities and responsibilities given to CSR managers, CSR coordinators or an officer in charge. As for the implementation aspect for those companies who do not have a CSR Foundation, it is being done through NGOs working with vulnerable groups.

In this section, four underlying themes emerging from the interviews will be discussed to provide a better understanding of the CSR practices of companies during the pandemic.

11.6.1 Finding 1: Diversification and New Interventions of CSR During COVID-19

Most companies interviewed highlighted on the fact that their employees have contributed towards the preparation and distribution of 'food packs' during the COVID-19 pandemic. Since the implementation of the national lockdown in 2020 and 2021, companies seek recourse to having '*work access permits*' for their employees. While during the first phase of the lockdown, the permits were primarily given to '*front liners*' including mostly people working in the health sector and those sectors termed as '*essential service providers*', companies who had all their relevant permits started contributing through distribution of food items to families in need and to the "*vulnerable groups*". As a result, it was noted that many employees started to distribute food packs.

Companies interviewed indicated that the amount of food packs distributed ranged from 100 to 300. This new intervention on the part of businesses depicts an effort towards the contribution for COVID-19 relief. The businesses responded to the societal demands and have been engaged with their non-for-profit partners which operate mostly within the vicinity of the businesses or their respective business clusters. The contribution towards the societal needs depicts the involvement of businesses either towards a new form of social responsibility or purely based on a humane approach.

CSR managers interviewed claimed that one of the fastest response action taken has been food distribution, and on the other hand, it was also noted that NGOs sought help from businesses and requested for collaboration. It has been largely acknowledged by CSR Managers that their NGO partners, whom some of them would term as their 'social partners' are the firm's trusted collaborators and have been carefully chosen to work on different projects with the company because of their social skills and expertise. Hence, companies would seek the latter's support for distribution of food packs during the pandemic.

> "*We have been engaged in the distribution of food packs for the needy and people around our company branches. We saw it as a need to intervene and help people in the community…especially poor families and those who lost their job during the pandemic*"—Extract from Interview

"The company workers joined hands to create food packs and this was largely distributed through our NGO partners... Well, it was the NGO partners who designated the beneficiaries because they operate at the grassroot level and know the community well... so our support was also important... to fund for the food packs...and our employees also provided help in terms of distribution"—Extract from Interview

"Previously before the pandemic, we were more focused on sponsoring health programmes and sports activities but with the impact of the pandemic, our interventions were limited because of limited mobility...also, the demand was something else...people who needed food had to be catered for to meet for their basic needs...we collaborated with our partners to make several food packs and hygiene packs"—Extract from Interview

11.6.2 Finding 2: COVID-19 and CSR Funds

With the COVID-19 pandemic, companies from the Top 100 Companies of Mauritius list who operated in the hotel industry faced severe financial loss with the closure of borders and travel restrictions. Two interviewees mentioned that the company's biggest share of CSR funds came from the hotels. As a result, with the closure of hotels, the CSR funds of companies were limited. Companies thus had to review their strategy for funds allocated to their NGOs and social partners. Some companies set up a list of NGOs with whom they would compulsorily fund since their areas of intervention matched directly with the vision and mission of the company, and on the other hand, some decreased the financial donation given to NGOs. It has been noted that among the 16 companies which were interviewed, one of them set up a corporate donation fund besides the CSR fund and the corporate donation fund was used for emergency societal demands that the company would respond to.

"We lost a lot of our CSR programmes and could not fund our NGO partners because our hotels' financial situation was not okay"—Extract from Interview

"We could no longer fund the same amount yearly..."—Extract from Interview

11.6.3 Finding 3: CSR s During COVID-19

Companies are using various platforms to communicate about their CSR actions ranging from social media, newsletters, websites and reports.

In terms of official reporting and financial details, most companies report about their CSR activities in the company's annual report. Three companies from the 16 interviewed have a separate report which is mostly axed towards CSR and sustainability due to the demand set by the United Nations Global Compact (UNGC) to provide a separate detailed report about CSR and the social investment of the company.

It is to be noted that there is a general perception that "over communicating" about the CSR actions of the company is not necessary. Companies claim that they take into account the ethical aspect and confidentiality regarding beneficiaries of their CSR projects. Nonetheless, when the action is aimed at providing visibility to the internal practices of the company, it is widely reported. From the interviews, examples of go-green practices related to eliminate environmental degradation through sustainable procurement process, eco-friendly bags usage or design of new sustainable products were highlighted by interviewees. Such practices are communicated on various platforms and are also linked with the CSR strategies and the CSR commitment of the firms.

> *"Given the fact that Mauritius is a small island, reporting on our CSR activities give us an edge in terms of the overall operations of the company as well as our CSR commitments. For example, when showcasing our eco-friendly actions through CSR, we also showcase our green purchasing policies"*—Extract from Interview
>
> *"There are multiple benefits about talking publicly about the CSR activities...it can be a great tool for the brand visibility but we should be mindful of abusive marketing when it comes to CSR"*—Extract from Interview

During the pandemic period, companies reported about their CSR actions aimed at providing relief and emergency response mainly on their social media platforms. As such, interviewees claimed that they focused on showing support more than capitalizing on their CSR actions for benefits.

11.6.4 Finding 4: CSR for Reputation and Competitive Advantage During COVID-19

With the pandemic, firms are re-aligning their strategies to mitigate risks and improve resilience. The sampled firms believe that aggressive marketing strategies cannot be used when showcasing the CSR actions of the company. Two of the firms interviewed do not even provide any public reports about their CSR actions and investments. As such, CSR is perceived as a more humane contribution towards elimination of social issues.

> "*Internal reports are provided to the board and shareholders. We do not focus on aggressive marketing because... well, we are mindful of... and respect the privacy of our beneficiaries, especially children*"—Extract from Interview
>
> "*We do not submit public reports. Our CSR activities are generally showcased in our Annual Report. Yes, it is important to present these activities because they show what the company is doing to address social issues*"—Extract from Interview

On the other hand, firms do believe that through effective communication about their CSR actions, strategies and practices, they may achieve competitive advantage. It is agreed by all the 16 interviewees that CSR actions can consolidate the brand's image and the further reinforce consumer trust. Moreover, there is a general agreement that 'social washing' and 'green washing' could lead to severe implication on the firm's reputation and should be avoided. Interviewees also agree that CSR can add value to actions of the company.

In terms of competitive advantage, interviewees claim that being recognized as a socially responsible company can help demarcate from competitors in the same industry and as such, both employees and consumers feel that the company's approach is more ethically and socially responsible.

> "*Other companies who talk a lot about their CSR actions and have their own CSR Foundation are able to do prolonged social programmes which can make an impact...it does allow the company to demarcate from others*"—Extract from Interview
>
> "*Showcasing our CSR programmes help us attain visibility and why not, competitive advantage...because it is part of an action that we are doing besides our usual operations*"—Extract from Interview
>
> "*Some international companies have certification of being socially responsible, why not Mauritius? This is something to think about and could also reinforce the CSR commitments of companies...to do good and be rewarded through an official body*"—Extract from Interview

11.7 Discussion

It is widely demonstrated through various research that there is a need for innovative approaches that aim at conceptualizing the values of multiple stakeholders through CSR (Crane et al., 2021). The approach of the Top 100 Companies in Mauritius remains significant and innovative because companies who have their set "*Foundations*" are equally taking up a stand against social issues beyond the mandatory CSR obligation towards the State. The very setting up of a non-for-profit branch/unit demonstrates the commitment that companies have towards elimination of diverse social issues and the promotion of good. Moreover, this strategic approach highlights on the belief that companies have on the benefits of CSR actions.

The findings of this research do not only prove the multi-dimensional CSR contributions of companies but also showcase on the capabilities of private companies to take a stand and put forward concrete CSR actions aligned with the SDGs. However, with limited human resources and failure to integrate CSR actions to the larger development plan of the organization, the CSR strategies of companies may fail (Frynas, 2005). The current CSR framework does not propose nor directly recommend the setting up of a specific CSR branch/unit by the company. Therefore, compulsory CSR is just presented as taxation by another name. Companies who have been able to set up CSR department coupled with full time personnel are able to thoroughly engage and align their CSR actions to the values and mission of the organization. The future of CSR in Mauritius will largely depend on several internal and external factors including—how much the company is willing to invest in social causes; what will be gained for the company; is the company financially capable of hiring specialized workforce the CSR department; and will there be projects established over a long-term duration?

CSR currently expands beyond social responsibilities of organization; the concept has evolved from being more philanthropic to being a sustainable approach to meet socio-economic needs (Navickas et al., 2021). Most companies have designed their CSR strategic plan in line with the company's vision and mission. Simultaneously, the actions/programmes run by companies are carried out in the vicinity of the business units or within the respective business clusters. Such an alignment showcases the strategic approach transcending compulsory CSR; it shows that companies are trying to achieve recognition of the CSR actions being taken and the ownership and affiliation of the company's name and identity to the social action. From the research findings, it is predictable that in future, new dimension of CSR strategies will unfold as the theme of "sustainability" is being linked and widely acknowledged by many companies including the Top 100 Companies. There is a possibility of perceiving CSR as embodying "sustainability" or vice versa in the near future as this new thematic continues to evolve.

Furthermore, studies demonstrate that with the reinforced CSR strategies of businesses, researchers are calling upon distinguishing between social and political "responsibilities" that businesses carry (Crane & Matten, 2021). Indeed, with the COVID-19 pandemic, the engagement of businesses in social actions highlights on the roles being undertaken by business to combat social issues which remains one of the major roles of the State rather than that of businesses (Scherer et al., @@2016). COVID-19 is one of the major environmental and social disruption in history which has prompted several businesses to reconsider their business strategies and operations, as well as consider whether or not to continue operating (Navickas et al., 2021). The substantial impact on the evolution of corporate social responsibility is therefore irrefutable (Navickas, et al., 2021). On a worldwide scale, companies have reinforced their CSR actions to tackle the pandemic outbreak and provided support to several institutions (Navickas et al., 2021). In Mauritius, social partners and NGOs helped facilitate the process. Officials from the World Bank and USAID believe that CSR is a sustainable solution for social and public development (Frynas, 2005). The sampled companies believe in social investment and recognize the need of philanthropic activities. Consequently, due to the COVID-19 pandemic, companies are becoming political actors who execute corporate social duties and retain their credibility by delivering answers to social issues and presenting their governance practices to ensure democratic accountability (Rhodes & Fleming, 2020).

On the other hand, one of the advantages of CSR is that the company's credibility and moral actions are promoted through CSR (Hur et al., 2014). With the structuring of CSR in 2009 in Mauritius, companies have been called upon to invest in social actions and interviewees of this research also believe that CSR is an opportunity for brand equity. Therefore, investing in social causes can also bring competitive advantage (Frynas, 2005). For example, consumers trust the brand when they analyse the moral actions of the companies through the CSR initiatives put in place (Hur et al., 2014).

Nonetheless, communicating to shareholders, employees, consumers and the community at large about the CSR strategies of the firm is crucial in itself (Rhodes et al., 2020). This research reveals that companies' lack of communication around the triple bottom line can represent an opportunity to further reinforce the shareholder's impact. With managers of CSR having diverse views regarding the definition and conceptualization of CSR, this in turn impacts on the strategies set in place (Zollo, et al., 2009). In general, CSR managers see CSR as either 'do no harm' or 'do good'. While both concepts can be closely related, one is more towards mitigation of harm while the other is more a proactive attempt (Zollo, et al., 2009). These two concepts can equally be analysed through the sampled organizations and largely define the CSR strategy of the firms including its defined areas of intervention and projects. The implication of COVID-19-related projects can be attributed to the 'do good' as the interviewees focused more on defining these actions as providing relief and emergency response to the COVID-19 pandemic.

Generally, the four important factors that drive companies to embark on CSR projects include gaining competitive advantage, maintaining a stable work environment, management of external perception and keeping employees happy (Frynas, 2005). Thus, the corporate performance, brand reputation and image are enhanced with investment in CSR (Hur et al., 2014). CSR can contribute towards enhancing corporate reputation and many companies justify their CSR actions as a means to build the brand image (Hur et al., 2014). While sampled companies believe that there is a need to remain cautious when communicating about their CSR actions, they do confirm that there can be positive brand associations. Indeed, since the value of brand equity has increasingly been emphasized, businesses concentrate on brand communication and developing brand image as well as positive brand associations through CSR actions (Hur et al., 2014). CSR reports and sharing public information about CSR demonstrate that a firm has extensive CSR expertise, and it depicts the company's ongoing engagement instead of being a one-off charity event (Navickas et al., 2021). Therefore, CSR can also be an extrinsic motivation to attain corporate reputation (Fombrun, 2005).

11.8 Conclusion

The research demonstrates a clear impact of COVID-19 on CSR strategies and projects of companies in Mauritius. It can be noted that one of the emergency actions taken by companies was the distribution of food packs. With the mandatory CSR, companies have re-structured their social interventions from mere donations to financing large-scale projects in line with the company's vision. It can be said that the social investment being made by companies in Mauritius is also supporting the governmental welfare programmes and aiding NGOs to implement projects in view of combating social challenges. While CSR is now perceived as a strategic investment in society, not much is being communicated about internal CSR programmes of companies aimed towards their employees or towards consumers. Nonetheless, it is widely accepted that CSR actions can boost the brand image of the company but should not be used as an aggressive marketing tool.

11.9 Limitations and Future Research

This research is subject to limitations because it considers a sample of companies from the Top 100 Companies list only. As such, the list does not constitute of any banks in Mauritius as well. Moreover, this research can be expanded to yield quantitative results focused on determining the impact of COVID-19 on CSR strategies of firms in a more global context and potentially focus on companies from diverse or a specific industry. Since it has been noted that the hotel industry has been massively affected by the COVID-19 pandemic, further research could investigate on the impact of the restructuration of CSR strategies of the hotel industry.

Further to that, the sample of this research consisted of CSR managers/coordinators of firms and as such other research extended to understand consumers' and employee's perception of CSR strategies of firms admits the pandemic could be undertaken. The relationship between the brand image and CSR could have been further explored as well given that the TPL and sustainability are now being perceived as an integral part of companies with the pushing forward of the UNGC agenda.

References

Ahmed, J. U., Islam, Q. T., Ahmed, A., Faroque, A. R., & Uddin, M. J. (2021). Corporate social responsibility in the wake of COVID-19: multiple cases of social responsibility as an organizational value. *Society and Business Review.*

Albitar, K., Al-Shaer, H., & Elmarzouky, M. (2021). Do assurance and assurance providers enhance COVID-related disclosures in CSR reports? An examination in the UK context. *International Journal of Accounting & Information Management, 29*(3), 410–428.

Bhattacharya, S., Smark, C., & Mir, M. (2021). COVID 19: Social, financial and economic implications. *Australasian Accounting, Business and Finance Journal, 15*(1), 1–4.

Clarkson, M., Starik, M., Cochran, P., & Jones, T. M. (1994). The Toronto conference: Reflections on stakeholder theory. *Business and Society, 33*(1), 82.

Cochran, P. L., & Wood, R. A. (1984). Corporate social responsibility and financial performance. *Academy of Management Journal, 27*(1), 42–56.

Crane, A., & Matten, D. (2021). COVID-19 and the future of CSR research. *Journal of Management Studies, 58*(1), 280.

Crane, A., Matten, D., & Moon, J. (2008). *Corporations and citizenship: Business, responsibility and society*. Cambridge University Press.

Doh, J. P., & Quigley, N. R. (2014). Responsible leadership and stakeholder management: Influence pathways and organizational outcomes. *Academy of Management Perspectives, 28*(3), 255–274.

European Foundation for Management Development. (2005). *Globally responsible leadership—A call for engagement.*

Fombrun, C. J. (2005). A world of reputation research, analysis and thinking—Building corporate reputation through CSR initiatives: Evolving standards. *Corporate Reputation Review, 8*(1), 7–12.

Frynas, G. (2005). The false developmental promise of corporate social responsibility: Evidence from multinational oil companies. *International Affairs, 81*(3), 581–598.

Greenwood, M. (2001). The importance of stakeholders according to business leaders. *Business and Society Review, 106*(1), 29–29.

Grewal, J. and Serafeim, G., 2020. Research on corporate sustainability: Review and directions for future research. *Foundations and Trends® in Accounting, 14*(2), 73–127.

Hamann, R. (2009). South Africa: The role of history, government, and local context. In *Global practices of corporate social responsibility* (pp. 435–460). Springer.

He, H., & Harris, L. (2020). The impact of Covid-19 pandemic on corporate social responsibility and marketing philosophy. *Journal of Business Research, 116*, 176–182.

Hinson, R.E. and Ndhlovu, T.P., 2011. Conceptualising corporate social responsibility (CSR) and corporate social investment (CSI): The South African context. *Social Responsibility Journal.*

Humphreys, K. A., & Trotman, K. T. (2022). Judgment and decision making research on CSR reporting in the COVID-19 pandemic environment. *Accounting & Finance, 62*(1), 739–765.

Hur, W. M., Kim, H., & Woo, J. (2014). How CSR leads to corporate brand equity: Mediating mechanisms of corporate brand credibility and reputation. *Journal of Business Ethics, 125*(1), 75–86.

Jamali, D. (2008). A stakeholder approach to corporate social responsibility: A fresh perspective into theory and practice. *Journal of Business Ethics, 82*(1), 213–231.

Japhet, K., Tawiah, V., & Benjamin, M. (2015). *Debate on mandatory corporate social responsibility*. Available at SSRN 2592880.

Karake, Z. A. (1998). An examination of the impact of organizational downsizing and discrimination activities on corporate social responsibility as measured by a company's reputation index. *Management Decision, 36*(3), 206–216.

Kurucz, E. C., Colbert, B.A., & Wheeler, D. (2008). The business case for corporate social responsibility. *The Oxford handbook of corporate social responsibility* (pp. 83–112). Oxford University Press.

KsiężaK, P., & FischBach, B. (2017). Triple bottom line: The pillars of CSR. *Journal of Corporate Responsibility and Leadership, 4*(3), 95–110.

Lawton, T. C., Dorobantu, S., Rajwani, T. S., & Sun, P. (2020). The implications of COVID-19 for nonmarket strategy research. *Journal of Management Studies, 58*, 1732–1736.

Lee, S. (2022). Corporate social responsibility and COVID-19: Research implications. *Tourism Economics, 28*(4), 863–869.

Mahmud, A., Ding, D., & Hasan, M. M. (2021). Corporate social responsibility: Business responses to Coronavirus (COVID-19) pandemic. *Sage Open, 11*(1), 2158244020988710.

Maheshwari, K., & Kumar, D. (2013, January 1). To create a positive brand image through corporate social responsibility. *To Create a Positive Brand Image Through Corporate Social Responsibility.*

Mauritius Revenue Authority. (2021). *Guide on corporate social responsibility.* [Online] Available at: https://www.mra.mu/download/CSRGuide.pdf. Accessed 15 January 2022.

Mohammed, S. (2020). Components, theories and the business case for corporate social responsibility. *International Journal of Business and Management Review, 8*(2), 37–65.

Muñoz-García, A., Lagos-Ortiz, K., Vergara-Lozano, V., Salavarria-Melo, J., Real-Aviles, K., & Vera-Lucio, N. (2016, November). Ontological model of knowledge management for research and innovation. In *International conference on technologies and innovation* (pp. 51–62). Springer.

National Social Inclusion Foundation. (2020). *Funding framework.* [Online] Available at: https://www.nsif.mu/wp-content/uploads/2021/03/Funding-Framework-2020.pdf. Accessed 10 January 2022.

Navickas, V., Kontautiene, R., Stravinskiene, J., & Bilan, Y. (2021). Paradigm shift in the concept of corporate social responsibility: COVID-19. *Green Finance, Issue, 3*(2), 138–152.

Panagiotopoulos, I. (2021). Novel CSR & novel coronavirus: Corporate social responsibility inside the frame of coronavirus pandemic in Greece. *International Journal of Corporate Social Responsibility, 6*, 1–12.

Ramdhony, D. (2018). The implications of mandatory corporate social responsibility—A literature review perspective. *Theoretical Economics Letters, 8*, 432–447.

Raimo, N., Caragnano, A., Zito, M., Vitolla, F., & Mariani, M. (2021). Extending the benefits of ESG disclosure: The effect on the cost of debt financing. *Corporate Social Responsibility and Environmental Management, 28*(4), 1412–1421.

Rhodes, C., & Fleming, P. (2020). Forget political corporate social responsibility. *Organization, 27*(6), 943–951.

Rugimbana, R., Quazi, A., & Keating, B. (2008). Applying a consumer perceptual measure of corporate social responsibility: A regional Australian perspective. *Journal of Corporate Citizenship,* 29, 14.

Ruf, B. M., Muralidhar, K., Brown, R. M., Janney, J. J., & Paul, K. (2001). An empirical investigation of the relationship between change in corporate social performance and financial performance: A stakeholder theory perspective. *Journal of Business Ethics, 32*(2), 143–156.

Saunders, M., Lewis, P., & Thornhill, A. (2007). Research methods for business students (4th ed.). *Financial Times.*

Schaefer, S. D., Terlutter, R., & Diehl, S. (2020). Talking about CSR matters: Employees' perception of and reaction to their company's CSR communication in four different CSR domains. *International Journal of Advertising, 39*(2), 191–212.

Sklair, L., & Miller, D. (2010). Capitalist globalization, corporate social responsibility and social policy. *Critical Social Policy,*30(4). https://journals.sagepub.com/doi/10.1177/0261018310376804

Slevitch, L. (2011). Qualitative and quantitative methodologies compared: Ontological and epistemological perspectives. *Journal of Quality Assurance in Hospitality & Tourism, 12*(1), 73–81.

Srivastava, A., Meena, A. K., Srivastava, K., Gupta, V., & Kaushal, K. (2020). Socio economic impact of COVID-A review. *Asian Journal of Research in Chemistry, 13*(6), 497–501.

Stahl, G. K., & Sully de Luque, M. (2014). Antecedents of responsible leader behavior: A research synthesis, conceptual framework, and agenda for future research. *Academy of Management Perspectives, 28*(3), 235–254.

Sustainability. 2021. The impact of CSR on corporate value of restaurant businesses using triple bottom line theory. *Sustainability 13*(4), 2131.

Thakkar, J. J., Mahanty, B., & Maiti, J. (n. d.). *TBL (Triple Bottom Line) sustainability and CSR (Corporate Social Responsibility) driven performance measurement systems.*

Voegtlin, C., Patzer, M., & Scherer, A. G. (2012). Responsible leadership in global business: A new approach to leadership and its multi-level outcomes. *Journal of Business Ethics, Issue, 105*(1), 1–16.

Windsor, D. (2001). The future of corporate social responsibility. *The International Journal of Organizational Analysis.*, *9*(3), 225–256.

Wood, D. J. (1991). Corporate social performance revisited. *Academy of Management Review, 16*(4), 691–718.

Zhao, J. (2021). Reimagining corporate social responsibility in the era of COVID-19: Embedding resilience and promoting corporate social competence. *Sustainability, 13*(12), 6548.

Zollo, M., Mario, M., Lourdes, C., Kai, H., Peter, N., Susan, S., & Antonio, T. (2009). Towards an internal change management perspective of CSR: Evidence from project response on the sources of cognitive alignment between managers and their stakeholders, and their implications for social performance. *Corporate Governance, 9*(4), 355–372.

Printed by Printforce, United Kingdom